DEATH BY PEDICURE

the dirty secrets
of nail salons

Dr. Robert Spalding, Jr.

Chattanooga Fu Fu Factory
Signal Mt., Tennessee

Cover Photograph by Greg Forehand. Type and design by Karen Stone, Waldenhouse.

DEATH BY PEDICURE *the dirty secrets of nail salons*

Published by Chattanooga Fu Fu Factory
1225 Taft Highway, Signal Mt., TN 37377 USA
Printed in the United States of America

Third Printing September 2007
Library of Congress Cataloging-in-Publication Data

Spalding, Robert, 1956-
  Death by pedicure : the dirty secrets of nail salons / Robert Spalding, Jr.
-- 1st ed.
    p. cm.
  Includes index.
  ISBN-13: 978-0-9711068-1-9 (alk. paper)
  ISBN-10: 0-9711068-1-9 (alk. paper)
  1. Foot--Care and hygiene. 2. Nails (Anatomy)--Care and hygiene.
3. Foot--Infections. 4. Beauty shops. I. Title.

  RD563.S63 2006
  617.5'85--dc22

                         2006027850

DISCLAIMER: The publisher does not accept any responsibility for the accuracy of the information or the consequences arising from the application, use, or misuse of any of the information contained herein, including any injury and/or damage to any person or property as a matter of product liability, negligence, or otherwise. No warranty, expressed or implied, is made in regard to the contents of this material. No claims or endorsements are made for any drugs or compounds currently marketed or in investigative use. This material is not intended as a guide to self-medication. The reader is advised to discuss the information provided here with a doctor, pharmacist, nurse, or other authorized healthcare practitioner and to check product information (including package inserts) regarding dosage, precautions, warnings, interactions, and contraindications before administering any drug, herb, or supplement discussed herein. There are no warranties expressed or implied.

Dedication

I dedicate this book to my wife Gina, daughter Katherine and my father, Dr. Robert T. Spalding, who are the three biggest sources of motivation I have in life. My wife provided me with the time and patience to dedicate to this project. My daughter has tasked me with the challenge to completion of this book. And finally, my dad, who is the eternal academician, provided me with the drive to succeed in medicine as well as his valued opinions in literature and life.

Acknowledgments

An acknowledgment page is an opportunity for the author to acknowledge the contributions of organizations and individuals who he or she feels helped with the book.

I must give the first review credit to Doug Schoon. I thank him for the generosity of his time. We, like many professionals, do not agree on everything, but we managed to find some excellent common ground that we both feel will improve this text. I can safely say we learned a great deal from each other, and for that alone, the reader should benefit. I agree with the statement that Doug has in his book, "No one can know everything."

Special appreciation to Janet Foliano-Kemp, owner of Bella Vita Spa, for allowing her foot to be photographed for the book cover.

The talent of Greg Forehand of Contemporary Portraits shows in his design and composition of the book cover photograph, where he combined his computerized graphic skills with his photographic abilities.

I very much appreciate my medical school dermatology professor and perpetual mentor, Bryan Markinson, DPM, for taking the time to review portions of my manuscript and offer his guidance.

Many thanks to Mark Anderson, MD and James Sizemore, MD who, as infectious disease specialists, reviewed the accuracy of the microbial information in the manuscript, as well as consulted on behalf of my patients.

Thanks to Athena Elliott who introduced me to the top echelon of nail techs in the country and who has helped me on writing projects in the past and including this one.

Kudos to Karol Singleton, who unselfishly provided nail technicians worldwide a wonderful opportunity to get together annually and share unique nail care techniques and friendship.

My thanks to Debbie Doerrlamm for her frank opinions and feedback. She operates the longest running bulletin board service for nail techs in the world.

Special thanks to David McKin, who took my long winded book project and magically condensed it overnight to a consumer friendly story.

Thanks to nail technician, Janie Soloff and Amber Lockhart who provided some excellent information for my book.

And finally, my special appreciation goes to Karen Stone at Waldenhouse Publishers, Inc. for expertly designing and formatting this book.

Contents

Figures / Illustrations

Introduction
Death by pedicure? Can it happen?
Yes, absolutely!

Here's how: Consumer injury occurs through the use of improperly sterilized, poorly disinfected or unsanitized equipment. One person's bacterial, viral or fungal organisms transfer to another person's body through pre-existing breaks in the skin, or through injuries that occur during improper nail (manicure/pedicure) procedures. The resulting infections, now increasing in number, vary in intensity from minor to deadly.

A recent incident in Fort Worth, Texas, involved the death of a paraplegic woman who allegedly contracted an infection during a pedicure treatment. The infective organism turned out to be the highly drug-resistant bacteria called MSRA, *Methicillin Resistant Staphylococcal Aureus*. The bacteria caused a systemic reaction called *sepsis* that her body could not overcome. Media coverage of this woman's death and a second recent death in Santa Clara County, California has called attention to serious problems in the nail industry. (See Chapter 4: "The Death of Kimberly Jackson and Jessica Mears".)

In this book, I'll share with you how I got involved with the beauty care business, and what we as consumers, nail technicians, salon operators, cosmetology schools and boards, medical professionals, equipment suppliers can do about the multifaceted problems now facing the industry.

Consumers need to protect themselves from infection by unsterilized or improperly disinfected equipment and dangerous procedures now common in nail salons.

Nail technicians, (nail techs) must learn how to protect their clients from harm, how to keep themselves within the law, and how to maintain their own health when faced with daily exposure to infection and inhalation hazards associated with nail industry chemicals and airborne debris.

Education of consumers, nail techs, and interested medical professionals regarding salon industry practices and hazards is paramount in addressing those areas which can effect harm to individuals. Products and industry practices that create dangerous health situations have to be exposed, and change must occur for the sake of public and personal health.

It is my intent that this book serve as an agent of change in this field.

Chapter 1
A serious problem

Millions of women, men, and teenagers want their fingernails and toenails to be clean, healthy, and well maintained. They may want decorations as well, with anything from nail polish to glitter, rhinestones, four-inch extensions, and original nail art. Basic and decorative artwork related to nails is the backbone of a multi billion dollar business in the United States of America alone.

At this time, an estimated one million unsuspecting clients walk out of their chosen salon with infections – bacterial, viral, and fungal. Depending on the state of their immune systems and overall health, they may experience an annoying itchy infection that requires drug treatment – or a life-threatening outbreak that requires a trip to the emergency room. Many may never connect their infections with a salon treatment. As a podiatrist, a doctor who specializes in the treatment of foot problems, it took me a while to make this connection.

During my first year of practice, I began to design foot care products. In the process of development and testing, I came in contact with many nail technicians. They wanted more information on the foot problems they encountered in their work. I discovered that resources for them are scarce, and that there is conflict and confusion in the industry overall.

As nail techs began referring more and more clients with foot problems to me, I began paying attention to the sources of my patients' nail infections. I hadn't connected the dots before. Neither had others – not primary care physicians, dermatologists, or orthopedists, I discovered. We all saw and treated nail infections without realizing how many originated from manicure and pedicure treatments.

Several nail techs suggested I serve as a professional medical resource for the national website, www.beautytech.com. I was invited to seminars and national beauty trade shows where I answered questions about nail health and nail disease from a medical perspective. Over a period of eight years, I discovered entrenched patterns, processes, and procedures in the industry that vary from untruthful and unhealthy to outright unlawful.

Change typically follows a pattern: a serious problem like a death leads to a crisis; crisis creates awareness; awareness leads to education; education leads to action; and action leads to change.

There is a need for change in the nail industry. In this book I'll share with you what I've learned, and include many chapters that go deep into specific areas, so that the big picture of what's involved is clear to all.

Right now let's start by visiting a nail salon where we'll see the problems unfold before our eyes.

Chapter 2
Let's Nail It!
A hypothetical nail salon - Part I

The Stage is Set. We'll call our hypothetical salon *Let's Nail It!* Their menu of services goes like this:

Basic Pedicure
Therapeutic foot soak scented with lavender softens the cuticles and calluses. After the nails are shaped cuticles are trimmed and calluses and corns are removed. Nails are complemented with your choice of French manicure or polish.

Spa Pedicure
The elements of the basic pedicure plus a super vitamin C enriched moisturizer followed by paraffin dip and polish.

Basic Manicure
Nails are shaped cuticles are softened, pushed and trimmed. Hands are massaged with herbal lotion and cuticle oil is applied. This manicure is topped off with your choice of natural nail buff or polish.

Spa Manicure
The elements of the basic manicure plus a super vitamin C enriched moisturizer followed by paraffin dip and polish.

Rosemary Peppermint Pampering

The elements of the basic manicure/pedicure plus a heavenly peppermint, rosemary lotion with a longer relaxing massage.

Enhancements

Your choice of UV gel or acrylic nails with optional French tips or choice of nail polish colors.

Rebalance

At a reduced rate, we offer bi-weekly maintenance to keep your acrylic or gel nails looking great.

Nail art

Your choice of nail art or rhinestones.

In the *Let's Nail It!* reception room, two clients are reading magazines waiting to be called for their appointments, and four more are on their way.

"Jack," a CEO, has active hepatitis C. He scratches the bumpy tiny lesions on the top of his head, then an itchy mosquito bite on his arm. In so doing, he acquires a small amount of pink serous fluid (infectious discharge) under his fingernails. He comes in regularly for a nail-maintenance manicure.

"Sara," a teenager, wants a natural manicure for a weekend dance date. She hopes the nail tech will do something about the rough hands and split cuticles she has from horseback riding and barn duties. She wants soft hands for her date.

"Mrs. Taylor" has diabetes, but no health insurance. Her daughter, nail tech Amy's best friend, requested that Amy cut her mom's thick toenails because she can't afford to see a doctor. Mrs. Taylor doesn't want her nails painted, just trimmed and sanded so that her feet fit comfortably in her shoes.

"Molly," a well-to-do sixty-year-old, is waiting to get her artificial nails backfilled (rebalanced), and to reattach the one on her thumb that broke during a tennis match. She comes in every two weeks to have her artificial nails kept in mint condition.

"Brenda" is a marketing executive who just closed a big account, is treating herself to a pedicure and manicure to relax at the end of a difficult week. She wants to soak her feet in the bubbling foot whirlpool. She eases gratefully into the comfortable "throne chair" (See picture page 157.) and closes her eyes for fifteen minutes before the pedicure. This morning in the shower, she shaved her legs so they'd look nice.

The last client is "Suzie," a polished administrative secretary with high heels, red toenail polish, tender bunions and cracked callused heels, who is coming in for a quick pedicure. She gets Amy to trim her calluses with a callus cutter know in the industry as a "Credo Blade" that looks like a potato peeler. She likes to wear the stiletto heels that she believes accentuate her legs and make them so attractive to others.

Inside, "Amy," the nail tech, has had a busy day. In addition to regular manicures, one booked an arty nail enhancement, and two more wanted artificial nails and fill-ins. She clears her table for the last clients, putting her nail nippers and the drill-bit-like burrs for her electric nail file in a new ultraviolet "sterilizer" box she'd bought at a recent beauty show. Between it and a new dry heat sterilizer, she's confident about protecting her clients from the nail salon infection problems publicized on TV and in her nail magazines.

Knowing she has one more acrylic nail treatment to go, Amy rows up the products in order of their use: 1) a fine grit nail file to sand the top of the nail; 2) dehydrating alcohol to dissolve surface moisture 3) acid nail primer to prepare the nail surface 4) adhesive (cyanoacrylate "glue") to apply nail tips (extensions) onto nails; and 5) liquid monomer and 6) powdered polymers that blend to form the dollop of acrylic that is spread and shaped on each nail bed, evenly, one-sixteenth-inch away from the nail edge. Amy micro-adjusts the dozens of polishes that sit neatly on wall shelves next to her nail table. The nail enhancements she uses – extensions, decals, glitter, artificial nails, rhinestones, nail art decals, the materials for air-brushing to create original art, and more – live in a clean drawer dedicated to their storage. She checks it quickly, sees adequate supplies, takes a deep breath, and lets the receptionist know she's ready for the next client.

Amy asks her first client, Jack, to go to the bathroom and scrub under his nails with a brush. This is standard proce-dure. Jack goes to the bathroom, relieves himself, and quickly washes his hands, but doesn't remember to use the scrub brush to clean under his nails. He sits at the table and offers his hands. Amy retrieves the nail nippers and a pointed nail instrument from the ultraviolet light box. She cuts Jack's nails and cleans under them, including the one harboring pink serous viral fluid, and finishes the manicure. After Jack leaves, she puts the nail nipper and the cleaning instrument in the sterilizer box for the required ten-minute treatment.

Sara comes in and is sent to the restroom to wash her hands, which she does, though lightly, as the soap stings when it gets into the cracked skin of her fingers. She sits down at the nail table. Amy retrieves the nail nippers that have been in the sterilizer for ten minutes and trims the dead tissue around the girl's fingers and nails. Some of Jack's hepatitis viral particles now reside in Sara's split cuticles. Amy recommends a certain oil to help the cuticles, and tells Sara to use a moisturizer on her hands and to not get them wet. Sara leaves happy with her softer, oil-massaged hands.

Mrs. Taylor walks in as Sara walks out. After giving her a hug, Amy settles her friend's mom in the special pedicure chair and tips it backwards so she can easily work with her feet. Mrs. Taylor likes to have her feet handled as they tingle and get numb; rubbing and warm hands feel great. Amy picks a sanding burr from the sterilizer box and sands Mrs. Taylor's cracked cal-luses. Then, as she trims the thick nails with the nipper she just used on Sara, Amy notices a soft black-green tarry substance and some redness under a big-toe toenail. As she clips more nail away, the now-exposed redness appears to be dried old blood and what looks to be a soupy mix "with a peanut butter smell." Concerned, Amy stops, puts the tools into the sanitizer, and lets Mrs. Taylor know that that's the best she can do, that to go deeper might hurt her toe. She washes the toes in soapy water and rubs them with softening cream. Mrs. Taylor immediately feels better with newly trimmed nails that allow her feet to sit painlessly in her shoes. She tips Amy, thankful that her daughter has such a nice friend.

The fourth client of the afternoon is Molly, who sits down and begins talking animatedly about the tennis move that broke her right artificial thumbnail. It looks a little dark under the chipped extension. Amy suggests to Molly she may need a bottle of "cleaning drops" for her artificial nails. To save time, Amy picks up the electric nail file she just used on Mrs. Taylor and sands off Molly's broken thumbnail evenly, then retrieves the nippers from the UV (ultraviolet) light box and begins the acrylic nail maintenance protocol. Five product applications later, during which Molly shared that her fingernails itch sometimes, Amy is complete and Molly is pleased. She tips handsomely and leaves.

Brenda sticks her head in the door and says she's headed for the whirlpool throne chair. Amy meets her in an adjoining room, settles her into the plush leather-upholstered chair, and turns on the warm-water whirlpool. foot bath. As Brenda relaxes with her eyes closed in the cushioned throne chair, millions of *mycobacterium fortuitum*, *mycobacterium smegmatis*, and other bacteria that call the whirlpool home begin to infiltrate the invisible tiny cuts on her freshly shaved legs.

And finally, Suzie, who came in for a quick pedicure, is soaking next to Brenda, (See pictures page 157.) and they are both relaxing in the plush whirlpool chairs with the soothing bubbles that are carrying more than just aromatic oils. Suzie gets Amy to trim her calluses with a Credo blade, because of the discomfort and irritation caused by her choice of footwear.

Amy, relieved to be going home in twenty minutes, buries the nippers and sanding burrs in the glass beads of her new dry heat sterilizer. Below the beads is a heat filament that unevenly heats to 215 degrees Fahrenheit, which she was incorrectly told sterilizes everything. Pleased, she flicks on its switch for the first time, cleans her table, and puts her nail products in order again.

What's not right with this day in "Let's Nail It!" salon?

To help us with our assessment, we need to be familiar with the key terms *sterilize, disinfect, sanitize*, and *antiseptic*. Here are the definitions Amy learned in her training program:

Sterilize: To sterilize is to completely destroy all bacteria on inanimate surfaces.

Disinfect: To disinfect is to destroy pathogenic and other kinds of microorganisms by physical or chemical means. Disinfection is preformed on fomite or inanimate (*i.e.* non-living) surfaces, generally by low to moderately effective disinfectant chemicals such as 70-90% alcohols, detergents called quaternary compounds, acids called phenols, or any combination of these agents. Disinfection does not kill bacterial spores.

Sanitize: To sanitize is to control the growth of microorganisms by various means of cleaning".

Antiseptic: An antiseptic, without damaging or irritating living tissue, destroys or stops the growth of germs on skin surfaces.

Chapter 3
Let's Nail It! Part II
"Nail techs are in the health business whether they know it or not."
Dr. Robert Spalding

Millions of people whose immune systems are compromised – by diabetes, HIV, cancer, hepatitis, and other infective organisms – book services offered in nail salons. Jack's arrival in the salon, infected as he is with active hepatitis C, alerts us to a nail salon's number one problem: infection.

But neither Jack nor his infection is the problem here. Jack is at the same or greater risk of infection as a healthy client. Indeed, having a second infective organism introduced into Jack's immune-compromised body could result in an unpleasant medical event.

The problem is the transmission of infection from one client to another. Breaks in the skin can be microscopic or highly visible. They can come in with the client – cuts, scratches, hangnails, bitten nails, insect bites, paper cuts, split cuticles – or be created in the salon. Nail techs using callus-cutting tools and nail nippers, files, cuticle pushers, and electric burrs and drills, can and do scratch and nick skin and draw blood. Called portals of entry, breaks in the powerful immune system organ called skin can allow infective organisms to enter.

Let's see how this happens. Sara, the teenager, was nail tech Amy's next client after Jack. Amy did not break Jack's skin, he had no obvious infections, and she had put the clippers and nail tools she used – both contaminated with microscopic amounts of Jack's hepatitis C material – into her brand new ultraviolet light sterilizer box for the required ten-minute treatment. She followed the rules. How is it, then, that young Sara walked out of the salon thirty minutes later with Jack's hepatitis C cells making themselves at home in her split cuticles?

Problems identified: 1. Inadequate interview with client: Amy didn't ask Jack if he had a blood-borne disease. 2. Basic sanitation: (a) Amy sent Jack to the restroom to scrub under his nails with soap, water and a nail brush. He didn't, and Amy didn't double check. (b) The nippers were contaminated. The serous fluid contaminated with Jack's hepatitis C virus stayed under his fingernails. Microscopic clumps of it were stuck on the nippers when Amy trimmed Sara's cuticles and nails. (c) Equipment was not sterilized. Amy put the nail nippers in her newly bought UV light "sterilizer" box. The ultraviolet light of a "sterilizer" box is not designed to kill 100 percent of all infective organisms.

Some infective microorganisms are easy to kill. Some are not. Thanks to the industry-wide confusion about the definition of the term "sterilize," Amy thinks her instruments are sterilized, when, in fact, she has no clue. She doesn't know that Jack has active hepatitis C, nor that his hep C virus material is on the nippers. To handle this essentially medical situation, she would have to know that the nippers are contaminated with hepatitis C virus, and know whether or not ultraviolet light is a powerful enough disinfectant to kill that particular virus. Is this part of her job description? No!

Is there a way to be completely safe for each client? Yes. It's called an autoclave. An autoclave kills 100 percent of all infective organisms. None of Jack's hepatitis C virus – nor any other microorganism – can survive the pressurized steam heat of an autoclave. In other words, there would be no transmission of infective organisms from client to client via contaminated instruments in a nail salon whose techs used properly autoclaved instruments. It's a simple solution.

However, the question still exists. Why aren't all nail salons equipped with autoclaves? What stops a salon owner from going straight to a solution which is 100 percent effective? The answer is the lack of sterilization training, economics, and a conceptual difference in the need for disinfection versus sterilization.

The third client, Mrs. Taylor, Amy's best friend's mother, has diabetes. Amy agreed to work with her as a favor to her friend. Mrs. Taylor came in right on Sara's heels, and Amy, caught up in the warm interaction with her friend's mom, forgot to put the nippers she just used on Sara back in the UV sterilizer box.

Problems identified: 1. Amy stepped outside the law when she agreed to work with a client with a medical condition, diabetes, and a classically related symptom – thick, fungus-infected nails. Most state laws forbid nail techs to touch clients who have nail or skin problems, and they are told to refer such clients to a doctor. Amy didn't. Most state regulations forbid nail techs to work on thick, fungus-infected toenails without written consent from a physician. Depending on what state she lives in, Amy may have broken the law by agreeing to work with her friend's mom. 2. She also forgot to put the nippers in the "sterilizer" box, and she may have exposed an immune-compromised older lady with no health insurance to Jack's hepatitis C virus.

Molly with the broken acrylic thumbnail, may have been exposed to both Jack's virus and Mrs. Taylor's fungus via contaminated nippers and sanding* burrs. Additionally, Molly has some *pseudomonas* under the old artificial nail. While Molly has no life-threatening problems yet with her artificial nails, long-term problems with both the procedure and the chemicals abound.

Brenda, relaxing with her eyes closed in the plush, cushioned, leather throne chair, her feet in the warm whirlpool bath, is exposing invisible tiny cuts from her freshly shaved legs to millions of *mycobacteria fortuitum, mycobacterium smegmatis,* and others that reside in the poorly disinfected filter, tub and hose assembly. As she rests, the microbes begin to infiltrate the minor lesions in her legs

Finally, Suzie with her tender bunions and thick callus over the ball of her foot and deep cracks in her heel, is getting treated with a callous cutter that never got disinfected. A tiny nick in her skin next to her heel callus has a faint capillary bleed that is now exposed to the *Myco bacterium* in the whirlpool foot bath.

Problems identified: 1.The receptionist didn't stipulate when she set the appointment that Brenda should not shave her legs before her pedicure. 2. Amy did not notice that, or ask Brenda if she had shaved her legs that day. 3. No one had properly cleaned the whirlpool bath equipment. Amy and the nail salon will be in trouble with the state cosmetology board and Amy could lose her license and/or be sued in the event Brenda contracts an infection.

Amy has spent hours breathing potentially harmful fumes from nail polish and artificial nail chemicals. The ventilation in the salon is marginal, but a cool breeze blows from her oscillating fan. Amy's lungs have also been exposed to potentially infected, airborne cellular debris from sanding real nails, artificial nails, and calluses with an electric burr.

Problems identified: The salon has not complied with the suggested requirements for ventilation which would have reduced her exposure. Amy is at short and long-term risk for disease.

Clearly there is room for improvement!

Now let's look at an actual situation in a real nail salon. This is where the title of this book comes from. This is truly a case of *Death by Pedicure.*

Chapter 4

Death of Kimberly Jackson and Jessica Mears- the perfect infections

An opinion by Dr. Robert Spalding

The following information about Kimberly Jackson is compiled from a series of articles by Brad Watson from WFAA TV News Channel 8, Dallas, TX. Additional information regarding Jessica Mears is complied from Alexa Tondreau from The Mountain View Voice, MSNBC.com and CBS5.com in San Jose, California.

On July 5th 2005, Kimberly Jackson didn't know she was going to be an unintended martyr when she directed her wheelchair into the Angel Nails salon owned by Dinh Tran on the 6200 block of McCart Avenue in Fort Worth, Texas. Now as a result of her unfortunate death, a major upheaval in Texas nail salon regulations descended statewide within two weeks. These newly enacted regulations have broad implications affecting the nation's state boards of cosmetology and nail salons across the United States.

Kimberly was a paraplegic a result of an unfortunate injury which created permanent damage to her lower extremities. Due to her inability to trim her own nails, Kimberly, like many other Americans with medical problems, relied on the services of a nail technician instead of a podiatrist to render delicate nail and foot care treatments.

As most people do, Kimberly looked forward to her regular visit to the nail salon. She came into the salon monthly to get relief from her painful foot and nail afflictions. Some paraplegics or others with neuropathy depend upon these services. They are unaware that certain foot and nail conditions can lead to amputations or life threatening infections.

As she had always done for several years, Kimberly rolled her wheelchair up to the foot bath. She then complied with the soaking process to soften her skin in the whirlpool bath while seated in her wheelchair. Suddenly, it was reported that blood appeared on the pumice stone while her foot was in the water. It is unclear whether she was treated with a pumice stone prior to her soaking.

Her close friend and neighbor, Patricia Mathis, stated, "She had said she had gone to get a pedicure and that they were all sitting there talking, and she looked down, and the girl had the pumice stone turned on the corner edge, and she pulled back, and Kim saw blood." Mrs. Mathis said, "She left the salon with an open cut on her foot."   No antiseptic was apparently on hand to treat the wound.

The combination of an alleged injury with a pumice stone on the typically frail, atrophied leg of a paraplegic and bacteria from a potentially improperly maintained whirlpool is a perfect recipe for a disastrous infection. Unfortunately, improperly maintained whirlpools have been linked across the country to a frequent cause of bacterial outbreaks. This case is no exception.

As reported by Brad Watson with Channel 8 News, a doctor and nurse at a JPS network clinic started treating Kimberly Jackson in early August for infected sores on her feet. Her medical records read, "[The] patient thinks these may be related to rubbing during pedicure."

Medical records obtained by News 8 showed that over the next seven months the JPS physician at a clinic treated Jackson for the MRSA *staphylococcal* (staph) infection on her foot from the cut.

MRSA is an aggressive staph bacterium resistant to common antibiotics and is reported to be found sometimes in the water of salon foot spas that are not disinfected properly. The doctor put Jackson on a cocktail of strong oral and intravenous antibiotics. "It got pretty big and she got pretty scared she was going to lose her foot," her friend, Patricia Mathis said.

Unfortunately, the 46 year old Kimberly Jackson died Feb. 12 2006 after seven long months of intensive medical treatment. The JPS Health Network doctor who signed her death certificate listed the cause as a heart attack from a blood infection brought on by a staphylococcal infection on her foot.

Mrs. Mathis filed a complaint with the state after her friend's death, which Mathis and others said they believe was caused after her injured foot was bathed in a whirlpool foot spa. Even after her death, the Angel Nails Salon initially denied even servicing Kimberly. The owner of Angel Nails was absent during the interview with the TV news reporter, but a nail technician who said she worked at the location for two years stated that they don't recall ever seeing Kimberly Jackson and claimed they run a sanitary salon.

"We're very clean here, so I don't think she would get infected," said Kim Chi Do, the Nail technician.

The likelihood that an employee who had been working for an establishment for 24 months had not noticed a highly visible paraplegic who had been getting a pedicure for the same two years is dubious, in this author's opinion.

Jackson's bank records showed she last made a check card purchase at Angel Nails on July 5, 2005, and while state records indicate there are 22 salons named Angel Nails in Texas, there was just one in Fort Worth on McCart Avenue.

In February 2006, following a surprise inspection from Texas Department of Licensing and Regulations (TDLR), state investigators found Angel Nails failed to disinfect tools and implements. There was no hot water in the salon and no antiseptic or disinfectant to stop bleeding from cuts. Also, according to investigators, the salon staff didn't sanitize the whirlpool foot spas that can breed bacteria if not cleaned properly before each customer.

Inspectors returned in April and found Angel Nails still didn't disinfect implements or have a disinfectant and antiseptic on hand to treat cuts. For these violations, the number and nature of them warranted a large penalty. In June 2006, TDLR proposed a fine of $16,500 and a six-month license suspension for Angel Nails. Neither Angel Nails owner, Dinh Tran nor his attorney would return phone calls or e-mails to News 8 for comment, but the owner did tell the news station via e-mail to stop disturbing his business.

In addition to the violations and proposed fine by the state, the family of Kimberly Jackson also filed a lawsuit against the salon. This case was settled out of court for an undisclosed sum this summer only a few months after it was initially filed

Patricia Mathis reflected on the loss of her friend and how her death might've been prevented. "This guy simply didn't do what he was supposed to do, and it didn't have to be this way," she said.

Kimberly husband, David Jackson of Fort Worth, said he still can't believe his wife is gone, and the cause of her death only adds to the agony. He said, "Something so stupid like a pedicure took her life." The Jacksons had previously divorced, and it was during this time Kimberly was shot by her ex-boyfriend. The Jacksons eventually reconciled to raise their boys. David Jackson is now finding it hard being alone.

Kimberly Jackson was the mother of a 17-year-old boy and twin 13-year-old boys. At her funeral, friends and family remembered her as the wife of a man who took care of her after she lost the use of her legs 6 years ago. "It's hard," Jackson said. "Nobody has a clue. I mean everybody can say, 'I can only imagine.' It's hard.... It's real hard."

David Jackson thinks less now about his plumbing business and more about the future of the three teenage boys. "All she lived for was to see these kids get an education, and she knew that would take them through the rest of their lives," Jackson said. Jackson hopes to win a judgment that will support the boys through high school and pay for their college education.

His attorney, Steven Laird, hopes the case sends a message to dirty salons. "Simply follow the rules and regulations," Laird said. "It's for the protection of the salons, but much more so for the protection of the public, so that a family never has to go through something like this again."

Outcome

Everything about this tragic death was wrong. It serves as a beacon for patrons of nail salons in the US and around the world. Regulations were grossly violated. In my opinion, the number one mistake, before the first instrument was used, was the fact that Kimberly Jackson should not have been treated in a nail salon without written permission from her doctor.

Many services are preformed in nail salons on individuals with certain medical problems. These people should not patronize these establishments without the written permission of a physician who is closely monitoring their care. Regulations in Tennessee stipulate that written permission from a physician must be obtained before clients with skin diseases or lesions can receive services from nail techs. Unfortunately these regulations are not being enforced.

In my opinion, skin diseases could imply loss of surface tissue integrity as a result of diabetes, neuropathy, or vascular problems. Routinely, every week, I also see patients walk into my office with nail fungus, athletes foot other foot/skin/nail infections in those who have just recently received the services of a nail tech.

Physicians nationwide are failing to get a history of these services with their patient population. Each treating physician should develop a referral protocol for patients with significant foot problems from having their nails trimmed in nail salons.

With the exception of Texas, many state boards of cosmetology across the nation have rag-tagged, mis-matched or even absent regulations to protect their citizens. The 28 states that have no laws against callus cutters are a perfect example. Also, there has been a historical resistance to sterilization because these states feel current disinfection protocol is sufficient. This is due to the fact nail technicians are not supposed to be working on medical problems or in situations that produce a blood field.

However, a significant problem exists like in the case of Angel Nails where existing disinfection rules are not being followed. Disinfection soaking times with intermediate liquids like 70% alcohol are almost impossible to monitor effectively. The minimum 10 minute soaking time is sometimes short changed. Disinfection regulations are not effective unless the solutions are changed on a daily basis. Disinfection times have to be extended if the pre-cleaning or proper sanitation brushing with soap and water are improperly performed. Unfortunately, not every salon follows this protocol.

When individuals without proper medical training and experience perform these services, regrettable issues can result as in the case of Kimberly Jackson.

Several other remedies can be instituted by state cosmetology boards who have been following this Texas scenario. One issue is particularly important. The state boards of cosmetology should not be using the word "treatment" in the cosmetology regulations without mentioning the fact that the word treatment specifically excludes medical treatment.

Additionally, most of the state boards do not have physicians on their boards as consultants nor seek the guidance of physicians to review health citations commonly found in salons. When individuals without proper medical training and experience perform these services, regrettable issues can result.

Most importantly, the state of Texas legislature and TDRL (Texas Department of Professional Licensing) should be highly commended for stepping up to the plate with this surprisingly unprecedented and meaningful self-regulated action.

Every tragedy or death should peel back a silver lining in the form of awareness. In this case, the sweeping new regulations implemented in Texas that may be adopted by other states should be named after Kimberly Jackson, in my opinion. My sincere condolences go out to the family of Kimberly Jackson. I hope they find that from her death comes direction for other states to improve conditions. Hopefully, this will be accomplished as quickly as Texas has recognized the need to do so.

To further illustrate another tragic preventable case of a immunocompromised nail salon client being served, I offer the Death of Jessica Mears. Jessica, a client with a medical autoimmune connective tissue disease called Lupus allegedly walked into the Top Hair and Nail Salon (renamed since the original) in San Jose, California in November of 2004 only to be one in a series of 140 victims of infections in 33 salons from multiple improperly disinfected nail salon whirlpools.

Jessica contracted a Mycobacterium infection that caused a deep persistent six inch lesion that did not heal over a period of 2 years. She won a personal injury lawsuit filed by Robert Bohn from the Attorney Firm of Bohn and Bohn (Bohn link, http://www.bohnlaw.com/case11.jsp to other settled salon lawsuits).

Jessica suffered with this non-healing wound for 2 years before her alleged death late June of 2006. Robert Bohn filed a wrongful death suit against Top Hair and Nails Salon August

8th in the Santa Clara County Superior Court. This death adds another specter to what can happen when improperly disinfected whirlpools can concentrate a bacteria common to most municipal water supplies to unsafe levels in combination with clients who shave their legs 24-48 hours prior to receiving salon pedicure services.

The final critique of both of these two incidents also highlights the question as to why any immunocompromised client or individuals with medical problems such as paraplegics, diabetics, or other individuals with serious medical problems should receive any nail salon services without a written physician's permission as should be required in many states.

IMPORTANT NEWS
Third Death Monday, March 26, 2007

SACRAMENTO – An infection contracted from a pedicure may have caused the death of Gerry Ann Schabarum, wife of former state Assemblyman and longtime Los Angeles County Supervisor Pete Schabarum. According to the *Pasadena Weekly*, Schabarum had been battling a staphylococcus infection for more than a year, and because she suffered from rheumatoid arthritis, it was able to take hold in her body.

"It is tragic that another life may have been lost because of an unsanitary nail salon," said Senator Leland Yee (D-San Francisco/San Mateo), the author of legislation signed into law last year to help clean up dirty salons. "While progress has been made to address these outbreaks, clearly more needs to be done to protect the health of nail salon consumers."

http://dist08.casen.govoffice.com/index.asp?Type=B_ PR&SEC=%7BEFA496BC-EDC8-4E38-9CC7-68- D37AC03DFF%7D&DE=%7B74547257-0190-4EFC-A2DF- 138C0092FFD8%7D

Chapter 5
Vital health practices for the consumer

Here we get into the crux of the nail salon problem: transmission of infective organisms from client to client via unclean instruments and equipment. To come to a point of clarity on this issue, we need to expand our definitions of and master the proper usage of the four key words: sterilize, sanitize, disinfect, antiseptic. Confusion about what they mean is a root cause of nail industry problems, particularly the confusion between sterilize and sanitize.

Thanks to the widespread incorrect use of these terms (even dictionary definitions vary), we here use the highest industry standard definitions as set by APIC, the Association for Professionals in Infection Control and Epidemiology (www.apic. org,) and the CDC, Centers for Disease Control. See the APIC brochure Disinfection and Sterilization Principles from which we quote below APIC Disinfection Guidelines (www.guideline. gov/summary/summary.aspx?ss=15&doc_id=2228&nbr=1454) and the CDC's Guidelines for Environmental Infection Control in Health-Care Facilities (www.cdc.gov/ncidod/dhqp/ pdf/guidelines/Enviro_guide_03.pdf) from which we also quote below. The first three terms – *sterilize*, *disinfect*, and *sanitize* – apply only to non-living surfaces. The fourth – *antiseptic* – applies to skin. Only one word – *sterilized* – describes a nail instrument that is 100% free of all infective organisms. Know these terms: *Sterilize, Disinfect, Sanitize*. These are terms that apply to non-living surfaces, such as nail instruments.

Sterilize

To be *sterile* is to be 100% free from living microorganisms. To *sterilize* is to completely destroy all microorganisms on non-living (inanimate) surfaces. The term does not apply to skin. One cannot *sterilize* skin without destroying the skin itself.

APIC's Disinfection and Sterilization Principles states: "The sterilization process completely eliminates or kills all microorganisms, and is done by using sterilizers that provide steam under pressure [as in an autoclave*], ethylene oxide (ETO) and other gases, or by using liquid chemicals for prolonged soaking times. Sterilized items are considered to remain sterile until the package they are in is torn, wet, or damaged. Sterility is a function of intact packaging and time."

*autoclave: A device that sterilizes by steam pressure, usually at 250°F (121°C) for a specified length of time. Every item in an autoclave is in a package that maintains its sterility until the package is opened.

Disinfect

Bear with us as we go more deeply into information that clarifies our understanding of what it takes to *disinfect/sterilize* nail equipment. It's important. This knowledge will make you a savvy consumer, an educated nail tech, an enlightened salon owner, and will encourage the industry to use medically accurate language. In the extreme, it could save your life; short of extreme, it could save you from infection; and at the very least, you'll be awake and aware of what's going on in the next nail salon you visit.

It is very important for the consumer to know that if nail techs would follow proper disinfection techniques, the risk of infections would be lower. This continues to be a factor in nail salons.

From APIC: *Microbes* – Different types of microorganisms vary in how easy they are killed by disinfectants. Some are very hard to kill with disinfectants, while others can easily be killed by many disinfectants and even soaps. This list of microorganisms starts with the hardest to kill and ends with the easiest to kill:

- Bacterial spores*: *Bacillus subtilis*
- Mycobacteria: M *tuberculosis*
- Non-lipid or small viruses: Polio virus, Hepatitis A virus
- Fungi: Aspergillus
- Vegetative Bacteria**: *Pseudomonas Staphylococcus aureus*
- Lipid or Medium-Sized Viruses: Herpes simplex virus, Hepatitis B virus, Human immunodeficiency virus (HIV).

*Medline Plus: A spore is a reproductive cell produced by plants (fungi, moss, ferns) and some protozoa and bacteria. The spore often fully develops after a state of dormancy or hibernation. Spores have thick walls and are very resistant to high temperatures, humidity, and other unfavorable conditions. Chemical disinfection kills bacteria, but does not destroy their spores. Sterilization destroys spores as well as bacteria, and requires high temperatures and high pressures. In health-care settings, sterilization is usually accomplished using an autoclave.

Remember the other meaning of *sterile*: "unable to reproduce." That's the idea here – rendering spores unable to reproduce. **CDC: Vegetative bacteria are bacteria that are actively growing and metabolizing.

Knowledge of this hierarchy – of easier, harder, hardest to kill microorganisms – will allow us to understand the hierarchy of measures needed – *cleaning, disinfection, sterilization* – to free nail-tech instruments of microorganisms.

Process Definitions from the CDC

Cleaning: removing all foreign material (i.e., dirt, body fluids) from objects by using water and detergents or soaps, and washing or scrubbing the object. Cleaning must be done before any disinfection or sterilization process so the foreign material will not keep the process from working.

Disinfection is a process that eliminates many or all microorganisms except spores, and is done with liquid chemicals or by pasteurizing objects. For the process to work, proper contact time and dilution of the disinfectant must be followed.

High-level disinfection can be expected to destroy all microorganisms, with the exception of high numbers of bacterial spores.

Intermediate disinfection inactivates M. tuberculosis, vegetative bacteria, most viruses, and most fungi, but it does not necessarily kill bacterial spores.

Low-level disinfection can kill most bacteria, some viruses, and some fungi, but it cannot be relied on to kill resistant microorganisms (e.g., M. tuberculosis or bacterial spores).

Environmental Cleaning

Environmental surfaces, such as bedside tables [read nail tech tables], are usually not sources of infection. However, when infective substances are on them, they could be a source of contamination to hands or objects that may have contact with a patient. Therefore, environmental surfaces should be cleaned regularly with an Environmental Protection Agency (EPA) approved hospital disinfectant.

Types of Disinfectants

Disinfectants and their use in a nail salon setting. Definitons by Wikipedia.

Disinfectants are chemical substances used to destroy viruses and microbes (germs), such as bacteria and fungi. The ideal disinfectant would offer complete sterilization, without harming other forms of life, be inexpensive, and non-corrosive. Unfortunately ideal disinfectants do not exist. Many disinfectants are only able to partially sterilize. The most resistant pathogens are bacteria spores but some viruses and bacteria are also highly resistant to many disinfectants. All disinfectants in nail salons must be EPA registered to kill bacteria (including M.tuberculosis), fungi, and viruses.

• *Alcohol* – Usually ethanol or isopropanol – Considered a low to moderate disinfectant. Wiped over benches and skin and allowed to evaporate for quick disinfection. Alcohols are more effective combined with water, 70% alcohol is more active than 95% alcohol. Alcohol is not effective against bacterial spores and must be changed daily. Common in salons.

• *Phenol and other phenolics* – The active ingredient in most bottles of "household disinfectant". Phenol is probably the oldest disinfectant (used by D. Joseph Lister, the father of Modern Sterilization) and was called carbolic acid in the early days of antiseptics. Phenol is rather corrosive to the skin and sometimes toxic to sensitive people, so the somewhat less corrosive substitute phenolic o-phenylphenol is often used as part of a disinfectant formula.

• *Quaternary ammonium salts* (quats) – such as benzalkonium chloride are a large group of related compounds. Some have been used as a low level disinfectant. They are effective against bacteria, but not against spores or some viruses.

• *Gluteraldehyde* – Is one of the highest level disinfectant liquid chemicals available. It is capable of destroying bacterial spores with proper contact time. Gluteraldehyde is not generally used in salons due to the need for precautions compared to other disinfectants.

Relative effectiveness of disinfectants

One way to compare disinfectants is to compare how well they do against a known disinfectant and rate them accordingly. Phenol is the standard, and the corresponding rating system is called the "Phenol coefficient." The disinfectant to be tested is compared with phenol on a standard microbe (usually *Salmonella typhi* or *Staphylococcus aureus*). Disinfectants that are more effective than phenol have a coefficient > 1. Those that are less effective have a coefficient < 1.

Sanitize

Basically, the word *sanitize* means "to clean." Usually this involves brushing instruments or surfaces with soap and water. Getting to a bedrock definition of *sanitize* is challenging. Stedman's Medical Dictionary defines *sanitary* as healthful; conducive to health; usually in reference to a clean environment, and sanitation as use of measures designed to promote health and prevent disease. The CDC defines sanitizer as an agent that reduces microbial contamination to safe levels as judged by public health standards or requirements. Merriam Webster defines *sanitary* as of or relating to health; characterized by or readily kept in cleanliness, and *sanitize* as to make sanitary (as by cleaning or sterilization). Taber's Cyclopedic Medical Dictionary defines *sanitize* as to make sanitary; to inactivate or remove microorganisms from equipment and surfaces, and adds that chemicals, heat, and ionizing radiation can be used for this purpose.

A microbiologist at APIC explained that professionals in the scientific community (of disease control and epidemiology) do not use the word *sanitize*. Sanitize, they say, is considered more a layperson's or a marketing term: professionals in the field use the terms *clean*, *disinfect*, and *sterilize* to describe how microbe-free an object is.

*All proper disinfection and proper sterilization protocols must start with proper cleaning (sanitization) to remove all visible debris. A problem may occur when this visible debris is not noticed due to poor eyesight, or the sanitation step is overlooked.

Antiseptic: A term that applies to living surfaces, such as skin. An *antiseptic* is a substance that prevents or stops the growth of microorganisms on skin surfaces without damaging or irritating living tissue, such as various soaps in bar or liquid form.

Dictionary *antiseptic*: Relating to antisepsis; an agent capable of producing antisepsis. Sepsis [Greek, putrefaction] A systemic inflammatory response to infection, in which there is fever or hypothermia, tachycardia, tachypnea, and evidence of inadequate blood flow to internal organs. The syndrome is a common cause of death in critically ill patients. Pathogenic organisms, including bacteria, mycobacteria, fungi, protozoa, and viruses may initiate the cascade of inflammatory reactions that constitute sepsis. The number of patients with sepsis has increased significantly in the last 25 years, as a result of several factors including: aging of the population, increased number of patients living with immune suppressing illnesses and multiple diseases, and increased use of invasive or indwelling devices in health care that serve as portals of entry for infection.

FIGURE. Decreasing order of resistance of microorganisms to germicidal chemicals

Source: Adapted from Bond WW, Ott 3J, Franke K, McCracken JE. Effective use of liquid chemical germicides on medical devices; instrument design problems. In: Block SS. ed. Disinfection sterilization and preservation. 4th ed. Philadelphia, PA: Lea & Gebger, 1991: 100.

Here recall the lady in Texas who died after exposure to microorganisms in a pedicure whirlpool bath. Immune-compromised, her body's immune system was not strong enough to overcome a drug-resistant strain of bacteria.

When challenged, the body's immune system mounts a variety of defenses, such as white blood cells and the antibodies they produce. Sometimes this battle goes on without our conscious awareness. Other times we can feel and appear quite ill while our immune system battles with the microorganisms.

The intention of this book is to prevent exposure to microorganisms in the first place.

Discussion

Nail technicians like Amy are neither schooled nor licensed to work in the presence of blood or to maintain a surgically sterile environment. They are not medical professionals. The standards for keeping instruments used by beauty industry technicians free from bacteria, virus, and fungal microorganisms have historically been more relaxed. There has been no requirement until recently by the State of Texas to sterilize, only to properly sanitize and disinfect. And as we have just seen, there is no consensus on what sanitize means. Even state cosmetology boards confuse the term *sanitize* with *disinfect* or *sterilize* in their own state regulations.

Additionally, all rules that govern disinfection with the state boards have, historically, applied only to normal nails and intact skin. We have seen in one day's worth of Amy's clients that people do come in with medical conditions (hepatitis C, diabetes), non-normal nails (fungal nails), and broken skin (split cuticles, newly shaven legs). We know as well that nail techs are at times inattentive to proper protocol, occasionally break skin with their instruments, and often exercise poor judgment in terms of whom they accept as clients.

The argument that exact proper sanitation and disinfection is effective in removing 99.9% bacteria of the time is true most of the time. Proper disinfection protocol is effective if followed exactly. The problem arises when sanitiation and disinfection steps are shortcut. Professional disciplinary boards demonstrate this fact monthly in nearly every state cosmetology board's violation hearings.

The main advantage that favors sterilization over disinfection occurs when proper protocol is broken and visible debris is not effectively removed from instruments. Soaking instruments in low and intermediate disinfectants becomes ineffective with higher debris loads. Whereas, autoclaves using steam under pressure can effectively destroy bacteria even in visible debris fields per the same unit of time for normal disinfection or sterilization protocols. In other words, if a mistake is made and visible debris is accidentally not removed or the sanitation step is skipped, sterilization favors disinfection in these instances. This is one reason the State of Texas went to sterilization and that sterilization is the benchmark for medical offices.

Sterilization steps can be also shortcut. Sterilization pouches that instruments are packaged in and autoclaved can have instruments that are sealed without being sterilized. But the heat activated color indicator on the sterilization pouch will determine if the pouch has been in a sterilizer. State inspectors and salon owners can readily check this package indicator to make sure the public is protected.

Given the inevitability of situations ripe for transmission of infection, the correct response is sterilization, the 100 percent solution. A nail salon manager who requires all technicians to use disposable liners in their whirlpool baths and clean and autoclave all instruments all of the time, could step out of the current fog of confusion into the clear air of correctness.

With the advent of drug-resistant strains of all of the following organisms HIV and staph, hepatitis A, B, and C, bacterial infections, and fungal and viral organisms, things have changed. The change is global. A new history is being written.

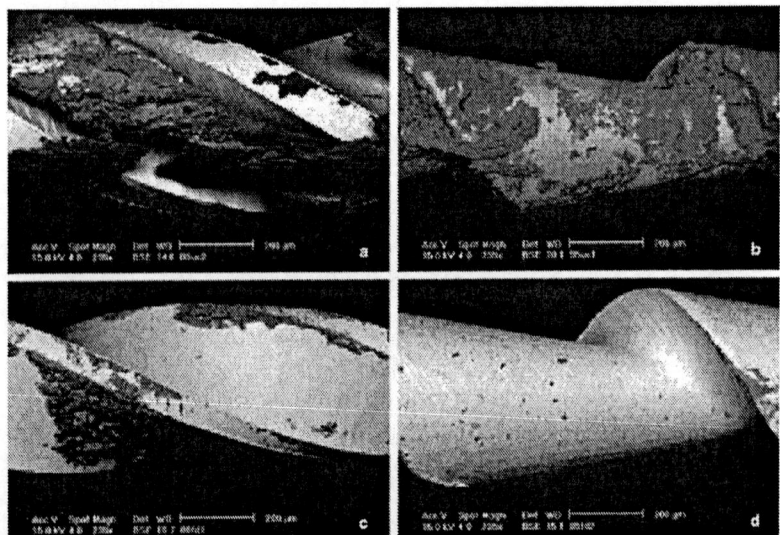

Fig 4a. Scanning electron micrograph of incomplete bioburden removal from a GT 0.08 taper file after cleaning by ultrasonication with a container. 4b. Scanning electron micrograph of a Hedström ISO size 35 file after cleaning by ultrasonication with a container. 4c. Scanning electron micrograph of incomplete bioburden removal from a GT 0.06 file after cleaning by a thermal disinfector. 4d. Scanning electron micrograph of a Hedström ISO size 35 file after cleaning by a thermal disinfector.

The top two photographs, above, show incomplete bioburden removal by ultrasonic cleaning. The two on the bottom show cleaning by a thermal disinfector.

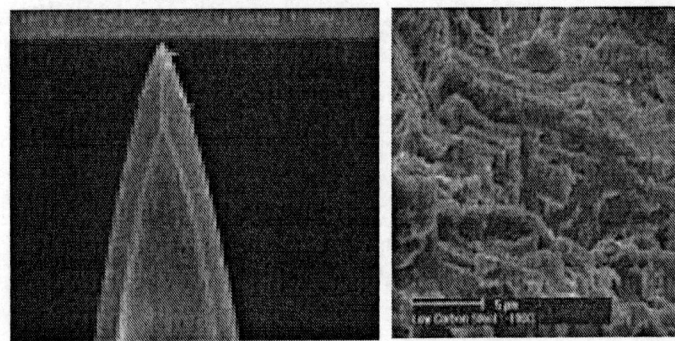

Electron microscopic view of cutting edge of low carbon surgical steel instrument/needle

Electron microscopic view of pitted surfaces of a "smooth" low carbon surgical steel instrument, demonstrating recesses where bacteria can adhere.

A SEM evaluation of debris removal from endodontic files after cleanign and steam sterilization procedures. Australian Dental Journal 2004;49:(3): 128-135 DA Van Eldik, * PS Zilm, ** AH Rogers, ***PD Marin

Chapter 6

The salon industry in perspective

Here are some important players and terms used in and by the beauty industry.

Nail Industry: The term "nail industry" as used in this book refers to a broad range of entities that have to do with regulation, instruction, licensing, certification, and continuing education. Also included are manufacturers and suppliers of nail products, magazines, and beauty trade shows. The industry interfaces directly with the public in nail, beauty, and hair salons, in spas and massage therapy businesses, and one-on-one with individual licensed nail technicians and cosmetologists.

Regulation: State cosmetology boards regulate beauty schools, the practice of cosmetologists, manicurists/nail technicians, and aestheticians. The boards provide training guidelines, certification, scope of practice, sanitation guidelines, and enforcement of regulations. The boards regulate all continuing education credits (CEUs), fines, and salon inspections.

Cosmetologist: By state definition, a *cosmetologist* performs, for compensation, arranging, dressing, curling, waving, cleansing, cutting, singeing, bleaching, coloring, or similar work on the hair. A cosmetologist may care for or service wigs or hair pieces; manicure; massage, clean, stimulate, manipulate, exercise, beautify or perform similar work upon the hands, arms, face, neck, or feet with hands or by use of cosmetic preparations, tonics, lotions or creams; place or apply artificial eyelashes, give facials, apply makeup, give skin care, or remove superfluous hair by tweezing, depilatories, or waxing.

My definition of *cosmetologist:* A licensed individual who performs beauty services to the hands, feet, face, and hair that include the application of artificial nails and facial makeup, cutting of nails and hair, smoothing and exfoliation of dead skin, and the massaging of hands and feet.

Manicurist (Nail Technician, Nail Tech): By state definition, a person who manicures or pedicures the nails of any person, or performs nail artistry.

My definition of *manicurist:* A licensed individual who performs beauty services to the hands and feet only, which includes the application of artificial nails, cutting and manicuring of nails and hair, smoothing and exfoliation of dead skin and the massaging of hands and feet.

The following is quoted from *NAILS magazine:*
"Six billion beauty customers have been served from 2004 to 2006. There are 125,000 nail salons in the US based on 1996 statistics from an Associated Press article. *NAILS* magazine reports that in 2005 there are 380, 000 licensed nail technicians in the

US. (A New York Times 2005 article reports that the number of nail techs in the US is 400,000 and the number of nail salons is 90,000.) Many of these hair salons have nail techs who also do also do nail services and enhancements. Nail magazine reports that there are 57,000 licensed nail salons in the US. Many are operated by minorities and new arrivals of Asian American immigrants.

"James Casteel, vice president of Amerispa LLC, a Rancho Cordova, Calif.-based manufacturer of pedicure thrones, estimates that 55% of his company's sales go to Vietnamese-owned nail salons. The number is significant even when taking into account NAILS' estimate that 38% of America's nail techs are Vietnamese. The estimated business associated with the nail industry in 2006 is about $6.43 billion dollars according to NAILS magazine. This figure is down from the previous year in 2004 where the industry made $6.8 billion. [Perhaps all the negative pedicure 'throne' chair news stories, sanitation issues and the variations in the economy have hurt the nail business.]

"Anyone, including newly arrived immigrants to this country can complete nail tech's training in less than 3-6 months depending how accelerated the program is. This immigrant worker, no matter how recently arrived in the United States, can be well on their way to earning a respectable income. A recent industry wide survey published in NAILS magazine listed manicurists' average income as $482 a week. Generally speaking, workers appear to be on their own once they get their license."

Aesthetician: By state definition, an *aesthetician* does one or more of the following; massage, clean, stimulate, manipulate, exercise, beautify, or perform similar work with hands or mechanical or electrical apparatus or by use of cosmetic preparations, tonics, lotions or creams; places or applies artificial eyelashes, does facials, applies makeup, provides skin care or removes superfluous hair by tweezing, depilatories, or waxing.

Schools: Schools are licensed by each state.

Qualifications of applicants: State qualifications vary from being at least 16 years of age, to having a tenth-grade education, a GED, or a high school diploma.

Training: Nationwide required hours for training programs, on average, are: Cosmetologist 1,600 hours, Nail tech 300 - 600 hours, Aesthetician 600 hours. A typical 600-hour nail technician curriculum looks like this:

• 150 hours of instruction on sterilization, sanitation, bacteriology, anatomy, physiology, ethics, salon management, and state law.

• 100 hours of chemical instruction on product knowledge, ingredients and usage of materials, manicuring, pedicuring, and EPA and OSHA requirements.

• 350 hours of physical instruction on massage, manicuring, pedicuring, nail care, nail artistry, nail wraps, sculptured nails, nail tips, gel nails, and nail safety.

Legal places of business: Every salon or business location where nail techs and cosmetologists provide their services must have a separate posted license near the cash register. Every nail tech and cosmetologist must post an individual license near his or her workstation.

State legislature: The state legislature gets involved when the cosmetology board members are unable to make a decision regarding trade, commerce, and livelihood of cosmetologists, nail technicians, and aestheticians. The board will defer to the state legislature or the attorney general's office, as happened in Texas February 2006 with the pedicure death of Kimberly Jackson. (See Chapter 4: "Death of Kimberly Jackson.")

Commerce department: The commerce department may become involved in the cosmetology regulations when new cosmetology laws unfairly restrict free trade.

Involved Medical Community: Podiatrists, dermatologists, family physicians, emergency room doctors, and surgeons become involved when they provide advice and medical care to clients who contract infections from contaminated instruments or equipment during nail salon services.

Podiatrists: Podiatrists specialize in medicine and surgery on the foot and ankle. They attend four years of podiatric medical school and must complete a residency to practice. In some states, a podiatrist's scope of practice includes the hands. Podiatrists prescribe medicine and perform surgery in private clinics or hospitals. They are experts in foot and ankle emergencies, all medical conditions and infections of the foot, wound care, diabetic foot care, and in all types of nail care, such as fungal and bacterial infections and hangnails.

Manufacturers: Manufactures or suppliers of nail products such as acrylic nails, throne chairs, ultraviolet light boxes, callous blades, nail nippers, electric nail files, nail polish, disinfectants, sanitizers, autoclave sterilizers, textbook publishers such as Milady Press, and more.

Beauty and Trade Shows: These venues promote the products and trends of the business and keep the industry vibrant

Trade Magazines: NAILS *magazine*, *Nailpro*, and *Salon* magazines provide information and education, and are progressive forums for discussion of new, interesting, and controversial issues facing the nail industry.

Consultants, Educators, Industry spokespersons: Nail technician educators crisscross the globe keeping interested nail techs current with better techniques and providing continuing education credit courses. Consultants, state salon inspectors, and industry spokespersons keep additional nail salon personnel informed about proper disinfection techniques.

Lawyers: Lawyers represent persons who have had unpleasant medical outcomes resulting from poor sanitation techniques.

Water department: Whirlpool footbaths, for example, are filled with city water, which may or may not be free of microbes. Some city water is unsafe for those with compromised immune function.

Health department: The health department gets involved when it responds to complaints that even supposedly clean water is contaminated, and when the design of and maintenance of whirlpools are in question.

Consumers: In the millions.

Industry giants

According to *Business Report* newsletter, Charlie Ton is the King of nail salons in the US with over 900, and growing by a rate of 3 per week. Many of these franchised nail salons are in hundreds of Wal-Marts across the nation. He additionally owns Alfalfa Nail Supply which make nail tips for nail polish brushes and manufactures whirlpool pedicure foot baths. Add this to the huge Regal nail salon franchise, and you have an empire. Ton apparently operates his empire from six buildings in Baton Rouge's industrial district.

"Wal-Mart builds roughly 225 stores per year, and we get in more than half of those with nail salons. ...We expect to add 125 stores per year," according to *Business Report*.

Ton has 10,000 nail supply customers and the Regal Nails franchise which market his nail salons that some are seen selling on the market for roughly $50,000 apiece, putting the total market value of the salons at more than $35 million, states *Business Report*.

Mr. Ton's salon foot bath manufacturing business improves profit margins by using quiet motors and in house assembly to lower cost of production by 33%. In Ton's businesses, Alfalfa buys the parts for the foot bath and assembles them on site, then marks them up for retail, improving its profit margin by 50%.

http://www.businessreport.com/newsDetail.cfm?aid=63

(See the corporate letter from Charlie ton in Chapter 26.) However, 10 states nationwide that have Internet state professional board disciplinary posting of nail salon violations report that Regal Nails have had MMA violations, infections, and owner license violations.

Organizations and associations:

ABA: American Beauty Association, renamed PBA below

APIC: Association for Professionals in Infection Control and Epidemiology, http://www.apic.org

CND: Council for Nail Disorders. www.nailcouncil.org

CIR: Cosmetic Ingredient Review Panel   www.cir-safety.org

EPA: Environmental Protection Association www.epa.gov

FDA: Food and Drug Administration. www.fda.gov

INTA: International Nail Technicians Association www.chicagomidwestbeautyshow.com/MEMBERSHIP/International

IPA: International Pedicure Association www.pedicureassociation.org

NIC National Interstate Council of State Boards of Cosmetology www.nictesting.org/

NIOSH: U.S. National Institute for Occupational Safety and Health. www.cdc.gov/niosh/homepage.html

NMC: Nail Manufacturing Council. www.probeauty.org.

PBA: Professional Beauty Association. www.probeauty.org

Chapter 7

Salon industry trade shows

Premier Beauty Show, Orlando, Florida, August 2000.

My involvement in the beauty industry began shortly after I established a podiatry practice in Chattanooga, Tennessee in the summer of 1998. After seeing a void of good inexpensive foot care products, I developed a proprietary line of foot care products – "Heel Pain Relief," a topical analgesic/counterirritant crème; "Cracked Heel Relief," a combination urea/lactic acid crème for cracked dry skin; and "Just for Toenails," a nail polish with tea tree oil – and marketed them on my website, in other podiatry offices, and in drugstores via a sales rep.

Through websites (beautytech.com) and the internet, I spoke with owners of beauty salons, cosmetologists, and nail technicians about my products. At the same time with phone calls and e-mails I provided information about my products. These nail professionals in turn approached me in my capacity as a medical professional about the medical problems they were dealing with in their work.

After seeing all the medical problems in the nail salon industry first hand, I started asking questions about where I could get more information about nail salons. One of my patients was a nail tech. She suggested I contact beauty schools to speak to their students about medical problems that could be seen in nail salons.

I was asked by these nail salon owners to speak at beauty schools and beauty seminars. Through these venues I was able to inform interested individuals about how to recognize foot care problems and how to care for the medical issues that surface unbidden in nails alone.

As I began to lecture, ask questions and learn about this industry, I was at the same time seeing patients in my practice who had visited these salons. I found my patients related some mixed experiences with nail salons. Many contracted nail fungus and/or infection from ingrown toenails as a result of visiting local salons. In these cases, either the clients had ingrown nails and the nail techs would work on them against established regulations, or the nails became infected from trimming the nails too close in corners or cutting them past the "quick" or hyponychium.

In 1999, I requested the current version of the rules, regulations and licensing requirements for nail technicians in the state of Tennessee. I studied their rules and sanitation requirements carefully. More and more patients with fungal bacterial infections came to my office with a history of going to nail salons. I became more concerned with the then current state of sanitation, with nail salon whirlpool designs, and with the use of Credo blades .

As I spoke to local audiences, these issues became primary lecture topics, and I began to show pictures of infections and amputations I had encountered in my practice. That same year, 1999, I was asked to speak at the Orlando Premier beauty show regarding medical foot problems found in nail salons. Unfortunately, that year I was unable to attend.

Karol Singleton and Athena Elliot were the first two nail techs I corresponded with on the internet regarding nail infections. They both invited me to lecture at a large beauty conference in Orlando, Florida, in August of 2000.

Karol Singleton told me she had organized a yearly gathering of the nail techs, and that Orlando was the place to be to meet nail techs who were top in the industry. Karol, also a nail tech, hosted a yearly sideline international nail conference breakfast that coincided with the larger Premier Beauty Show in Orlando. Her intent was to meet and introduce nail techs n an effort to improve the industry worldwide. She hoped they could address the industry's problems in a forum over the next three days.

My invitation to speak at this conference was a result of my being outspoken about problems in the nail industry. I basically discussed what needed to be changed to avoid the medical problems I was seeing in my practice: Upon arrival, I was impressed with meeting nail technicians from all over the country, many of whom I had been advising over the Internet. I was also curious to see what these beauty trade events were all about.

In addition to being asked to speak about medical problems to interested nail techs, I was invited to appear with a panel for a local TV affiliate conducting interviews about issues in nail salons. Someone thought it would be good to get a physician experienced with foot care to comment regarding the medical perspective on the nail industry.

If you have never been to one of these beauty shows, I highly suggest you find a way to befriend a nail tech and attend. The Orlando show is a very expensive beauty expo, and there are some very colorful booths. A number of beauty manufactures make large investments in their booth displays and staffing. (See picture page 158.) The shows hosts contests on apply-ing artificial nails; there are nail product demonstrations; and a galaxy of beautiful models occupying booths and demonstrating other products.

When it was time for the television panel, I was ushered to a private room where TV cameras were set up in front of several long tables. Nail techs from around the country were already seated. The lights from the camera came up, and I found myself sitting in the middle of the nail techs.

I did not have a prepared text or know what the line of questions was going to be. As I listened for several minutes to the conversations with the moderator, I suddenly realized why I was asked to be there. All questions were seemingly staged to support the industry. I felt my presence there was to show my "tacit" support.

Having formed this opinion, I interrupted and began to list the top ten things that needed to change. I probably made a few people uncomfortable with what I said. Suddenly, the cam-era lights shut down. I don't know what got filmed or how it was edited. I never saw the final cut.

I was approached by several nail techs after the panel/ press event. These nail techs wanted to find out more about my suggestions for the industry. We talked at a dinner held later that night at Walt Disney World. They shared horror stories about Credo blades, and I told them I was going to talk more about these problems in my seminar.

They were surprised I was even there, and they were happy that I had mentioned several issues like sterilization and disinfection on the TV panel. These nail techs were relating their own fears about the industry and gave me even more rea-sons to be concerned. I found these first face-to-face series of conversations very helpful. That first trip to Orlando solidified my understanding of this industry and where the focus of my involvement should lie.

The next morning at the beauty show exhibit hall there were a few other medical doctors who were lecturing. These physicians mainly talked about skin and hair related issues. A few were showing "cold" lasers for reducing spider veins and demonstrating microdermal abrasion units for exfoliation therapy. There were also several sideline lectures on fungal nail products that were directed for sale in nail salons and designed to be dispensed by nail techs.

One humorous episode occurred. I attended a "private" lecture series given by a company that sold Varisi nail treatment. Their booth exhibit banner made some powerful claims, and the booth operator made verbal claims about how safe and effective this treatment was in treating nail fungus and the "greenies." I was encouraged to hear more information on this product, so I left the exhibit floor and went to a private room away from their exhibit booth.

I listened as this individual remarked that the Varisi product was so safe he would drink it in front of people. He looked around saying, "I'm not supposed to do this because my boss would get mad," but he turned that little blue bottle up and swallowed it in front of 70 people or so. Everyone was silent.

After the lecture, we were given additional information on how we could be distributors. I went up to the podium after the marketing pitch was over and asked him to name some ingredients in his formula, He told me it was a secret, but if I ordered a case he would see what he could do. I asked for any proof that this product worked. He said he had hundreds of testimonials and that if I gave him my name he would send me some "proof."   He then passed out some additional literature. I never did get any "proof" even though I did give him my business card. The experience reminded me of a modern day snake oil salesman.

In my opinion, his product is a perfect example of deceptive marketing on the general public, FDA misbranding, and is very misleading. Diabetics with serious nail infections may purchase this product from nail techs who dispense this in their salons, and could suffer from a more serious infection by delaying proper medical treatment.

After the Beauty Show in 2000, I encountered a series of unfortunate medical nail events. These experiences confirmed several issues I had spoken about in my seminar.

First, only a few weeks after the Premier Beauty Show, the Watsonville pedicure disaster in California occurred during September 2000. This incident infected the extremities of 110 people and really brought focus on the topic of the nail salon industry. This was very interesting and timely, and I was now ready with a new topic for the next year at the beauty show. I called the Santa Clara office of public health and spoke to a Dr. McNutt. He relayed basic information about these infections over the phone. Dr. McNutt then faxed me a press release from his office regarding this "new" problem that had surfaced. The release was very informative about the mycobacterium that was responsible for this outbreak.

Second, a series of outbreaks of the same organism occurred in 2003 and 2004. That incident affected over 140 people in San Jose, California.

Next, in 2005, Paula Abdul's bacterial infection from a manicure made national news. In February 2006, a death occurred in Texas from a MRSA staph infection. Shortly thereafter, two more cases of *Mycobacterium fortuitum* showed up in Spartanburg, South Carolina, and there had been two other *Mycobacterium* cases in Atlanta, Georgia in 2004. The infections have plateaued since the publishing of this book, until the recent *Mycobacterium* death of Jessica Mears in June of 2006.

Interestingly enough, even though I was told no one has ever contracted a viral infection in a nail salon, I found out through a May 2002 ABC News announcement of a judgment for 3.2 million dollars, that the first known recorded viral infection from a manicure was a herpes infection (*herpetic whitlow*) in 1998 in Aurora, Colorado.

Chapter 8

Violations at the Tennessee Board of Cosmetology

I had been lecturing to beauty schools and trade shows as a guest of the Nail Tech industry for about three years-before I made a request to speak with the Tennessee Board of Cosmetology in the spring of 2002 as a physician. I talked to the staff attorney representing the Tennessee Cosmetology Board, Sandra James, and was surprised to find out that she was as concerned about sanitation and Credo blades as I was. She said she needed some medical support to bring the issues up with the Board. She invited me to appear, and we finally arranged a November meeting.

I was slated to talk to the Board in a state office building a couple of blocks from the state capital in Nashville. I got there at 8:00 am for the 9:00 am meeting. Once past security, I found the conference room and sat in the first row to watch the proceedings. The agenda started with a discussion about the

Tennessee Department of Commerce representative, who had been invited to discuss the issue of reducing the difficulty of the nail technician's licensing exams. Apparently, many cosmetology schools had become concerned about the level of difficulty of the cosmetology exams. The owners and operators of the beauty schools claimed that the exams were too tough. They wanted the Cosmetology Board to cancel the existing testing exam contract and to hire a different testing company so more students could pass the exam.

It crossed my mind that this was an attempt on the part of beauty schools to legitimize less stringent exams. The result would allow more students to pass, and the schools would, therefore, not lose federal Pell grants or loans that financed some students' training.

What happened minutes later shed light on why we are having so much trouble passing these students – and it's not the difficulty of the tests. The board had asked that I wait to speak so they could start violation hearings, and I was therefore present for those proceedings. About a dozen nail techs, salon owners, and beauty school operators had been cited for a large list of violations. Several of the nail techs appeared to be Asian. One brought a friend to interpret the board's questions since she spoke minimal broken English. This Asian nail tech had been accused of having another person take the licensing exam for her. Following are the Cosmetology Board minutes from the November 4, 2002 meeting.

"Appearing before the board: Bich Ngoc Nguyen Nashville, TN – Present – Ms. Griffin received an incident report from 'Experior' [a testing company] on someone trying to test for a candidate in Nashville. The report stated a person came in the testing center to retake the manicure theory. Ms. Nguyen presented an ID that the office manager and Ms. Johnson from 'Experior' felt was not the person in the ID. The report stated this candidate had tested several times, so they pulled all her answer sheets. The handwriting on the most recent answer sheet was different from all the other sheets. Ms. Nguyen presented the board with her identification. Ms. Nguyen wasn't able to understand the board, and had someone speak for her. Ms. Nguyen attended school at Lyle's Middle Tennessee School of Cosmetology. The board is concerned about Ms. Nguyen attending the school when she can't speak English well.

"MOTION was made by Ms. Kathy Rochelle and seconded by Ms. Frankie Eaves Pratt to have the owner of Lyle's Middle Tennessee School of Cosmetology appear before the board with Ms. Nguyen at the next meeting. Motion carried unanimously."

After this complaint was heard before the board, there remained fourteen other nail techs/cosmetologists in violation of state cosmetology regulations. Some were practicing without a license. Some salon operators were cited for having sanitation violations, dirty towels present, not posting information, and allowing unapproved persons to perform beauty services in a work area.

The board handed out $300 to $1000 dollar fines for almost every violation.

Again, it struck me that if these people could not understand simple questions from the board, how could they read labels, understand sanitation laws, or even deal with the public? The answer is obvious. They can't. And no amount of reducing the difficulty of tests will help these individuals. For nail techs who speak English, the tests should be hard enough to prevent anyone from acquiring a license without merit – not to simply churn out poorly trained individuals to flood the market ostensibly to create more jobs.

Finally, the individual from the Tennessee Commerce Dept. showed up. Basically, he was brought in on behalf of the beauty schools. The school operators were making the argument that the more difficult exams were interfering with the trade and commerce of these hopeful nail students and preventing them from starting a business to pay back their loans.

The board voted to recess for lunch and asked if I would come back at one o'clock to speak.

I said, "Yes."

I didn't want to waste my entire day. I also didn't want to let the board off the hook by not hearing my statement about sanitation laws that desperately needed changing. While I wished I had not let them talk me into waiting, viewed in retrospect, I learned valuable information and saw even more about the salon industry that needed correction.

At 1:30, I gave my speech about foot-related medical conditions resulting from nail salon treatments. I delivered case studies about artificial nail problems, told the board about the Watsonville California whirlpool outbreak information, and finally discussed the top ten things that needed changing in the industry. The board thanked me for coming to Nashville. I drove home to Chattanooga, and a week later called Sandra James. She told me that the board had approved a ban on Credo blades and that she would fax a copy.

It reads as follows:

From Sandra A. James, Staff Attorney, Tennessee Board of Cosmetology

Date: November 14, 2002

At its meeting on November 4, 2002, the Tennessee Board of Cosmetology voted to ban the use of sharp blades to remove calluses or dead skin.

The board has been informed by numerous physicians and their board that this procedure should be performed by a medical professional.

Failure to comply with this policy will be considered a violation of Tenn. Code Ann. 62-4-127(5), which states your license may be suspended or revoked for unlawful invasion of the field of practice of any profession.

There in print was the ban and it was being enforced!

Then, about six months later, a nail tech I know told me the board had reversed the ban. I called the board immediately, and sure enough, in the April 2003 board meeting, they rescinded the callus cutter ban. The new staff attorney told me the board did not have the approval to make a ban after all, and it would take legislation to change it.

I then asked to speak to Sandra James but was told she no longer worked there. They didn't know how to get hold of her.

I eventually notified my Board of Podiatry about this issue and was told to write it up and submit it. I have done just that. To date, no other medical group has taken on the issue of Credo blades in Tennessee.

Chapter 9
Your nail anatomy

The human body produces – from twenty living, breathing nail beds – a continuous supply of hard nail off the tops of our soft fingers and toes. This firm, flexible substance strengthens and protects them.

What we call "nail" is medically referred to as "the nail plate". The nail plate slides along on its "nail bed", and is held in place by nail ligaments and skin.

Skin folds over the top 20 percent of the nail plate, mostly over the base, called the "matrix" (Its root word is mother, parent: *mater, matr-.*). The longer the matrix, the thicker the nail. The matrix is the active part of the nail bed. It gives birth to the keratin protein cells that form the nail plate.

A channel of groves and ligaments holds this active nail plate in a track that allows the nail to move forward, yet stay firmly attached. The nail plate has microscopic channels that are conduits for water and water vapor that keep the nail moist.

Cells that make up the nail bed, and the skin that folds over the nail plate, respire or "breathe," making water as a by-product. In addition, water, oil, electrolytes, minerals, chemical vapors, and liquids move through the nail plate freely by simple diffusion, osmosis, chemical reactions with water, chemical reactions with keratin, and by transonychial (across the nail) evaporation, or "insensible water loss", water loss we don't notice or feel. Skin, lungs, eyes, mucosal membranes, and nails all lose water by evaporation.

The combination of evaporation, diffusion, osmosis, and chemical reactions with water can be thought to the layperson as "breathing," a type of movement of water. Knowing about this breathing movement is one key to understanding how improperly applied artificial nails, produce an environment conducive to the growth of bacteria.

A nail can hold up to one third of its weight in water – as is evident to those who stay overlong in the bath. A strong, damage-resistant nail plate has 10 to 25 percent water content. A nail with less than 10 percent will become brittle. A nail with over 25 percent will lose natural oil, get too soft, and be vulnerable to damage.

Too-frequent use of acetone and other "acetone free" or "non acetone" nail polish removers, like methyl ethyl ketone and ethyl acetate, can dehydrate the surface of the nail plate, or cause splitting and some forms of ridging.

A proper balance of water and oil will help maintain optimal nail health. Avoid problems by paying attention to how much time nails are in water, protect them from harsh chemicals like bleach and detergents, and use protective cuticle oils when necessary.

Nails are composed of many substances. Amino acids, iron, copper, silver, gold, titanium, phosphorus, zinc, calcium, sodium, and aluminum are all found in very low concentrations. While present at less than five percent, sulfur is the next largest constituent after the carbon atoms of the nail's elemental makeup.

Sulfur in the nail combines with the nail's amino acids to form disulfide bonds. The cross-linkage of disulfide bonds between amino acids forms polypeptides that give amazing strength and rigidity to the nail plate. Such bonds are hard to break. But certain chemicals can do it. Some chemicals used to straighten or curl hair, style the hair by breaking disulfide bonds.

Nails are actually a form of modified hair, which is also made of keratin protein cells.

The cells on the topside of the nail are older than the ones underneath it, which can account for baklava/layer-cake-type splitting. There are about 100 layers of stacked keratin nail cells in the average fingernail, and about 150 in a toenail.

Nail infections will affect the shape of the nail plate. Trauma will affect its growth, as will tight-fitting shoes. Serious illnesses not only affect the nail, the nail will act as a time line to record the event like rings in a tree.

Fingernails grow an average of 0.1 mm per day, 0.5 to 1.2 mm per week, or 1 cm every 100 days, and 6 months to grow out completely. Toenails average half that fast, taking a year to grow out. Generally speaking, the longer the finger or toe, the faster the nail will grow. Right-handed people grow nails faster on the right hand, and vice versa. Nails tend to grow faster in summer, slower in winter. Actual growth rate varies with age, season, exercise level, and hereditary factors.

Anatomical terms:

Nail plate: what we call nail, the hard translucent plate composed of the protein keratin.

Nail bed: the adherent connective tissue that underlies the nail.

Lunula: the crescent shaped whitish area of the nail bed.

Nail matrix: "The root," the growing part of the nail under the skin at the nail's proximal end.

Skin: covers 20 percent of the nail plate

Eponychium: the fold of skin at the proximal end of the nail.

Cuticle: the protective seal of non-living tissue that protects the eponychium

Paronychium: the fold of skin on the sides of the nail.

Hyponychium: the attachment between the skin of the finger or toe and the distal end of the nail.

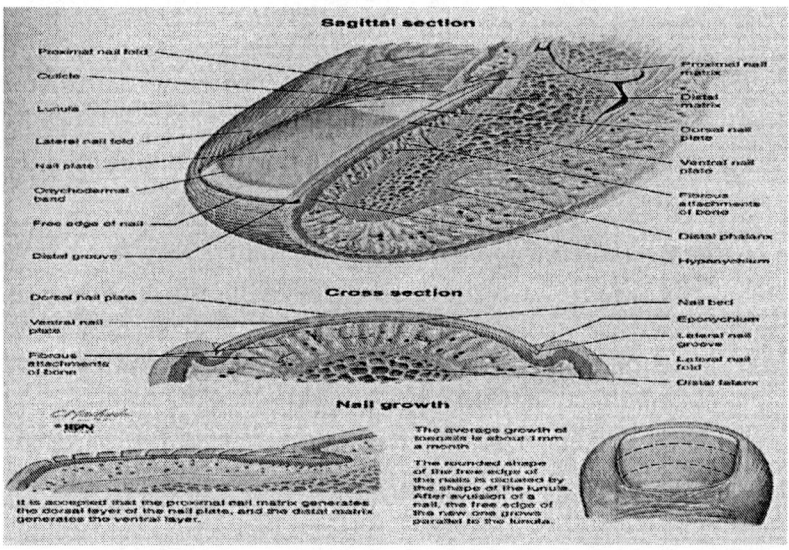

Chapter 10
War of the microbes in nail salons

Bacteria (e.g., *pseudomonas* - "Greenies" See page 146-147.) are responsible for 90% of fingernail nail infections contracted from artificial nail applications in a nail salon. Other infections such as staph from manicure injuries represent the other 10%. Many of these infections are "treated" by nail techs or clients without seeking physician services.

Nail fungus accounts for approximately 90 % of nail infections from pedicures in nail salons. (Above statistics are based on my office practice figures, interviews with nail techs, and nailsaloninfectionsurvey.com)

Bacteria that cause harm are called pathogens. We'll examine seven of the top offenders in nail salons. How do bacterial infections get transmitted in salons?

Bacteria can be present on or under all nails – natural, painted, and artificial – when the client or the nail tech has not properly washed his or her hands. Who knows where those hands have just been! Proper washing involves soap, water, scrubbing, and, in the case of nails over a needle's-width long, scrubbing under them with a nailbrush. Protect yourself.

Basic cleaning kills most bacteria.

Artificial nails and nail polish present unique opportunities for bacteria. When the artificial nail product is not applied appropriately, and when the nail develops micro leakage from improper bonding to the nail, bacteria can enter via capillary action under the artificial nail or chips in nail polish.

Water-loving bacteria live, well, all over the planet – in pond, river, lake, and ocean water, and in hot tubs, well water, standing water, and even in the dirt in one's garden. Our immune systems, which include the skin and nails, provide ample protection from water-borne bacteria. Bacteria – and infective organisms generally – do no harm to the body unless they find a way in.

Improperly-applied artificial nails present such an opportunity, and one may not notice the new house mates until they've multiplied into what they call a thriving community and we call an infection.

Bacteria enter through the skin via scratches, cuts, nicks, and the like. Even so, the immune system is designed to battle these invaders. A strong immune system will kill the bacteria; a weak immune system will either take longer to do it or fail.

Here are seven pathogenic bacteria most likely to house-hunt in a nail salon:

Pseudomonas aeruginosa, Staphylococcus aureus, Streptococcus, Mycobacterium fortuitum, Actinomyces, Eshericheria coli, and *Klebsiella Pneumoniae*

1. *Pseudomonas aeruginosa*
Pseudomonas, the number one cause of bacterial fingernail infections in nail salons, is also the number one bacterium

responsible for deaths in burn wards. These water-loving bacteria can be found in sources such as poorly chlorinated water, well water, hot tubs, and improperly disinfected whirlpool foot baths or whole body baths. It is typically present in many areas that typically support mold. Damp, wet, moist, even soil and sod areas are environments that can have *pseudomonal* growth

Pseudomonas bacteria produce a staining green pigment as they multiply on skin surfaces or under artificial nails. Nail salon personnel have seen so many pseudomonal infections from improperly applied acrylic nails, gel nails and nail wraps, that they have given the bacteria a nickname: the "greenies." (See pictures on 146-147.) The cute name is a distraction from the seriousness of a pseudomonal infection. Many whose immune systems were not strong enough to overpower the bacteria have contracted infections that resolved only with extensive nail surgery.

Pseudomonas bacteria produce a slime coat that makes them tough to get rid of once they enter the bloodstream via breaks in the skin – or get trapped in ear canals, skin lesions, or under artificial nails with micro leakage problems. The green pigment they produce will permanently discolor the nail, and disappears only as the nail grows out. With pseudomonas nail infections, the quicker you remove the damaged artificial nail or chipped nail polish the less full thickness staining you will get. Most women hide this with nail polish until the nail grows out. Acetic acid is toxic to pseudomonas. Oral (and sometimes intravenous) antibiotics are often necessary if the infection is systemic or in the blood stream. The slime coat produced by pseudomonas protects the organism from many antibiotics.

Nurses, doctors, and other personnel who work in hospitals, intensive care wards, newborn intensive care centers, and burn wards should not have artificial nails or polish when working with these high risk patients, even when wearing gloves. Gloves can break especially using long sharp nails in latex gloves.

2. *Staphylococcus aureus*

Staphylococcus aureus is the number one cause of bacterial foot infections and ingrown nails seen in doctor's offices. These round, gram-positive bacteria called cocci look like a bunch of grapes under the microscope. Walled off to protect themselves, the bacteria multiply and form pus pockets that sometimes have to be lanced. Classic treatments are oral antibiotics and topical antibiotic creams.

Certain *staphylococcus* organisms are now resistant to antibiotics. As a result, pus samples are cultured, then tested to see which antibiotics work best. As this can take several days, an oral antibiotic active against most of these "staph" bacteria is usually given immediately.

When the culture sample tests positive for the *superbug* MRSA—Methicillin Resistant Staphylococcus aureus—oral antibiotics like trimethoprim-sulfamethoxazole, clindamycin and levofloxin (Levaquin®) are often given, with hope that the infection will subside. When it doesn't resolve with oral antibiotics, big-gun antibiotics like vancomycin are introduced intravenously.

Unfortunately, VRSA – Vancomycin-Resistant *Staphylococcus aureus* – a new super, superbug, can sometimes spell disaster. A new drug called linezolid (Zyvox®) is now being given to fight VRSA, as are other combinations of IV drugs.

Staphylococcus infections can also produce scalded skin syndrome (SSS). Infected, blistered skin falls away in sheets, giving the appearance of a large-scale burn over the entire body. Staph can produce toxic epidermal necrolysis (TEN), also known as Steven-Johnson syndrome which can be progress to a fatal systemic infection that presents with blisters, red rash, sheets of tender skin that falls away with additional massive tissue destruction and finally, multi organ system failure.

Remember toxic shock syndrome, TSS? Those well-publicized cases of tampon use are another example of how *Staphylococcus aureus* bacteria can be deadly under certain circumstances. The infections caused massive blood pressure changes that led to shock, and, in some cases, death. Staph infections, now more than ever, can be life-threatening.

Other forms of staph, like *staph epidermidis*, are common skin flora. Such organisms normally don't affect humans and are called non-pathogens or colonizers. Nonetheless, these simple organisms can be part of a "mixed," multiple-bacteria infection that can cause serious problems for people who have conditions like diabetes, chronic medical problems like HIV, or other immune diseases. Breaks in the skin—scratches, itchy areas, ulcers, mosquito bites, and accidental cuts by nails techs—are portals for bacteria to enter the body.

Both clients and nail techs must know that a medical problem can arise from simple bacteria and can develop into a big problem that is not normally or always perceived as a medical problem by some nail techs.

3. *Mycobacterium fortuitum*

This is the highly publicized bacterium found in all the pedicure chair whirlpool articles that have been surfacing in the news the last few years. *Mycobacterium fortuitum* is called an atypical *mycobacterium* (with typical being the mycobacterium causing tuberculosis) that is commonly found in most US municipal water supplies and in most drinking water plumbing.

Normally it is not a pathogen or disease causing organism but increase concentrations of this organism can enter small lesions in the skin such as previous cuts, lesion, insect bites or skin that has been recently shaved. The difficulty in culturing this bacteria and proper timing to request an acid fast staining technique may delay proper treatment. Course of treatments may last 6 months of longer. Azithromycin®, Levaquin® and some other fluoroquinolones like Cipro® have been used successfully in the past.

Mycobacterium bacteria have been linked to hundreds of infections from the expensive pedicure chairs that have been increasingly popular in the last 7 years. The Watsonville, CA incident and San Jose, CA high profile bacterial incidents in the media are the best recent examples. Improper disinfection, faulty plumbing designs, gravity flow systems, drain systems, basin material and filter designs found in pedicure chairs have been directly responsible for heavy accumulations of bacterial growth that expose the skin of feet and legs to a soup of concentrated microbes.

4. Escherichia coli

Escherichia coli, popularly known as E. coli, is an intestinal colon bacterium. These bacteria are almost always present in the alimentary canal of humans and other animals. E. Coli is a gram negative rod bacterium that is a benchmark measurement of fecal material in our water supply. It can also be injected in contaminated meat during processing, in contaminated food or water and has been responsible for deaths in the fast food industry. It is also found in soil and high concentration in waste material. Following broken skin or trauma the organism can enter the protective surface of the body. Callus cutters and nail nippers can injure skin and this organism can enter after the injury has already occurred. Examples exist that show that this organism can be acquired under the natural finger nails or artificial nails.

5. Actinomyces

Actinomyces species are principally soil bacteria that cause infections usually found in livestock or horses and not humans. But they can occur in humans after being inoculated in the skin or after salon services that injured skin that has not been adequately cleaned or even after you have left the salon. This organism is rod shaped facultative aerobe.

For example, if you receive a pedicure or manicure that unknowingly injured the skin of the foot or hand and you walked barefoot in the house you could acquire the bacteria through the open wound. No matter how clean the instruments, no matter how much the nail salon washed your feet or hands you can come down with an infection because the skin was broken during the salon services.

I have been directly consulted to render a medical opinion as a result of this particular organism in the above example. If the nail tech would just notify the client an injury occurred and practiced protocol set forth by the state, the infection may have been avoided. This was settled out of court and will never be heard of in detail in public records.

6. *Klebsiella Pneumoniae*

Infections caused by the bacteria *Klebsiella pneumoniea* affect people in hospital settings. Such infections are call nosocomial, from the Greek word *nosokomos*, one who tends the sick. This opportunistic bacteria flourishes in the bodies of patients who are debilitated, and the mortality rate is elevated, even with antimicrobial therapy. The mortality rate is higher for persons with alcoholism and *Klebsiella pneumoniae bacteremia.*

Community-acquired *Klebsiella (Friedländer) pneumoniae* bacteria favor the bodies of debilitated middle-aged and older men with alcoholism.

Nosocomial infections may affect adults or children, and they occur more frequently in premature infants, patients in neonatal intensive care units, and hospitalized individuals whose immune systems are compromised.

Documented cases of transmission from hospitals have been seen with nurses wearing artificial nails and demonstrating poor hand washing techniques in 19 neonatal cases documented by Dr. Gupta in Infection Control Hospital Epidemiology 2004; 25:210 – 215.

7. *Streptococcus bacteria*

Strep is a gram positive round cocci that produce chains of bacteria.

Strep also makes an enzyme to help it spread rapidly through the body tissues hence the rapidly advancing streaking. The bacteria can fully spread throughout a person in 24 hours in rare cases. Immediate IV therapy may stop it. Amputation may help stop it or sometimes only death will stop it. Not everyone's immune system reacts to strep bacteria the same way. Some people can fight it better than others.

Beta hemolytic Streptococci are the most dangerous of the streptococcal bacteria. *Beta hemolytic streptococcus* is also the bacteria responsible, under certain conditions, for the "flesh eating disease" or necrotizing *fasciitis*.

Streptococci also come in other variant forms. *Strep pneumoniae S. pneumoniae* is a lancet-shaped diplococcus. *Streptococcus pyogenes* or group A strep is another common variant. *Strep faecalis*, also known as *enterococcus* or group D strep is an intestinal flora bacterium and can be responsible for endocarditis and urinary tract infections. VRE or Vancomycin Resistant *Enterococcus* is a consideration when treating serious Group D Strep infections. http://www.cehs.siu.edu/fix/medmicro/strep.htm

Differences in bacteria

Aerobic bacteria need oxygen to grow. All of the above are aerobic.

Strict Anaerobic bacteria grow only in the absence of oxygen. Some of these anaerobic bacteria belonging to the genus *Clostridium* cause infections like gas gangrene and tetanus.

Under certain conditions, soil-based anaerobic clostridial bacteria form protective spores, and can be present on skin. A puncture wound (stepping on a nail, having skin broken by a nail instrument) can drive these bacteria into the body where oxygen is not readily present, creating an opportunity for them to multiply.

Bacteria called facultative anaerobes grow with or without oxygen. They too can enter the body via punctures, skin nicks, and abrasions.

In all cases, basic sanitation practices – soap and water – are crucial in reducing the likelihood of bacterial infection.

Chapter 11
Fungus, molds, and yeast

Fungus, Molds and yeast are responsible for fungal nails, and treatments for nail fungus are very popular on TV. "Digger®" the fungal cartoon character in the Lamisil® TV commercials is a "dermatophyte" that can be seen under a special stain or microscopic technique to see the presence of *hyphae* or branches that are characteristic of certain fungal organisms.

The dermatophytes are not a particular fungus but rather a common short-hand label for a group of three genera of fungi that commonly cause skin disease of people and animals. These are the genera *Epidermophyton*, *Trichophyton*, and *Microsporum*. Please refer to these individual fungi for more details.

Some fungi can grow on your skin, causing several different conditions including jock itch, athlete's foot, and ringworm. These fungi are known as dermatophytes. There are about 40 species in three genera.

Cutaneous Infections

These fungi are not really parasitic in the sense of attacking living tissue. They attack the dead cells of the epidermis, and cause a kind of dermatitis. The irritation caused by the fungus stimulates the skin cells to divide more rapidly. This means that more flakes of skin containing infective mycelium will be shed.

Twenty of the dermatophytes grow only on people, causing diseases called 'tineas'. These occur on various parts of the body. They may affect the scalp 'tinea capitis' (ringworm of the scalp), the groin 'tinea cruris' (jock itch), and the feet 'tinea pedis' (athlete's foot).

'Tinea capitis' is often caused by Microsporum audouinii or Trichophyton tonsurans. Ringworm of the scalp is recognized as round, spreading patches of irritation and/or baldness.

'Tinea cruris' - jock itch and 'tinea pedis' athlete's foot is caused by Epidermophyton floccosum. This produces short-lived infections and relies on shed skin for quick spread to other hosts.

Usually these fungi are contracted in change rooms from small pieces of shed skin, but spores can survive in carpets and upholstery for up to two years.

Microsporum canis has its reservoir in the cat. It can cause ringworm of the scalp or body. It can be transmitted to dogs or people but will die out after one or two person-to-person transfers.

Trichophyton rubrum causes chronic infections of the foot and toenails and can produce infective material for several years.

There are non-dermatophytes like candida or yeast as well that look like round spheres under the microscope. Individuals who constantly get their hands or feet wet can be subject to these infections. Individuals who have decreased immune function, such as those with HIV or diabetes, can present with nail fungus more frequently than other individuals.

Fungal organisms are a frequent cause of infections in nail salons. Inadequate sanitation/disinfection techniques and contaminated instruments beg the question why the nail industry still does not require the use of sterilized instruments.

Nail fungus sometimes is confused with other nail problems. Discolored nails from smoking, *pseudomonas* stains, artificial nail damage from methacrylate adhesives, formaldehyde, tolulene, sulfonamides, and the colored pigments in nail polish stain can all look like the beginning stages of nail fungus. Nail techs have used bleaching agents and peroxides to treat fungal nails. This may temporarily "whiten" the nail plate, but will not eradicate fungal organisms from the nail bed.

Several things happen when you get a fungal nail. First, the fungal organisms multiplying under the nail lift the nail from its bed, breaking attachments just like "Digger®" on TV. Next, the nail thickens. Toenails become uncomfortable in shoes during the day and sensitive to the weight of bed covers at night. When you bathe or shower, water gets trapped under the nail, making a warm, moist habitat for yet another organism.

When water-loving *pseudomonas* bacteria take up residence in this friendly habitat, they begin to produce a staining green pigment – which is often mistaken for yet more of "Digger's®" work

There are many myths about what will cure fungal and bacterial nail infections. Sometimes vinegar or Vick's VapoRub® (menthol) will kill the *pseudomonas* bacteria and temporarily decrease staining. Here, the riddance of pseudomonal bacteria is confused with a cure for nail fungus. But nothing could be further from the truth.

I have been asked if bleach, urine, or over the counter nail products will cure fungus. Ninety-five percent of the time it won't. The other five percent is pure luck. The only real cure is the oral medication like Lamisil® (terbinafine), 250 mg, which works about 70% of the time. The only approved FDA topical agent is Penlac®, which works 10 to 30% of the time depending on the area of nail plate involvement, based on my office experience. Other oral antifungals are available.

Chapter 12

Viruses responsible for health problems worldwide

Nail salons, pedicurists, and manicurists are in most every country in the world. Many countries have no sanitation or sterilization laws for cosmetology services or nail services. Viruses circulate globally, and can move from any one place on the planet to any other in less than 24 hours.

Hepatitis A,B,C,D,E, HIV, viral plantar warts, herpes, chicken pox, and other signs of disease can all appear directly or indirectly on the hands and feet .

The hepatitis virus is contagious, virulent, and has a high rate of transmission. It can survive for seven days on surfaces like manicure tables, instruments, bathrooms and pedicure chairs, outlasting the survival rate of the HIV virus, which is about 10 minutes outside the body. An estimated 300 million people have hepatitis C worldwide, and one million are infected every year.

There are 90 million active cases of hepatitis B, and it is estimated that one health care worker contracts it every day. Hepatitis A is transmitted by a virus in fecal material. That's why people who work in restaurants need to wash their hands well after using the bathroom, and before preparing or serving food. All hepatitis viruses attack the liver, making hepatitis the single largest cause of liver transplants and death from liver failure. There has been one case in California where a hepatitis C patient may have received the virus from a nail salon. (See Chapter 18.)

Preventing Hepatitis A

Historically people have used their bare left hand or index finger to wipe themselves. This fact is one of several reasons it is customarily universal to shake hands with the right hand. Traditions carry over. America is a diverse country that advocates washing hands before food is handled or eating.

Hepatitis A can be caused by not washing one's hands effectively after using the bathroom before eating or serving food. The correct protocol for nail salons is to request that clients wash their hands thoroughly and scrub under their fingernails for 30 seconds to prevent contamination. Washing the feet and hands will reduce 99 percent of most germ contact.

Left hand unclean See http://www.msc.navy.mil/msccent/taboos.htm for the free government information on Right and Left Hand traditions and cleanliness.

Herpetic Whitlow and Herpes

Herpetic whitlow is an infection of the herpes virus. It is found commonly on the fingers of health care worker and dentists; www.emedicine.com reports the following information.

"Herpetic whitlow is an intense painful infection of the hand involving 1 or more fingers that typically affects the terminal phalanx. Herpes simplex virus 1 (HSV-1) is the cause in approximately 60% of cases of herpetic whitlow, and *herpes simplex virus 2* (HSV-2) is the cause in the remaining 40%.

"In children, HSV-1 is the most likely causative agent. Infection involving the finger usually is due to autoinoculation from primary oropharyngeal lesions as a result of finger-sucking or thumb-sucking behavior in patients with *herpes labialis* or *herpetic gingivostomatitis*.

"Similarly, in health care workers, infection with HSV-1 is more common and usually is secondary to unprotected exposure to infected oropharyngeal secretions of patients. This easily can be prevented by use of gloves and by scrupulous observation of universal fluid precautions.

"In the general adult population, herpetic whitlow is most often due to autoinoculation from genital herpes; therefore, it is most frequently secondary to infection with HSV-2."

The first case of a viral transmission of herpetic whitlow in a nail salon was in Aurora, Colorado, in 1998. The victim contracted herpetic whitlow from a nail file and successfully proved her case in a lawsuit where she collected 3.2 million dollars in 2002. Viral herpetic infections, though rare in nail salons, can occur.

Viral Plantar Warts

Plantar Warts, formally called *verruca plantaris*, are from the Human Papilloma Virus or HPV. Contagious plantar warts can look identical to calluses. These potentially painful warts are spread by walking barefoot on well-trodden floors. Warts gain access through small imperfections in the feet via shared shoes, from carpet or tile surfaces in hotels or motels or your own home, or from visitors in your home. Plantar warts can also be found on the top of toes, between toes and in the top of feet.

However, plantar warts can look remarkably like small or large calluses to all but the trained eye of a specialist. They can even resemble cancers on the foot. To determine if a wart is a wart or, in fact, a callus, a physician must carefully scrape it with a sterilized surgical blade, and that only after the skin has been cleaned with an antiseptic.

Capillary bleeding is a diagnostic symptom of plantar warts. Sometimes broken capillaries leave dried blood (under the skin surface) and it looks like small "dots". They are mistakenly referred to as "seed warts," a misnomer. Once the virus reaches a blood supply, the wart will grow a protective skin surface to protect it while the virus increases in size and establishes a better vascular supply. Topical acid, blistering agents, injections of anti-neoplastic cancer drugs like 5FU or bleomycin, hyphercation/burning with electricity/ laser, surgery, or combinations of several approaches at once, are all accepted treatments.

If your nail tech treats, cuts, or shaves plantar warts, whether intentionally or unintentionally, be aware that the warts can spread, get infected, and create increased morbidity. When nail techs are willing to treat plantar warts, they are in effect also willing to expose you to contamination. Does your state allows callus shaver blades in the hands of nail techs? If so, lobby your state medical associations and state cosmetology boards until they forbid the practice.

Chapter 13
Global parasitic threats

Just like viruses, parasites come from around the world. Parasites include protozoa that travel through the blood stream by vectors or transmission sources like mosquitoes, fleas and ticks, as well as other insects.

Scabies

Common parasitic diseases like scabies are caused by parasitic organisms like mites/head lice which can be associated with close living quarters with other infected individuals, as in nursing homes. These critters can jump from skin surfaces by intimate or close contact from massages, rubbing, or utilization of other contaminated hygiene implements like combs, hats, scarves, brushes, clothing, pillows and bedding. Nail techs who performs these services in hospitals, private home and nursing homes should wear gloves to help stop the transmission source of these organisms.

http//www.medem.com/MedLB/article_detaillb.cfm?article_ID=ZZZYNDYJ 1AC&sub_cat=107

http://medlib.med.utah.edu/kw/derm/pages/ni12_5.htm

Confirmed cases of *cutaneous leishmeniasis* have been associated with service men coming back from Iraq and Saudi Arabia. It can take less than 24 hours to bring these organisms back to the US from any country in the world and introduce them into a nail salon.

http://www.cdc.gov/mmwr/preview/mmwrhtml/mm5242a1.htm

Most people who are diagnosed with these organisms have visible small lesions or small bites that indicate a parasite may have taken residence. It may also be noticeable by the symptom of intense itching that an infestation has occurred.

Some parasites have surface blood meals. Little balls of "brown dirt" discovered under your bed sheets with corresponding bites on your legs, could even mean a simple flea infestation. If certain parasites burrow, they will consume blood and defecate under the skin and create infected, itchy tracts.

The message again is that gloves should be worn to help protect the client and the nail tech from harsh chemicals, bacteria and parasites.

Chapter 14
Nail disease and treatments

A client presenting with any of the nail pathologies listed in this chapter needs first to be sent to a doctor for evaluation. Then, with written permission and only after treatment by the podiatrist/physician, they can be seen by the nail tech. If a nail tech treats first, the nail symptom-based evidence of the problem may temporarily be destroyed and the patient will go undiagnosed. It is very important for both consumers and nail techs to recognize this fact.

Clients showing advanced nail pathology to nail techs for diagnosis open the cosmetology industry to lawsuits if the nail techs proceed to treat the problem. Education of the nail techs and the nail industry about medical nail problems is important. They must study nail problems to determine what to refer to physicians. Techs need to learn about the conditions they should not treat themselves. Nail industry professionals could protect themselves if they would refer such problems, and would perform their services only with written permission from a physician. Unfortunately this is not always the case, and many nail techs sell and provide treatments in their salons.

Who's most at risk?
The following are risk factors for nail disorders.

- Genetic predisposition
- Excessive exposure to water, heat, and humidity
- Tight-fitting shoes
- Chemical damage
- Diabetes
- Skin diseases
- Tumors
- Over-manicuring
- Habits involving picking at the skin surrounding a nail
- Soil contamination
- Human immunodeficiency virus (HIV), the virus that causes AIDS
- Other systemic metabolic disorders seen below

Some causes of nail disorders
Trauma:
- A crush injury to base of the nail or the nail bed may produce a permanent deformity.
- Nail biting can be a sign of anxiety, chronic tension, or uncontrollable compulsion.
- Chronic picking or rubbing of the skin behind the visible portion of the nail can produce a washboard nail.

• Chronic exposure to moisture or to nail polish can produce brittle nails with peeling of the edge of the nail.

• Over aggressive filing of the nail plate

• Improper removal of nail enhancements

Infection:

• Fungus or yeast produce changes in the color, texture, and shape of the nails.

• Bacterial infection may cause a change in color (green nails with *pseudomonas*) or painful pockets of infection under the nail or in skin surrounding the nail. Severe infections may cause loss of the nail plate.

• Viral warts may cause a change in the shape of the nail or ingrown skin under the nail.

Internal diseases:

• Disorders that affect the amount of oxygen in the blood (such as abnormal heart anatomy and lung diseases including cancer or infection) may produce clubbing , in which the nail looks like the back of a teaspoon.

• Kidney disease that causes a build-up of nitrogen waste products in the blood

• Liver disease including chronic liver failure

• Thyroid diseases including hyperthyroidism or hypothyroidism may produce brittle nails or splitting of the nail plate from the nail bed (*onycholysis*)

• Infection (especially of the heart valve) may produce splinter hemorrhages (red streaks in the nail bed)

• Systemic amyloidosis Primary amyloidosis is a disorder in which insoluble protein fibers are deposited in tissues and organs, impairing their function.

- Severe illness or surgery may produce horizontal depressions in the nails (Beau's lines)
- Vitamin deficiency can cause a loss of luster or brittle nails
- Malnutrition of any sort can affect the appearance of nails

Nail function

The primary function of the nail is protection. Nail concerns are common, but the exact prevalence of nail disease is unknown. Nail disease occurs with certain skin diseases (psoriasis, eczema), often follows external trauma, may be an adverse effect of medication, and may occur with certain illnesses. The most common cause of nail disease is infection, usually fungal (*onychomycosis*) and less often bacterial. In many respects, the nails may indicate or reflect medical illness.

See a Physician

If you develop a nail problem see your physician as soon as possible. Early treatment may help the eventual outcome of a nail disorder. See a podiatrist for toenail disorders.

Remember that If a nail tech treats a condition first, the nail symptom-based evidence of the problem may temporarily be destroyed and a serious health issue may go undiagnosed.

The following links represent the source of the information in this chapter:
http://www.clevelandclinicmeded.com/diseasemanagement/dermatology/naildisease/naildisease.htm
http://www.som.tulane.edu/courses/clinicaldx/Year_III_syllabus_2003-4_Wiese.pdf
http://www.patient.co.uk/showdoc/40024530/
http://www.umm.edu/altmed/ConsConditions/NailDisorderscc.html#Signs#Signs
http://www.netwellness.org/ency/article/003247.htm

Chapter 15

If your nails are discolored

Environmental and medical considerations for discoloration of the nail plate

Causes of Nail Discoloration -

White

- Excessive use of nail polish removers creates pseudoleukonychia by removing water and oil

- A superficial white nail fungus, *Candida albicans*, can appear on the nails of those who have HIV/autoimmune disease, cardiac, gastrointestinal, or renal disease, metabolic disorders, psoriasis, and neoplasia/cancer.

- White bands across the nails are caused by protein deficiency.

- White spots are the result of insufficient zinc.

- White lines and horizontal ridges can result from arsenic poisoning.

Gray or Silver

Formaldehyde and quinine sulfate can turn nails grey or silver.

Yellow

Many sources: Nail polish, fungal infections, formaldehyde, excess vitamin D, psoriasis, disinfectants, tetracycline, gluteraldehyde, insecticides, weed killers, hydroquinone, bronchitis, diabetes, arthritis, hyperthyroidism.

Green

Pseudomonas aeruginosa bacterial infection ("the greenies" from artificial nails), *aspergillius* mold, *blastomyces* mold, grass or chlorophyll stains, chlorhexidine.

Blue

Oxygen starvation, absence of oxygen (cyanosis), silver toxicity, ink, fluoride, tetracycline, metal cleaners, silver intake.

Pink to Red

Nail polish, carbon monoxide poisoning (cherry red), cardiac failure (atrial fibrillation/splinter hemorrhages), *lichen planus*.

Brown

Melanoma, henna ink from tattooing, mercury, dyes, iodine/Betadine, nictone from smoking, chronic nail infections, radiation therapy, pregnancy (hormonal surges), tetracycline (stains teeth and nails), malnutrition, gluteraldehyde.

Black

Melanoma, blood under nail from trauma, *aspergillus* (mold), *penicillium* (mold), drug use, nevi (mole), silver nitrate.

Other nail plate changes reviewed

• Selenium or lack of selenium can cause onycholysis or lifting of nails

• Dry, brittle nails can be a sign that you lack vitamin C, vitamin B12, or calcium

• Loss of fingernails or brittleness, malnutrition, vitamin deficiency, heavy metal selenium toxicity, insecticides/weed killers like paraquat dichloride, and environmental exposure

Systemic Drugs that induce nail changes

DRUG	NAIL FINDING
Antineoplastic drugs	Hyperpigmentation, leukonychia, splinter hemorrhages, onycholysis, onychomadesis, Beau's lines
Arsenic	Mee's lines
Azidothymidine	Melanonychia
Beta-blockers	Thickening and pitting, Beau's lines, ischemic changes
Chloroquine	Blue-grey to yellow pigmentation
Chlorpromazine	Blue-purple pigmentation
Indinavir	Paronychia, pyogenic granuloma
Minocycline	Blue-grey pigmentation
Psoralens/ PUVA	Photo-onycholysis sun sensitivity that causes lifting of the nail
Retinoids	Brittleness, pyogenic, granuloma-like growths
Tetracycline	Photo-onycholysis or lifting of the nail plate by sunlight reactions

Note. If the offending drug is discontinued, the abnormality typically disappears, except for *pyogenic granuloma* caused by Indinavir®.

Infections of the Nail Plate

Onychomycosis or *tinea unguium,* the most common nail disorder, is a fungal or yeast infection of the nail. Predisposing factors for infection include heat, moisture, trauma, *diabetes mellitus,* and *tinea pedis.* Affected nails are dystrophic and hyperkeratotic (thickened), often with yellow-brown discoloration. Discomfort may occur. Onycholysis or lifting of the nail may also occur. See photos on page 154.

There are four types of *onychomycosis:*

• Distal and lateral subungual onychomycosis (DLSO) is the commonest form and is virtually always caused by dermatophytes. Infection starts under front of nail or nail fold and extends under the nail to involve the whole structure. Can either affect a healthy nail or one already diseased, e.g., by psoriasis. Approximately 80% of cases occurs on the feet, especially on big toes often affecting both toe and fingernails. Initially presents as white patch on the under surface of the nail and nail bed but becomes discolored to brown or black. Progression can incur within weeks or more slowly over months or years with the nail becoming opaque, thickened and cracked, friable and raised from the nail bed.

• Superficial white onychomycosis (SWO) Usually caused by dermatophyte invading surface of dorsal nail plate presenting as white chalky plaque on proximal nail plate almost exclusively on the toenails. Nail plate may become eroded and even lost.

• Proximal subungual onychomycosis is almost always associated with immunocompromised patients, and presents as a white spot beneath the proximal nail fold which eventually fills the lunula, occurring most commonly on toenails. Eventually can involve whole of the under surface of the nail plate.

- Candida onychomycosis occurs in 3 different types:

- Candida paronychia – initially appears as edema, erythema and pain of the nail fold from which pus can be expressed at times. Also nail plate becomes dystrophic with patches of opacification or discoloration (white, yellow, green or black) with transverse furrows. Usually, pressure on the nail causes pain. Most cases are on fingernails, usually the middle finger.

- Subungual abscess with DLSO occurring in the setting of onycholysis (see above).

- Total nail dystrophy – affects all or large proportion of nails associated with chronic *mucocutaneous candidiasis*. Entire fingernail may become thickened and dystrophic.

Diagnosis of all four types of *onychomycosis* is by direct microscopy KOH, PAS (Periodic Acid Shift) stain, or DTM (Dermatophyte) culture.

Causes

- Dermatophytes like *Tricophytum rubrum*, *T. mentagrophytes*
- Non dermatophytes (yeast) like *Candida albicans*
- Molds like *Aspergillus, penicillium*

Treatment

Treatment is warranted for onychomycosis of the fingernails and whenever discomfort occurs. Diagnosis of above is by direct microscopy KOH, PAS (periodic acid shift stain or DTM (dermatophyte) culture. Without treatment, condition often spreads to multiple toenails and can form a portal for recurrent bacterial infections. Common in diabetics and can contribute to foot problems.

Need to trim dystrophic nails with the aid of a podiatrist for toenails. In DLSO, remove nail and hyperkeratotic nail bed

with clippers. In SWO debride abnormal nail with a curette.
Because of slow growth of nails, they do not appear normal
even after effective treatment, and treatment can be stopped
when culture and KOH preparations are negative. Patients
should practice long term prophylaxis with benzoyl peroxide soap for washing feet, antifungal cream daily, antifungal sprays or powder for shoes. Treatment is with systemic
antifungal agents – terbinafine, itroaconazole, fluconazole.
Success with either agent is less than 65%, and recurrences
are common.

Several systemic disorders may present clinically in a form
that resembles onychomycosis or onycholysis. The following
medications can mimic onychomycosis:
  bleomycin, doxorubicin, 5-fluorouracil, retinoids, cap-
  topril, chlorpromazine, chloramphenicol, tetracyclines,
  psoralen phototherapy agents, thiazide, diuretics, and
  quinine. Intermittent cycles of chemotherapy may cause
  multiple transverse lines called Beau's lines.

Other diseases mimicking onychomycosis:
  Lichen planus Nails involved in approximately 10% of
  cases of disseminated lichen planus. However, may be only
  presentation of disease. With matrix causes thinning,
  brittleness, crumbling of the nail with accentuated surface
  longitudinal ridging and color change to black or white.
  Typically, the lunula is raised more than the distal part
  of the nail. Severe chronic inflammation causes either
  partial or complete loss of nail plate and formation of
  pterygium with partial loss of central nail plate seen as
  distal notch or completely split nail. Involvement of nail
  bed causes onycholysis, distal subungual hyperkeratosis,
  formation of bulla or permanent anonychia (loss of nail.)
  Can affect any number of nails.

Treatment
Injection of steroid into proximal nail fold.

Onychocryptosis (ingrown nail) with acute parony-chia is an inflammation of the proximal and lateral nail folds characterized by erythema, edema, and pain. Purulent drainage with compression behind the cuticle may also occur. Trauma is often the initial event with secondary infection.

Causes

- Numerous bacteria including
- *Staphylococcus aureus*
- *Streptococcus pyogenes.*
- Tight shoe friction
- Improper nail trimming resulting in protruding sharp nail spicules or injury to the skin nail fold borders

Treatment (basic)

Basic treatment usually requires compresses and an oral anti-staphylococcal antibiotic.

Chronic paronychia is usually a non-infectious disease that follows irritant or allergic contact dermatitis of the proximal nail fold. The cuticle is invariably absent. Affected individu-als often trim the cuticles aggressively and meticulously and/ or do "wet work' with their hands. Secondary infection with Candida albicans is common. Treatment involves aeration, topical corticosteroids, and perhaps an oral antifungal agent, for example, terbinafine, for secondary infection.

Treatment (surgical)

Local anesthesia of the affected digit and surgical removal of the offending nail plate or nail spicule.

Warts, *verruca vulgaris,* are an infection of the proxi-mal and lateral nail folds caused by human papilloma virus

(HPV). Types 1, 2, and 4 are primarily responsible for periungual warts. Because of the location, these warts are particularly difficult to treat, especially if they extend subungually. Subungual warts may cause deformity or discoloration of the nail plate. Affected patients are often 'nail biters.' Plantar warts are HPV virus found on the bottom of weight-bearing surfaces of the foot.

Cause

HPV virus

Treatment

Salicylic acid, 10% formalin, injected bleomycin, Aladara® cream (imiquimod), Canthacur® or blistering agents, Electrocautery/Hyfrecation surgical excision

Mucous or myxoid cyst is a soft nodule at the proximal nail fold, which may intermittently drain viscous fluid; less commonly, it may occur subungually. The cyst, a collection of degenerative collagen, may cause a longitudinal depression or groove in the nail plate from compression of the nail matrix. Occasionally, it may connect to the underlying joint space and is often associated with osteoarthritis of the distal interphalangeal joints.

Cause

Mucous or myxoid cyst

Treatment

Surgical excision

Subungual exostosis is essentially a hard, painful, subungual tumor, most commonly on the great toe. The exostosis typically occurs with trauma and often causes elevation of the distal nail plate. Exostosis is an outgrowth of normal bone or bone spur.

Cause

Bone spur under nail

Treatment

Treatment is symptomatic, for example, orthotics and analgesics, though surgery may be necessary for some patients. **See photo of xray on page 152.**

Periungual fibromas or Köenen's tumors, are

flesh-colored to pink papules that originate from the nail bed and cause a longitudinal depression in the nail plate. These fibromas may occur spontaneously, but are often associated with tuberous sclerosis.

Causes

Fibromas on or near the skin nail folds

Treatment

Treatment is often unnecessary; however, excision is curative.

Pyogenic granuloma is a benign vascular tumor that

usually develops after irritation of chronic infected tissues seen commonly in infected nails. Characterized by rapid growth and a blue-red color, the nodule/tumor bleeds easily with minimal trauma.

Causes

• Chronic inflamed infected tissue from ingrown nails

- Trauma to skin or nails
- Pregnancy
- Medication allergies

Treatment

Surgical excision is the treatment of choice.

Glomus tumor is a benign vascular growth, arising from glomus cells of the nail bed. The tumor is usually a red-blue macule (patch) within the nail bed visible through the nail plate. Pain or pressure and sensitivity to changes in temperature are common.

Cause

Growth near glomus nail cells

Treatment

Treatment, via excision, is often necessary for symptomatic relief.

The following links represent the sources of information for this chapter:

http://www.clevelandclinicmeded.com/diseasemanagement/dermatology/naildisease/naildisease.htm

http://www.som.tulane.edu/courses/clinicaldx/Year_III_syllabus_2003-4_Wiese.pdf

http://www.patient.co.uk/showdoc/40024530/

http://www.umm.edu/altmed/ConsConditions/NailDisorderscc.html#Signs#Signs

http://www.netwellness.org/ency/article/003247.htm

Chapter 16
Minerals, food and vitamins that may help nail growth

The main message to get with this chapter is that when you are healthy, your nails will be healthy. Nails are an indicator and a time line of medical events in your body. If you have a severe illness, trauma, injury to the nail, certain drug therapies or surgical procedures your nails may record this event with a deformity in the nail. The vascular insult to the nail matrix by way of the blood steam or physical pressure can cause the nail to deform where the living cells reside that produce the nail.

The old traditional suggestions by your mother that extra intake of calcium and drinking milk actually will not help the nails grow faster. Nails have almost no calcium in their composition. The health and nutritional factors are simple. If you are in good general health then your nail health will generally be good baring any environmental factors or medical pathology. There is some limited evidence that larger doses of biotin, one of the B class vitamins, in several studies did help growth by 25% in several patients. I have had direct experience with patient reporting improvement with brittle fingernails with this vitamin taken at 2500 mcg per day for 90 days (Rx Appearex®).

Andrew Weil, M.D., who is the preeminent author of many integrative (alternative medicine combined with traditional medicine) medical books is founder of the only US approved residency/fellowship in integrative medicine at the University of Arizona in Tucson. He suggests that the active essential fatty acid, **gamma linolenic acid**, found in *primrose oil* is helpful for healthy nails.

As you get older (generally over 50), sometimes fewer nutrients may be absorbed by your intestines in some individuals, so supplements are many times suggested.

Gelatin (made from boiled animal protein) has been suggested for many decades to combat brittle nails, although with very little supportive evidence that it directly strengthens nails. There are other sources of protein that negate the need for gelatin. Perhaps historically, gelatin was a replacement for protein due to severe economic conditions. In those times, gelatin was an inexpensive source of protein, and in the absence of protein in the diet during times of hardship, it may have improved nail health. It is not necessary for nail health as a supplement.

Keratin is made up of protein, and keratin forms the nail plate. You must remember, no supplement produces nail keratin or makes them grow faster. No supplement converts directly to nail. Supplements may only help in the overall healthy metabolism of some individuals who are deficient in certain trace minerals, which in turn may help nail development.

The following is for informational purposes only and is not suggested unless you speak to a physician to determine the need for optimal nail health.

Nutrition

Consume adequate protein and minerals for general nail health. Increase the amount of nuts, seeds, whole grains, legumes, fresh vegetables, sea vegetables, and cold-water fish that you eat. Avoid sugars, alcohol, caffeine, and refined foods.

When nails do not grow properly or have abnormalities, the cause can be associated in some cases with a nutritional deficiency stemming from an unbalanced diet, digestive problems, absorption problems, or eating disorders. The following list includes nutritional factors affecting the nails when there is a lack of vitamins, minerals, and trace elements in the diet. Check with your physician to confirm this information.

• A lack of vitamin A and calcium may cause dryness and brittleness.

• A vitamin B deficiency may cause fragility of the horizontal and vertical ridges in the nail.

• A vitamin B12 deficiency may lead to rounded and curved nails.

• A lack of protein, folic acid, and/or vitamin C may cause hangnails.

• A lack of "friendly bacteria" (*Lactobacillus sp.*) may lead to fungus under and around the nails.

• A deficiency of hydrochloric acid may contribute to splitting nails.

• Low iron may cause concave or "spoon" nails (kolonychia) and/or vertical ridges.

Iron Deficiency

Iron deficiency anemia affects 20% of women, 50% of pregnant women, and 3% of men. It can be caused by too little iron in the diet, poor bodily absorption of iron, heavy menstrual bleeding, or other loss of blood. In addition to pregnant or lactating women, children in rapid growth stages have an increased requirement for iron. People with a diet consisting of little or no meat or eggs for a sustained period may also suffer from iron deficiency. Symptoms of anemia are pallor, fatigue, weakness, shortness of breath, low blood pressure, decreased appetite, and brittle nails. Iron deficiency anemia can also cause a condition called Koilonychia in which the fingernail is thin and concave, and has raised ridges. If these symptoms are present, dietary iron supplements should be taken. Have a blood test to measure ferritin levels in order to ensure that supplementing with iron is necessary prior to taking any iron supplements.

Gamma Linolenic Acid

The following is from www.drweil.com

Want healthy skin, hair and nails? Try taking the essential fatty acid gamma linolenic acid (GLA). This essential fatty acid offers a wide range of benefits, from acting as an effective anti-inflammatory agent (with none of the side effects of anti-inflammatory drugs) to promoting the healthy growth of skin, hair and nails. GLA can also be used effectively for other conditions such as brittle nails and hair, arthritis, autoimmune disorders, and premenstrual syndrome.

Unfortunately, GLA is hard to come by in the diet, so supplements may be necessary. Three good, natural sources are evening primrose oil, black currant oil and borage oil. Each comes in capsule form, and vary in the amount of GLA they supply as well as in their cost.

Do not expect immediate results when taking GLA: it takes six to eight weeks to see changes after adding GLA to the diet.

Biotin

Biotin, a B-complex vitamin, has been shown in several studies to improve nail firmness, hardness, and thickness in test subjects with fragile and brittle fingernails (Hochman et al. 1993). After a 6-month treatment regimen consisting of oral administration of 2.5-10 mg of biotin, most test subjects show a marked improvement in the condition of their nails, often with complete clearing of nail fragility (Floersheim 1989; Bardazzi et al. 1993).

In a placebo-controlled, double-blind clinical study, 60 patients with reduced nail quality without a known biotin deficiency were treated for 6 months with a daily 2500 mcg dose of oral biotin. The changes in nail quality were documented by measuring the swelling behavior and water loss through the nail keratin after incubation with sodium hydroxide (NaOH), as well as by the clinical judgment of the investigator and the patients. All evaluation parameters showed improvement of nail quality (Anon. 1996).

Summary

The condition of our fingernails reflects our overall good health. Many factors contribute to the condition of nails, some of which are related to serious medical conditions. Studies repeatedly show that a diet that includes an adequate amount of essential nutrients is necessary to keep nails healthy.

The following links represent the source of the information in this chapter:
DR Weil Foundation www.drweil.com
Linus Pauling Institute http://lpi.oregonstate.edu/infocenter/vitamins/biotin/
University of Maryland Medical Center
http://www.umm.edu/altmed/ConsConditions/NailDisorderscc.html#Signs#Signs

BIOTIN CASE STUDIES: http://www.appearex.com/pdfs/
Appearex_Monograph.pdf
http://www.lef.org/protocols/prtcl-081.shtml

Disclaimer

This book provides scientific information on health aspects of micronutrients for the general public. The information is made available with the understanding that the author and publisher are not providing nutritional counseling services on this site. The information should not be used in place of a consultation with a competent health care or nutrition professional.

The information on micronutrients contained in this book does not cover all possible uses, actions, precautions, side effects, and interactions. It is not intended as medical advice for individual problems. Liability for individual actions or omissions based upon the contents of this book is expressly disclaimed.

Chapter 17

Whirlpool infection outbreaks

This is a governmental press release found on the link http://www.dca.
ca.gov/press_releases/2006/0627_attachment1.pdf

This chapter deals with the California Department Of
Consumer Affairs Recommendations of the Working Group on
Footspa Safety

Background: Consumer health issues associated with
pedicures have become a matter of increasing nationwide concern in recent years. Outbreaks of mycobacteria infections and
staph infections resulting from pedicures have caused injury,
disfigurement and even death.

In California, there was an outbreak of skin boils in
Santa Cruz County in October 2000. More than 100 pedicure
customers were affected by the outbreak, which was traced back
to a single Watsonville salon where footspa equipment was not
properly cleaned and disinfected.

As a result, the Department of Consumer Affairs (DCA)
Board of Barbering and Cosmetology (BBC) adopted new regu-

lations in the spring of 2001, which required more thorough cleaning and disinfecting of footspas.

In November 2004, however, there was another outbreak of serious pedicure-related skin infections in Santa Clara County. This outbreak involved 33 different salons and 143 customers.

Another outbreak occurred in March 2005 in Contra Costa County involving seventeen people.

In 2005, AB 1263 (Yee) was introduced in the California Assembly. The bill would have set minimum safety standards for pedicure equipment and required BBC to adopt regulations regarding proper cleaning and disinfection of pedicure equipment. The bill was vetoed by Governor Arnold Schwarzenegger in October 2005. However, in his veto message the Governor directed " . . . the Department of Consumer Affairs to convene a working group consisting of BBC, county health officials, consumer groups, pedicure equipment manufacturers and other interested parties, to determine how to improve the safety of pedicure equipment and ensure appropriate consumer protection."

In late 2005, DCA began contacting stakeholders and compiling information the group would need for its work. The Working Group on Footspa Safety was created. It included the following individuals:

Charlene Zettel, Director, DCA – Working Group Chair
Leah Alberto, Jerry Lee Beauty College
Marcia Bonawitz, Instructor, Sacramento City College
Adam Borut, Vice President, European Touch
Paul Bryson, Director of Research and Development, O.P.I. Products, Inc.
Dee Dee Carlson, San Francisco Institute of Esthetics and Cosmetology
Jim Casteel, Vice President, AmeriSpa
Joyce Chung, Epidemiologist, Santa Clara County Health Department
Sara Cody, Deputy Health Officer, Santa Clara County Health Department
Gary Duke, Legal Counsel to DCA / BBC.
Richard Hedges, Vice President, BBC
Russ Heimerich, Chief, DCA Office of Public Affairs,
James Jacobs, Supervising Inspector, BBC

Denise Johnson, Assistant Executive Officer, BBC
Fred Jones, Legal Counsel and Lobbyist, Professional Beauty Federation of California
Theresa Kimura-Yip, Enforcement Manager, BBC
Nancy King, Nail Care Consulting
John Lockamy, Jerry Lee Beauty College
Travis McCann, Manager of Customer Satisfaction Improvement Unit, DCA
Alex Ninh, National Sales Manager, AmeriSpa
Stephen Rhoads, Lobbyist, Strategic Advocates
Dustin Rodriguez, Cosmetologist and Establishment Owner
Doug Schoon, Vice President for Science and Technology, Creative Nail Design, Inc.
Julie Taylor, Legislative Analyst, Division of Legislative & Regulatory Review, DCA
Marcie Tidd, U.S. Environmental Protection Agency
Kristin Triepke, Deputy Director, Division of Legislative & Regulatory Review, DCA
Jerry Tyler, President, BBC
Kristy Underwood, Executive Officer, BBC
Candi Zizek, Health Program Specialist, California Department of Health Services

The group met five times in early 2006 – on February 2, February 15, March 15, April 5 and April 27. After the final meeting, work continued via telephone and e-mail, leading to the final recommendations.

Main Tasks and Recommendations by the Working Group on Footspa Safety

1. To review statutory and regulatory provisions regarding standards and protocol for cleaning and disinfecting footspas, and to determine the areas that need to be improved to ensure customer safety.

After deciding that existing Board cleaning and disinfecting regulations were insufficient, the Working Group proposed new procedures to clean and disinfect footspas. (See

Appendix A)

2. To review the Board's existing inspection and enforcement program and determine areas in need of improvement
The Working Group agreed to the following recommendations:

• Fines that are not waivable.

• $500 fines for violations per footspa or cleaning log.

• The $5,000 maximum on fines per inspection should
remain.

• Require repeat inspections for violators, possibly at the
owner's expense.

• A probationary period for one year per licensee and per
owner found to be in violation of health and safety laws.

• Board-approved remedial training on footspa cleaning and
disinfection for licensees in violation.

• That a licensee shall not perform services on a client
if the licensee has reason to believe the client has an unhealthy condition; communicable disease; contagious condition; inflamed, broken, raised or swollen skin or nail tissue;
or an open wound or sore in the area to be worked on that
would contraindicate the efficacy of the service.

Note: Some Workgroup participants felt it would be beneficial if the
above recommendation included those that are believed to be diabetic because for many diabetics, foot care is an important preventive
measure (due to decreased vascularity in their feet and increased risk of
infections).

However, it may be over-reaching to prohibit anyone with any degree
of diabetes from having a pedicure, as it should be the responsibility of the diabetic and their physician to determine what kind of foot
care is appropriate for them. The responsibility of the pedicurist is to
recognize physical signs of conditions that should preclude providing a
pedicure, not medical diagnoses.

• That licensees shall ask whether the client has shaved their legs or received waxing services on their legs within the past 24 hours. If so, the licensee shall not perform a pedicure service on that client.

3. To review current school curricula regarding cleaning and disinfection of footspas and determine areas in need of improvement.

The Workgroup developed the following policy directives regarding current school curricula and footspa disinfection:

• Recommend that cosmetology schools incorporate the footspa disinfection protocols into existing curriculum requirements.

• Recommend that the Board's licensing exam include a written component that tests footspa disinfection knowledge as determined by the occupational analysis.

Education/Outreach

The Working Group on Footspa Safety also recommended that DCA and BBC conduct education and outreach efforts targeted to both the salon industry and to consumers. The group specifically recommended that salons be required to post a "Consumer Footspa Tips" sign that includes the following text:

FOOTSPA TIP FOR CONSUMERS

Don't shave or wax your legs 24 hours before a pedicure. Shaving and waxing increase the risk of infection. If you have broken skin or open sores on your lower legs, do not get a pedicure.

Mycobacteria in Nail Salon Whirlpool Footbaths, California

April 2005

Mycobacteria in Nail Salon Whirlpool Footbaths, California
Duc J. Vugia,* Yvonne Jang,† Candi Zizek,* Janet Ely,† Kevin L. Winthrop,*‡ and Edward Desmond† *California Department of Health Services, Berkeley, California, USA; †California Department of Health Services, Richmond, California, USA; and ‡Centers for Disease Control and Prevention, Atlanta, Georgia, USA   Vol. 11, No. 4
http://www.cdc.gov/ncidod/EID/vol11no04/04-0936.htm

In 2000, an outbreak of *Mycobacterium fortuitum furunculosis* affected customers using whirlpool footbaths at a nail salon. We swabbed 30 footbaths in 18 nail salons from 5 California counties and found mycobacteria in 29 (97%); M. *fortuitum* was the most common. Mycobacteria may pose an infectious risk for pedicure customers.

In October 2000, we investigated the first known outbreak of *Mycobacterium fortuitum* cutaneous infections acquired from whirlpool footbaths, also called footspas, at a nail salon in northern California [1]. Over 100 pedicure customers had prolonged boils on the lower legs that left scars when healed [1,2]. In the investigation, we swabbed the area behind the screen of the recirculation inlet in each of 10 footspas at the nail salon and recovered strains of M. *fortuitum* from all 10. Isolates from 3 footbaths and 14 patients were indistinguishable by pulsed-field gel electrophoresis and by multilocus enzyme electrophoresis [1].

Before this outbreak, M. *fortuitum* and other rapidly growing mycobacteria (RGM) caused localized cutaneous infections but usually in a healthcare-associated setting with surgical or clinical devices contaminated with water from the hospital or from the municipal water system [3]. In the nail salon outbreak, we suspected that the mycobacteria entered the footspas through the municipal tap water and thrived in the large amount of organic debris accumulated behind the footspa recirculation screens. However, cultures of tap water at that nail salon later in the investigation yielded RGM in the M. *chelonae-abscessus* group but not M. *fortuitum* [1].

Since RGM are commonly found in municipal water systems [4-6], and since the nail care business is a $6 billion and growing industry in this country [7], we hypothesized that similar whirlpool foot bath–associated RGM infections occurred sporadically but went unnoticed. Soon after we alerted the health communities to this outbreak, 3 cases of lower extremity RGM infections associated with 2 different nail salons were documented from southern California [8].

No study has been published on the prevalence of mycobacteria in whirlpool footbaths. To determine the prevalence of nontuberculous mycobacteria in this common nail salon equipment, we undertook a mycobacteriologic survey of footspas in nail salons in California from November to December 2000.

The Study

Five large counties from different parts of California (Alameda, Sacramento, Orange, Riverside, and San Diego) participated in the survey. Counties chosen served large populations and had multiple nail salons with whirlpool footbaths. In each county, a team including the regional investigator of the California Bureau of Barbering and Cosmetology and a local public health professional visited selected nail salons. They assessed footspa equipment, cleaning solutions, and cleaning techniques and frequencies. Swab samples were also collected.

In each participating county, a convenience sample of 3 different nail salons equipped with whirlpool footbaths located in the town's main business section was randomly selected for the survey. Salon managers were questioned about cleaning and disinfection regimens of their footspas. Pedicure equipment time in service within the salon and make and model numbers of whirlpool pedicure equipment were noted. For each salon, 2 separate footspas were sampled, unless that salon only had 1 footspa, in which case only 1 swab was collected. Using a screwdriver, investigators removed the grate or filter screen covering the recirculation port in each footspa basin and inspected the area behind the screen for debris. A sterile, cotton-tipped culturette was used to swab this area and placed in standard transport medium.

At the California Microbial Disease Laboratory, each swab was removed from the transport medium, placed into a 50-mL tube containing 5 mL of sterile water, and the contents vortexed. The swab was then removed from the tube, and the remaining suspension was decontaminated with an equal volume of N-acetyl-L-cysteine-sodium hydroxide for 15 minutes, followed by neutralization with phosphate buffer and concentration by centrifugation [9]. The sediment was spread onto Middlebrook 7H10 and Middlebrook 7H11/Mitchison 7H11 selective agar plates, Lowenstein-Jensen slants, Bactec 12B, and Bactec Mycobacteria Growth Indicator Tube 960 system (Becton-Dickinson, Sparks, MD, USA) liquid media.

The mycobacteria isolated were identified by 1 of the following methods: rapid DNA probes using nucleic acid hybridization [10], high performance liquid chromatography that produces mycolic acid patterns [11], and biochemical tests [9]. M. simiae and M. lentiflavum were differentiated by urease activity and photochomogenicity; for both of these, M. simiae is positive and M. lentiflavum is negative [12]. M. smegmatis group organisms were not differentiated to the species level. M. mageritense was identified by polymerase chain reaction restriction analysis at a Mayo Clinic laboratory and by DNA sequencing at the University of Texas Health Center in Tyler.

Thirty-one swabs were collected from 30 whirlpool footbaths in 18 nail salons from the 5 California counties. Twelve salons had 2 footspas; 6 had only 1 footspa. Of these 30 footspas, nontuberculous mycobacteria were cultured from 29 (97%). From 15 (50%), >1 mycobacterium species were isolated. No mycobacteria or other acid-fast organisms were isolated from 1 footspa that had only been in use for 11 days, whereas the positive footbaths had been in use for an average of 22 months (range 3–84 months).

Isolated from the whirlpool footbaths were 10 species of mycobacteria, 6 of which were RGM: M. fortuitum, M. mucogenicum, M. smegmatis group, M. mageritense, M. neoaurum-like RGM, and a pigmented unidentified nontuberculous mycobacterium (Table). M. fortuitum was the most frequently isolated mycobacterium, found in 14 (47%) of the 30 footspas surveyed and from all 5 counties. Rapid growers, including M. fortuitum, were found in 23 (76%) of the footspas. Slow-growing mycobacteria species were also recovered, including M. avium complex, M. gordonae, M. simiae, and M. lentiflavum. These species were less frequent than the rapid growers, except for M. avium complex, which was found in 5 (17%) of the footspas.

Mycobacterial species vary in their ability to survive the selective NaOH decontamination step that was used in this study [13]. Some solid media cultures that grew M. fortuitum had only a few colonies of this species; others had nearly confluent growth; and still other cultures grew in broth only, not solid media, making it impossible to determine the quantity of growth. For these reasons, quantitative information about the number of colonies present on solid media is not reported.

The whirlpool footbaths sampled came from 3 manufacturers. Disinfectants reportedly used included a variety of brand name products and chlorine bleach, used at intervals of 1 to 14 days. Five (17%) footspas reportedly did not go through any disinfectant process. Twenty-five (83%) of the surveyed footbaths had collected visible debris or slime behind the recirculation screen cover, either on the screen itself, on the tub surface, or both. Fifteen (50%) of footspa operators reported never having cleaned behind this screen. One footspa had no screen or visible debris; nevertheless, it tested positive for mycobacteria.

Conclusions

Mycobacteria were isolated from virtually all pedicure spas surveyed, the sole exception being the footspa that had only been in service for 11 days. Mycobacteria were recovered whether or not disinfectants were reportedly used and whether or not debris was visible behind the recirculation screen.

RGM, M. *fortuitum* in particular, were the most frequently isolated mycobacteria. Our survey suggests that potentially pathogenic mycobacteria are widespread in these footspas across California. These organisms most likely were introduced into the footspas through the municipal water supply, where they colonized parts of the spas and probably the plumbing. Given that these whirlpool footbaths are widespread in California but similar infections known to date are rare, the presence of such mycobacteria alone may not be sufficient to cause pedicure customers to get cutaneous infections from using these spas.

Our 2000 outbreak investigation noted an unusually large amount of debris behind the footspa recirculation screens, which might have provided a niche for mycobacteria to colonize and proliferate to large numbers. In that outbreak, customers who shaved their legs before using these implicated footspas were at higher risk for *furunculosis* than those who did not [1]. However, some customers in that outbreak were infected even though they reportedly did not shave their legs before using the pedicure spas. Thus, while we documented the widespread presence of potentially pathogenic mycobacteria in footspas, the risk for infection remains unclear.

A limitation of this study is our inability to quantify the risk for cutaneous infection to pedicure customers despite finding widespread presence of RGM. We could not quantify reliably the amount of mycobacteria in each footspa with a positive culture. Furthermore, what we found in these footbaths may not be representative of other California counties or other states.

Nonetheless, our findings document the ubiquitous presence of potentially pathogenic mycobacteria among footspas of nail salons in California. The 2000 outbreak might have been a warning of what can happen again if this emerging infection is not adequately addressed. In 2004, a case report documented 2 cases of M. *mageritense furunculosis* associated with using footbaths at a nail salon in Georgia (14).

The California Board of Barbering and Cosmetology adopted new regulations in May 2001 requiring nail salons to follow specific cleaning and disinfection procedures to ensure that their footspa equipment is properly cleaned and maintained [15]. Since our survey was conducted before these new regulations were implemented, further monitoring and research are needed to determine whether complying with the regulations will decrease the potential risk for mycobacterial cutaneous infections among pedicure customers.

Acknowledgments: We thank Leslie Hall and Barbara Brown-Elliott for identifying the M. *mageritense* cultures and the public and environmental health staff from the participating local health departments and the regional inspectors of the California Bureau of Barbering and Cosmetology for assisting us with this survey. Dr. Vugia is an infectious disease epidemiologist and chief of the Infectious Diseases Branch, California Department of Health Services. His research interests include traditional and emerging infectious diseases.

Chapter 18
Hepatitis in nail salons

Reprinted with permission from the Hepatitis C Support Project (HCSP) at www.hcvadvocate.org.

PREVENTING TRANSMISSION IN HCV PERSONAL CARE SETTINGS

Hepatitis C Fact Sheet

Hepatitis C is a disease of the liver by a virus called the hepatitis C virus, or HCV. The U.S. government estimates that about three million Americans have chronic HCV infection. The virus is spread by blood-to-blood contact; primarily through use of shared needles for illicit injection drug use. Sexual transmission and transmission from mother to child are also possible, but less common. Although many people with hepatitis C have no symptoms, over time, the disease can cause serious liver damage, including cirrhosis (scarring) and liver cancer. There is no vaccine to prevent HCV infection, but there are several important measures people can take to reduce the risk of transmission.

How is HCV Spread?

Hepatitis C is a blood-borne infection, which means it is spread through contact with the blood of an infected person. The most common method of transmitting HCV is through sharing needles used to inject drugs. Health care workers may contract HCV infection through needle-sticks with contaminated needles or other accidental exposures on the job. In at least 1 in 10 cases, people have no identifiable risk factors for infection; in other words, it is not known how they got hepatitis C. Since HCV is a blood-borne virus, it can – at least in theory – be transmitted by contaminated personal items, such as razors or nail care equipment.

Any equipment used by manicurists, aestheticians, barbers, and cosmetologists who may come into contact with HCV-infected blood might transmit the virus. This can happen when a small amount of HCV-containing blood – even a tiny amount, too small to see – stays on the equipment after it is used on one person, and then comes into contact with the bloodstream (through a cut or other open area on the skin) or mucous membranes (such as the mouth or nostrils) of another person on whom the same equipment is later used.

Shared personal equipment that comes into contact with blood can spread HCV. This includes tattooing and body piercing needles and other equipment; cuticle scissors, nail files, and emery boards; razors and hair clippers; hair removal tools such as tweezers and electrolysis equipment; and even hair-cutting scissors and combs.

The transmission of viral hepatitis through personal care procedures has not been well studied. The U.S. Centers for Disease Control and Prevention (CDC) has not reported documented cases of HCV being transmitted this way.

Nevertheless, the agency issued health and safety guidelines for personal care professionals in 1985. State laws regarding health and safety standards in personal care settings vary widely. **••The California Department of Health Services recently released a report about a woman whose only known risk factor for getting hepatitis C was regular visits to a nail salon.••**

Keeping it Safe

DISPOSABLE ITEMS

Some tools used by tattooists, piercers, manicurists, and barbers should be used only once, on a single person. Most professional tattooists, piercers, and electrologists use new, disposable needles for each customer; disposable ink pots should also be used. Paper emery boards, files, orangewood sticks, cotton balls or swabs, sponges, neck strips, and other items that cannot be cleaned should be used on only one person and then thrown away. Whenever possible, substitute single-use items for reusable items.

RISKY ITEMS

Blade or scraper tools used to trim calluses (such as Credo blades) are especially likely to come into contact with blood. The California health code prohibits the use of such tools in nail salons. Needle-like instruments used to extract skin blemishes are also prohibited. Cutting cuticles presents a risk for contact with blood, and many experts recommend that nail salon workers not cut cuticles. Straight razors are also likely to draw blood; therefore, disposable blades or safety razors should be used and discarded after each customer.

CLEANING AND DISINFECTING

Equipment that is used for more than one person should be properly cleaned and disinfected between users. For procedures that pierce the skin, disposable tools should be used unless they can be completely sterilized (that is, made completely germ-free). Sterilization can be done using steam or dry heat. An autoclave machine sterilizes using both heat and pressure.

Other types of tools should be cleaned using a disinfectant solution. Commercial products such as Barbicide disinfect rather than sterilize. Although not well studied, research suggests that commercial solutions may not kill HCV. Look for an EPA-registered hospital grade product that kills bacteria (bactericide), viruses (virucide), and fungi (fungicide).

Immerse items in the solution for at least 10 minutes (some experts recommend 20 minutes). Small items may be stored in the disinfectant solution between uses. Commercial solutions should be changed at least once per week or when visibly dirty. Alternatively, alcohol, chlorine, or a 10% solution of bleach and water may be used for disinfection. Although the effectiveness of bleach has not been studied, most experts recommend soaking items in a bleach solution for 10 minutes. Bleach solution should be made fresh daily and kept away from sunlight.

Although the actual needles and blades are disposable, tattoo guns, razor blade handles, and electrolysis machines should be cleaned with a disinfectant solution between users.

WORK SPACE PRECAUTIONS

Workspaces should be set up so that new or clean, and used or dirty equipment is separated and cannot be mixed up. Cover work surfaces with a clean cloth or paper towel or sheet before each customer. Lotions, powders, and other products should be kept in containers that allow for dispensing a portion of the product without contaminating the container, and sanitary applicators should be used for cosmetics.

Work surfaces should be disinfected between users. Manicurists should not use soaking water for more than one customer. Soaking bowls and foot spas should be disinfected after each user. Counters, chairs, lamps, and other surfaces should be cleaned regularly with a disinfectant solution. Used razor blades and other sharp items should be discarded in a puncture-proof container. Nail and hair cuttings should be disposed of properly. Used towels, sheets, and gowns should be placed in a covered receptacle and washed in hot water with detergent.

Personal care professionals should be educated about disease transmission and trained to use proper health and safety procedures. Manicurists, cosmetologists, barbers, aestheticians, and electrologists must be licensed in most states. Workers should wash their hands with soap and water before each customer and, when appropriate, wear disposable gloves. Any cuts or sores should be covered with waterproof bandages.

PERSONAL USE ITEMS

To be as safe as possible, some customers prefer to bring their own equipment with them to the nail salon or barbershop. This is especially important for items like cuticle scissors and razors that are likely to come into contact with blood. Some professionals will keep personal client packs or kits at the salon with tools to be used only for a specific customer.

Finally, as is the case with equipment used in nail salons, hair salons, and barbershops, personal health and beauty items used at home, including nail files, razors, toothbrushes, and pierced earrings, should not be shared.

The information in this fact sheet is designed to help you understand and manage HCV and is not intended as medical advice. All persons with HCV should consult a medical practitioner for diagnosis and treatment of HCV.

Executive Director, Editor-in-Chief, HCSP publications: Alan Franciscus

Medical Writer: Liz Highleyman

Medical Reviewer: Norah Terrault, MD, MPH, Assistant Professor, Medicine/Gastroenterology, University of California, San Francisco

Design and Production: Paula Fener

126 DEATH BY PEDICURE

Contact information:

The Hepatitis C Support Project
PO Box 427037
San Francisco, CA 94142-7037
alanfranciscus@hcvadvocate.org

This information is provided by the Hepatitis C Support Project • a non-profit organization for HCV education, support, and advocacy • © 2002 The Hepatitis C Support Project • Reprint permission is granted and encouraged with credit to the Hepatitis C Support Project.

Important Comments/Clarifications: Only one case of Hepatitis C has been alluded to in a nail salon, so the risk is minimal as long as proper disinfection or sterilization protocols are followed. However, this letter clearly demonstrates the risk of potential hepatitis infection from multiple sources of injury if precaution is not taken. Credo blades (callous cutters) are illegal in 22 states including California and should not be advocated in any form under any circumstances. Twenty-eight other states pose a grave risk of injury and infection. The term cuticle used in nail salons refers to dead skin, not living skin such as the eponychium.

Personal use items must be not be shared. Personal nail kits must be disinfected like any other salon tool, and it is up to the customer who chooses to use a personal nail kit to insure proper disinfection or sterilization is accomplished. Nail salon clients should wash their hands and feet before every salon service. Nail salon clients should not shave their legs 24 hours prior to nail salon services.

Chapter 19
What is in nail polish?

Most nail polish formulas have in common some of the basic following ingredients. Nitrocellulose, Sulfonamides, toluene, formaldehyde resin, titanium dioxide, pigments to impart color, and phthalate. All of these ingredients except the pigments have been links to studies that show allergic potential, toxicity, or dermatitis. *However, with a risk based analysis there are very little current large scale incidents with these products unless improperly used. Some of the formaldehyde and toluene free products are available to individuals who have known sensitivities to these chemicals.

The polish without formaldehyde resin and toluene do not have the same luster, adhesive or lasting properties as those made with formaldehyde resins and toluene. Nail polish has almost no free formaldehyde which is a gas and is more reactive but rather formalin in the form of resins which release almost no free formaldehyde.

The nail industry has reduced the amount of free formaldehyde used earlier an as adhesion promoter at 0.5% to less than 2 thousandth of a percent (0.002%) free formaldehyde now days. The 0.002% could possibly cause dermatitis in some individuals who are already sensitized to formaldehyde but un-likely to cause new sensitivities. Nail hardeners, not nail polish, can legally have up to 3% formalin which can sensitize some individuals to the smaller amounts now found in nail polish.

Toluene is a vapor and contact hazard. It is scored by the Indiana Manufacturing society on it's SCORECARD (See www.scorecard.org). Individuals who huff or inhale paints or aerosols products will use nail polish to get high or intoxicated by the polish vapors of toluene. The key with all beauty product solvents like acetone, toluene and the liquid catalyst monomer products in acrylic nails is good ventilation. One would have to get several nail polish bottles in a plastic bag to obtain enough toluene to get the intoxicating vapors that cause the debilitat-ing effects addicts crave.

Nitrocelluose: The primary ingredient in nail polish is nitrocellulose (cellulose nitrate) cotton, a flammable and ex-plosive ingredient also used in making dynamite. Nitrocellulose is a liquid mixed with tiny, near-microscopic cotton fibers. In the manufacturing process, the cotton fibers are ground even smaller and do not need to be removed. Nitrocellulose acts as a film forming agent. For nail polish to work properly, a hard film must form on the exposed surface of the nail, but it cannot form so quickly that it prevents the material underneath from drying. By itself or used with other functional ingredients, the nitrocellulose film is brittle and adheres poorly to nails. http://www.madehow.com/Volume-1/Nail-Polish.html

After nail polish is applied, some of the ingredients vola-tilize and leave behind a film that is the coating over the nail. Dibutyl phthalate (DBP) is one of the ingredients left behind, reducing brittleness and cracking in the polish.

Phthalates have been named as causing birth defects with the use of some cosmetics. but this has been discounted by many extensive studies by the Cosmetic Independent Review panel.

Nail polish uses 8% or less amounts of phthalates as an ingredient. The plasticizing and film-formation properties of DBP make the chemical particularly useful for nail polish. Too much phthlates would make the nail polish so soft it would not adhere. A normal healthy nail plate that is not damaged or thinned by filing or external damage offers a good barrier to many chemicals including phthalates.

Phthalates in nail enamel testing results have been reviewed extensively by the Cosmetic Independent Review Panel. Even at a 100% concentration (as opposed to the required 10% for testing) phthalates are present at only .0008 ppm. It is very unlikely that a healthy nail plate will absorb most toxic chemicals unless the nail is exposed to long term higher percentage phthalate liquid products not found in nail polish.

Small children are attracted to color and the small bottles of nail polish. (See link of poisonings with nail primers) http://pediatrics.aappublications.org/cgi/content/full/102/4/979. Nail polish products can mimic candy to children. Parents need to be aware of this fact.

Skin can develop can develop various sensitivities to nail polish so a 1/16 border margin from the skin of the nail folds should be used to avoid prolonged contact. This 1/16 border is even more important with acrylic nails..

Women want pretty nails and will go to extremes to accomplish this task. I know this very well as a developer of a nail polish and by treating female patients who want pretty nails. Most nail products are just to cover imperfections, enhance appearance and improve looks.

Important Note "3 free"

Major self initiated changes in the nail manufacturing industry and nail polish manufactures are already underway to eliminate 3 highly controversial ingredients in nail polish ie; formaldehyde, toluene and phthalates. The new formulations are known as "3 Free." Two specific regulations in this country and Europe promoted these recent changes.

OPI started to enact these regulation several years ago see http://www.opi.com/PDFs/WVOEarth_Letter.pdf.

California passed a state law several years ago stating that nail polish formulations would have to be toluene free if sold in salons or other retail establishments in that state. Curiously, the legislator that presented that piece of legislation had a connection to the nail industry. Many companies started to design formulas that could meet this restriction. Toluene is one of the chemicals used in the manufacture of some paints, paint thinners and in small concentrations in nail polish. All three of these ingredients – toluene, formaldehyde and phthalates – were not found to be significant problems in nail polish unless they were improperly actually touching the skin near the nail plate.

Resistance to the fact that "3 free formulas" do not adhere to natural nails as well as regular nail polish formulations have been used as reasons by the nail industry for not changing their best formulations. But in actuality, for over a decade, "formaldehyde free and toluene free formulas have been available to the general public. The public will still purchase what has been recommended by their nail salon technicians and what they have personally experienced as best polish adherence to the natural nails. The nail salon industry additionally downplays any risks by referring to information from the (CIR) Cosmetic Ingredient Review Committee, the cosmetic industry's only self-policed scientific industry group.

Chapter 20
Just for fun - the history of nail polish

Reprinted with permission from NAILS magazine, February 1993

The First Colored Nails

Nail polish originated in China, at least as early as 3000 BC. The Chinese created varnishes and lacquers using ingredients such as gum arabic, egg whites, gelatin, and beeswax. The Chinese wore black and red nail lacquers.

The Egyptians used henna to dye their nails and fingertips orange or yellow. Women in India used red henna to color their hands and feet.

Modern nail polish has been referred to as a variation of car paint and was first sold in this country by Revlon in 1932.

History of Nail Beautification in the U.S.

1800- Almond shaped nails, short and slightly pointed, are the ideal. Nails are sometimes tinted with scented red oil and buffed with a chamois cloth.

1830- In Europe, a foot doctor named Sitts develops the orangewood stick, adapted from a dental tool, for nails. Before this invention, metal tools, acid, and scissors were used to manicure nails.

1879- The trade magazine *American Hairdresser* is published in the U.S.

1892- Dr. Sitts' niece brings nail care to women, and the Sitts method reaches the U.S. Salons spread and cater to women of different incomes.

1900- Women clip their nails with metal scissors and file their nails with metal files. Tinted creams or powders are massaged into the nails to create shine. A glossy nail varnish is available and is applied with a camel-hair brush, but wears off in a day.

1904- The Barber Supply Dealers Association of America, which becomes the Barber and Beauty Supply Institute in 1921, holds its first convention at the World's Fair in St. Louis, Mo., where manufacturers and distributors meet and develop business relationships.

1907- Fromm Industries is founded as Illinois Razor Strop Company.

1910- Flowery Manicure Products is established around 1910 in New York City. The company manufactures metal nail files and invents and introduces the emery board (garnet abrasive on a wood center).

1914- Anne Kindred of North Dakota files a patent for a fingernail shield, a covering for the nails designed to protect them from discoloring while the wearer works with chemicals or other discoloring agents.

Wilde, the parent company of Light Concept Nails, is formed as a dental supply company.

1917- "Don't cut the cuticle!" warns a November 1917 Vogue ad. Instead, suggests Dr. W.G. Korony in Louisville, KY., "Employ the Simplex Method of Home Manicuring –

requires no tools." The Simplex Sample Manicuring Outfit includes "Cuticle Remover, Nail Polish, Nail Enamel, Nail Whitener, Orange Stick, Emery Board, also Booklet of Home Manicuring Lessons."

Women buff their nails with cake, paste, or powder. One formulation is Hyglo Nail Polish, claimed to be brilliant, lasting, and waterproof.

Cutex is busy in the nail department, offering Cuticle Remover, Nail White, Nail Polish (in cake, paste, powder, liquid, or stick form; the color is pink), and Cuticle Comfort. A complete manicure set can be ordered for $.14.

For the New York woman disinclined to do her own nails at home, Miss Frederick at 500 Fifth Ave. "Specializes in Manicuring," according to Vogue Shoppers' & Buyers' Guide.

1918- Morris Flamingo, a supplier of beauty and barber products, opens for business as E. Morris Manufacturing Company in Detroit, manufacturing razor strops.

1920- Screen stars are known for a total look that is almost childlike, with short hair and slender figures. Nails are still unpolished, but soon the development of automobile paint provides the basis for fingernail paint.

1921- The National Hairdressers Assoc. (later to become the National Hairdressers & Cosmetologists Assoc., then the National Cosmetology Assoc.) is formed.

1922- Beauty Culture magazine is published in New York, N.Y.

1924- The Assoc. of Accredited Cosmetology Schools (AACS) is founded. It's a non-profit organization created to bring together all facets of the cosmetology industry, and to further education in cosmetology arts and sciences.

1925- Nail Polish enters the market in a sheer rosy red shade and is applied only to the center of the nail. The moon and the free edge are left colorless. The mid-twenties and thirties are the age of what Beatrice Kaye, manicurist at MGM, calls the "moon manicure." The cuticles are cut, the free edges filed into points, and polish applied to the nail but not to the moon. Sometimes the tip is left uncovered as well. However etiquette books of the time warn women against painting their nails with "garish colors."

Max Factor produces Max Factor's Supreme Nail Polish, a metal pot of beige-colored powder that's sprinkled on the nails and buffed with a chamois buffer. It gives nails shine and some tint.

1927- Max factor introduces Society Nail Tint, a small porcelain pot containing rose-colored cream. Applied to the nail and buffed, it gives a natural rose color. Society Nail White also hits the market. It's a tube of chalky white liquid that's applied under nail tips and left to dry. The end result resembles the modern French manicure. Max Factor also offers cuticle cream and cuticle remover.

1929- Polish with perfume is introduced, but its popularity is short-lived.

1930- Ladies of the silver screen bring polish into vogue. The overall look is one of cool sophistication and elegant, immaculate grooming. The moon manicure thrives in various tints of red.

Gena Laboratories premieres its polish remover, Warm-O-Lotion, cuticle oil, and cuticle remover.

1932- Charles Revson, with his brother and chemist Joseph Revson, and Charles Lachman, creates an opaque, non-streaking nail polished based on pigments rather than dyes, making a variety of colors available. Revlon is created; in the thirties, the company invents the fashion of matching lip and nail color.

1934- Anna Hamburg of California is granted a patent for acolored artificial nail that can be applied and removed easily without damage to the natural nail.

Maxwell Lappe, a dentist in Chicago, creates Nu Nails, an artificial fingernail for nail biters.

Max Factor's Liquid Nail Enamel is introduced and is similar to nail polishes of today. The company uses a limited number of pigments, which means its enamel is available only in red, dark red, vermilion, and crimson. The fashion is to cover the entire nail with polish.

1935- Eugene Rohrbach of New Jersey patents a nail covering that can be applied to the nail without glue. It is slipped over and under the nail's free edge.

1936- A finishing stencil, designed to be placed on top of the fingernail to ensure a consistent coat of polish, is patented by Stella O'Donnell of New York.

1937- A patent for a method using tips to repair and lengthen the nails is granted to Harriet Fligenbaum of Minnesota.

1938- Manicures cost from $.25 to $3.50, depending on whether or nor polish is applied. Base coat is created, which in turn leads to the entire nail being polished. Toenails receive attention, too—by 1938, they're getting a coat of polish along with the fingernails.

1940- Rita Hayworth's long red nails bring new shape to nail fashions. Hers are longer than previously worn, more oval than pointed, and fully covered with red polish. The look is glamorous, that of a worldly seductress.

During the first half of the twentieth century, men who frequent barbershops often receive a manicure as well as a haircut, shave, and shoeshine. For the women, there are bright colors such as Schoolhouse Red Nail Polish from Elizabeth Arden, $.75 a bottle. Clear polish brushed over and under nail enamel extends the life of the manicure.

Frank Nolon of New York patents an applique for nail designs. Other patents issued in 1940 include manicure shields, cuticle guards, and protective nail coverings. Manicure shields allow the manicurist to paint the client's nails while she sits under the hair dryer without the heat reaching the fingertips and ruining the manicure.

In the days before there were fiberglass or silk wraps, there were teabags, coffee filters, and Duco cement, says Beatrice Kaye. Donna Kohl of Boise, Idaho, a nail technician for 16 years, says cigarette and perm papers and airplane glue were used for wraps.

1942- The Charles G. Spilo Company offers hair products and a small selection of nail products.

1943- The Long Beach Hairdressers' Guild holds its first show.

1945- M.A. Kraft patents a stand-up easel with a hole cut in the bottom for the client's hand. This allows the manicurist to work on the client's hand, protected from the hair dryer's heat.

Max Factor offers Satin Smooth Nail Polish to consumers. An improvement upon its earlier Liquid Nail Enamel, the polish is available in reds, pinks, and other colors.

1947- Menda Scientific Products introduces its Babytime Dispenser for baby oil. By 1982, the company enters the beauty market, and obtains a patent on its purity Protector acrylic liquid dispenser in 1986.

1948- Noreen Reho of Missouri creates a manicure apparatus that contains and supports the instruments used in manicuring.

1950- Many more nail colors come on the scene, and with them, a more delicate-looking nail. Nails go from pointed to oval and pale. Eyes are emphasized, with perhaps less attention paid to lips and nails.

There's an explosion of nail polish colors, including Sunny Side Up, a cream red from Revlon. A box containing nail polish, lipstick, and lip liner costs $1.60 plus tax, according to a Vogue ad.

In the fifties, the invention of aerosol hair spray is borrowed by the nail industry to create spray-on nail polish dryers.

Juliette Marglen markets a wrap material resembling a matchbook with the wrap material in sheets, says Beatrice Kaye. Only the top third of the nail is covered. Having the nails wrapped this way is referred to as a "Juliette" manicure.

1957- Excelta Corp. begins importing tweezers and wire cutters for the electronic assembly industry under the name Swiss Army Precision Imports, later under the name Erem. The Danielle Division is formed in 1989 and introduces precision nippers, tweezers, and implements for the nail industry.

Thomas Slack is issued a patent for a "platform" that fits around the nail edge, designed to help manicurists apply extensions to the natural nail. Made of foil, it is used to apply the first acrylic for nails, called Patinail, which is manufactured in the fifties by the Slack family. The product is named after Patricia Still, who developed and demonstrated the technique in department stores.

1959- Max Factor's Nail Enamel is introduced.

1960- The look for a nail is pale. Coral is the rage, but nearly every color under the sun is used by somebody. False nails make their entrance, and they are longer than ever. Silk and linen wraps are found to be stronger than paper wraps. Manicures cost around $7 to $12.

Mona Nail, a Dallas Co., manufactures one of the early acrylic systems available for nails.

Melvco, founded by a professional manicurist, develops the company's Nail Magic, a nail strengthener and conditioner.

1962- WR Medical introduces its Therabath and wintergreen Theraffin.

1970- Age of the artificial nail. Acrylic nails look and feel real, but are much stronger. The square nail evolves. The salon is the place to get your nails made to order. By 1978, nails are very long and worn mainly by the rich. Artificial nails that cover the entire nail plate are available, including the Eye-Lure Nails brand. These are inserted under a lifted cuticle to make them look as if they grow out of the finger. Glue holds them on but not for long—water dissolves the glue.

C.R. Manufacturing Company goes into business.

International Beauty Distributors is founded and starts with a diverse group of beauty products, including eyelashes, nail guards, and wigs. In 1990 the company changes its name to International Beauty Design.

1971- SuperNail is founded and provides No Lite Gel, Stick It Nail Glue, and Electra Nail.

Antoine de Parsi opens for business, offering hair shears and cuticle nippers.

GG's Nails System is founded and starts with linen and fiberglass wraps.

1973- IBD develops the first adhesive especially for finger-nails.

Wilde-Light Concept Nails develops an acrylester resin that is cured by UVA light. In 1985, the material is introduced to the European market as Light Concept Nails.

1974- IBD creates nail tips for professional nail technicians.

Lee Pharmaceuticals begins testing its design for artificial fingernails.

1974 & 1975- The FDA seizes and recalls products containing methyl methacrylate, a chemical considered to be hazardous, and forces manufactures to reformulate acrylics for the nail that are gentler.

1975- The National Association of Nail Artists (NANA) is founded, and its first newsletter, NANA News, is published. Phyllis Monier, one of the founders, wanted to help salon clients realize that nails are just as important as hair. The last issue of NANA News is published in 1983.

Orly international is founded, offering Orly Nail Paint, Romeo liquid fiber wrap, and Ridgefiller primer base coat. The name "French Manicure" originates in 1978 when Orly introduces the first French manicure kit.

Pacific Airbrush starts making a line of paint.

Lee Pharmaceuticals introduces Lee Nails to the consumer market.

Supercuts is founded, making inexpensive haircuts available to salon patrons. The company franchises in 1979.

1976- Square nails become fashionable around 76-77, probably due to nail competitions—judges can easily critique a c-curve in a square nail. Exceptionally long nails are accepted and popular. Nail tips are used more and more, a relief to nail technicians who have difficulty applying forms.

Arius Eckert Company opens its doors, offering industrial shears and scissors.

No Lift Nails evolves from a skin care company established in 1964.

1977- Brucci Ltd. is established with a line of Nail Hardener Shades. Beatrice Kaye manufactures Soak 10 and a manicure owl, the first items in her line of MGM STUDIO 10 natural nail care products.

1978- Creative Nail Design offers its first product, non-yellowing Solarnail, a liquid and powder resin.

Hair Care Service Center is founded, and by 1987, the company's name changes to Hair Care Nail Supplies and markets products to the nail technician.

Salon Interiors takes root when its founder begins to knock on salon doors selling furniture and equipment.

Sogo is founded with a small nail repair kit known as "Patch 5" and a liquid dispenser called "The Pump."

1979- Mehaz International brings manicure sets from Germany to the U.S.

Origi-Nails is founded, offering sculpturing systems and education.

Simply Elegant's roots lie in a beauty supply store that opens in 1979.

Soft Touch opens for business, manufacturing the first cushioned foamboard file, the cushioned Grinder.

Sogo introduces fiberglass to the nail industry.

Lee Pharmaceuticals offers Sculptured Nails in an acrylic powder and liquid form to the consumer market.

1980- The eighties see the use of nail drills (adapted from dental, hobby, and jewelry drills) become common when working with acrylic nails. Fiberglass is the newest wrap system – light, strong & flexible. Nail charms and gold nails begin to decorate some clients' hands, and nail art, worn by the Chinese as early as 5000 B.C., and much later by the Gypsies, finally makes its appearance in the U.S.

The trade newspaper Mainly Manicuring reaches salons in the eighties.

Alpha 9 offers acrylic powders, liquid, and primers.

Beauty Supply San Francisco opens with six product lines.

Dina-Meri brings rollabouts and other salon furniture.

Set-N-Me-Free Aloe Vera Products starts selling aloe-based products to beauty salons nationwide.

Snails Italian Jewelry provides gold-posted initial charms for the fingernail.

Tweezerman begins business, offering the slant eyebrow tweezer.

World International Nail and Beauty Association (WIN-BA) holds its first tradeshow for nails, as well as its world championship competitions.

1981- Essie Cosmetics is founded and offers nail technicians 12 different nail colors.

OPI Products is established and develops 4 NP Powders and L-2000 Liquid especially for the nail industry.

Star Nail Products is born on Venice Beach, Calif. Its first nail products are Star Original acrylic, polish, and cosmetics.

1982- Develop 10 begins business, offering nail color and treatments.

Finger Mates offers Formula 10 Nail Hardener.

Kimberly Clark introduces Handsdown Nail Care Towels to the industry.

Tammy Taylor, a manicurist and salon owner, offers her own line of nail products, beginning with liquid, powder, and primer.

1983- Heken Gourley is the first in her area to offer one of the new gel systems on the market. Her lamp, invented by James T. Giuliano, an expert in plastic research, also creates a process for making artificial eyes.

NAILS magazine opens its first offices in Huntington Beach, Calif., and the first issue is distributed at the Long Beach Hairdressers' Guild Show.

Odorless systems are available.

Ladyfingers is one company offering it.

H & H Products opens, manufacturing emery boards. The first Nail and Skincare Array (NASA) Show is held.

TruNails is purchased by Gabel Holding Co.

1984- Backscratchers is started in a school environment.

Lasco Diamond Products offers drills to the nail industry.

NaturalGlass is begun, with fiberglass, adhesive, and spray accelerator.

Nail Systems International (NSI) is formed.

Worldwide Cosmetics-Winning Nails opens shop with a variety of nail care supplies.

1985- A Show of Hands begins offering stripping tape, paints, and rhinestones for nail art.

Nailco Salon Marketplace opens its doors, providing more than 1000 manicuring items.

Digits International emphasizes reflexology.

Realys Inc. begins making abrasive implements.

Lee Pharmaceuticals introduces Lee Press-On Nails, which are applied with adhesive tabs.

2000 Watsonville California whirlpool incidents.

2003 San Jose whirlpool incidents.

2006 NMC and INTA releases new whirlpool guidelines, Texas goes to full sterilization

The company history and products of the three largest nail companies in the United States: Creative Nail Design, OPI, and NSI.

Creative Nail Design

The company history of Creative Nail Design is taken from its Web site, http://www.creativenaildesign.com/about_companyhistory.asp.

In the 1970s, Dr. Stuart Nordstrom – dentist-by-day, chemist-by-night – began to work on an invention in his garage/lab sparked by an idea from one of his patients. This idea changed the future of the nail industry.

As Dr. Nordstrom mixed dental liquid and powder to create a temporary cap, his manicurist patient recognized an odor similar to the materials used to sculpt porcelain nails. When prompted by his patient, Dr. Nordstrom was

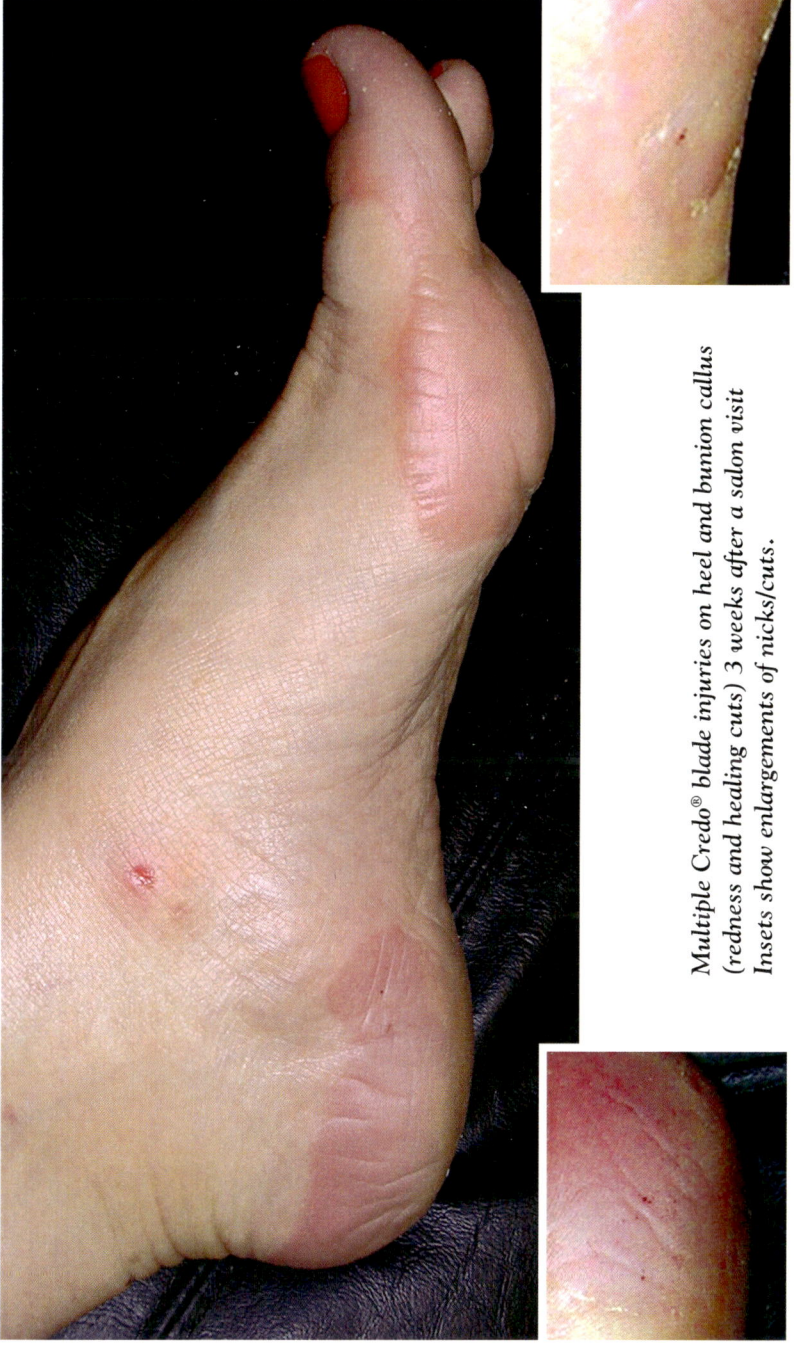

Multiple Credo® blade injuries on heel and bunion callus (redness and healing cuts) 3 weeks after a salon visit Insets show enlargements of nicks/cuts.

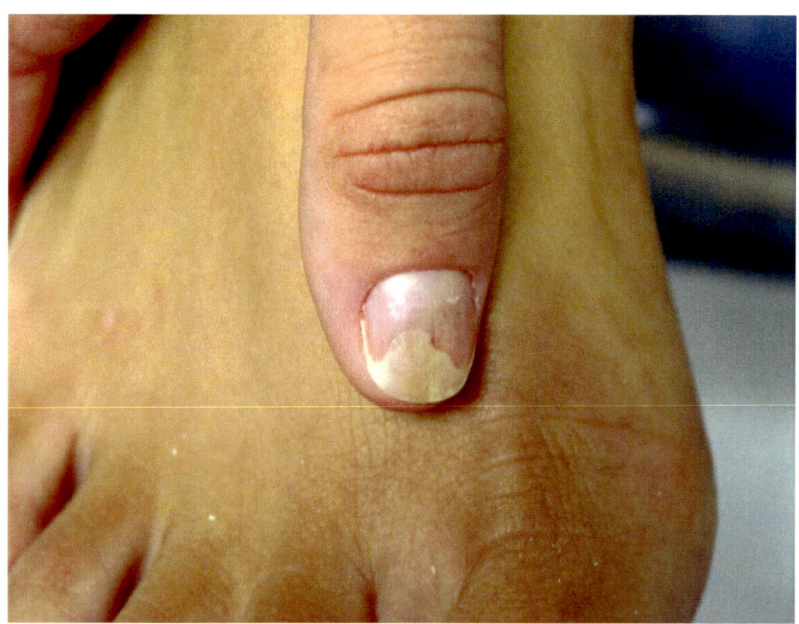

Patient who received a manicure and pedicure 4 months prior to podiatrist office visit

Nail fungus from a pedicure 4 months prior to podiatrist office visit

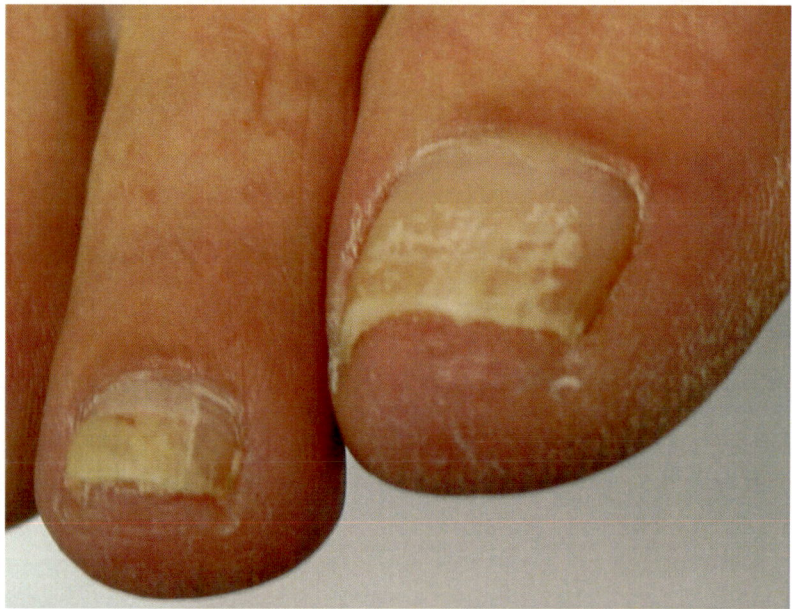

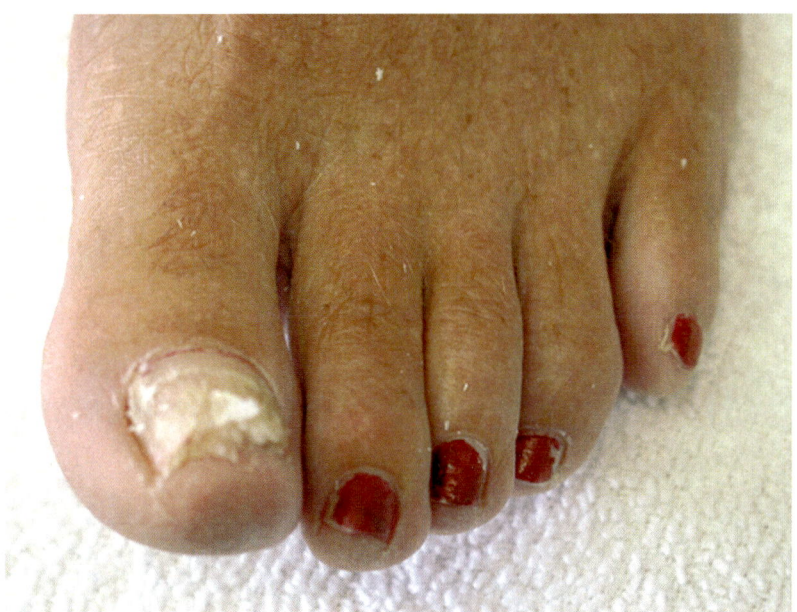

Nail fungus from pedicure 6 months prior to podiatrist office visit.

Fungal infection: Nail "darkened" after pedicure

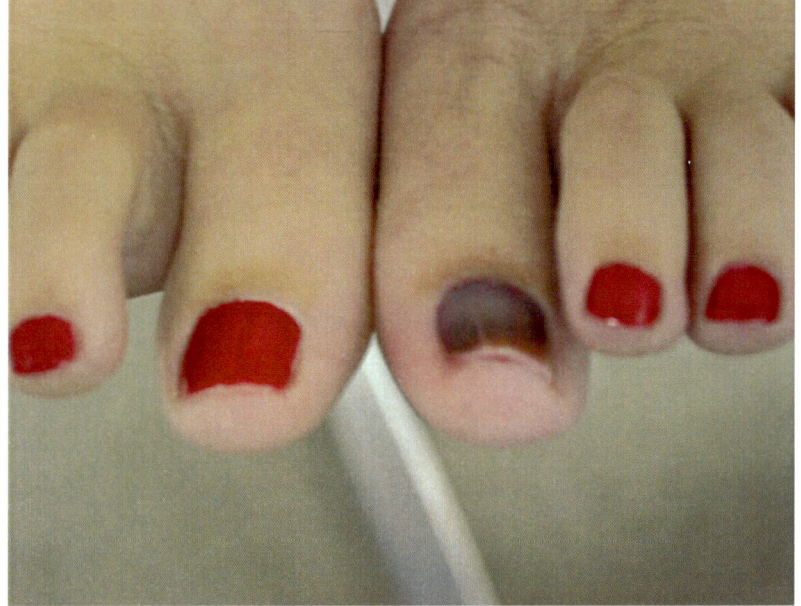

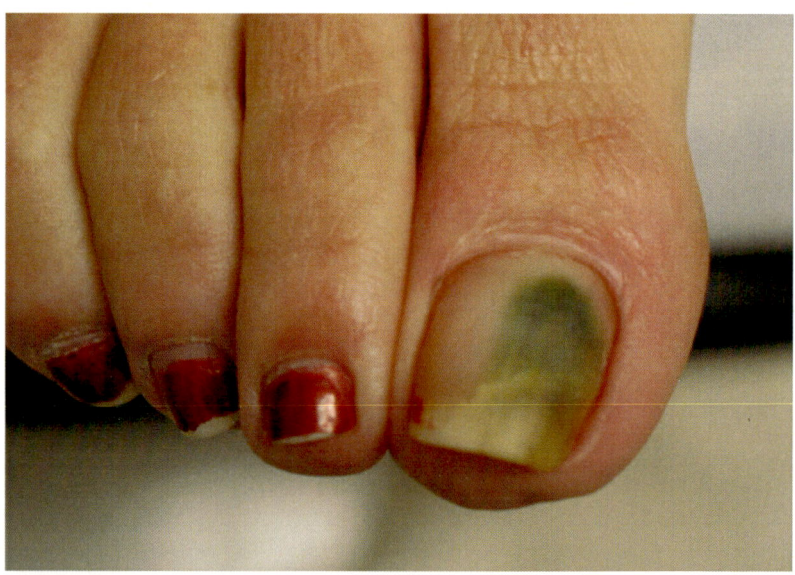

Pseudomonas ("Greenies") on two different patients (above and below) who had pedicures even though they had ongoing cases of fungal nails.

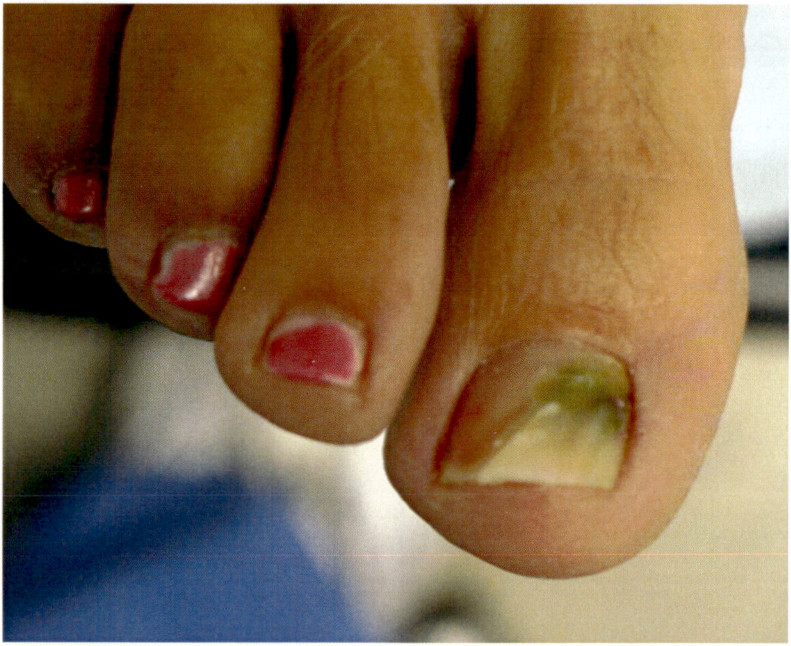

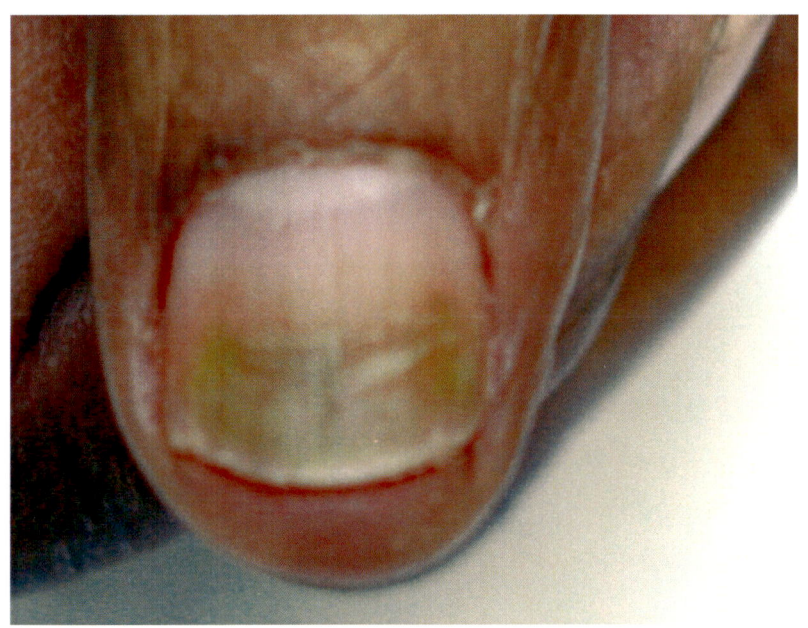

Pseudomonas ("Greenies") from artificial nail on thumb

Nail fungus under polish from a pedicure

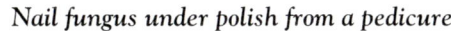

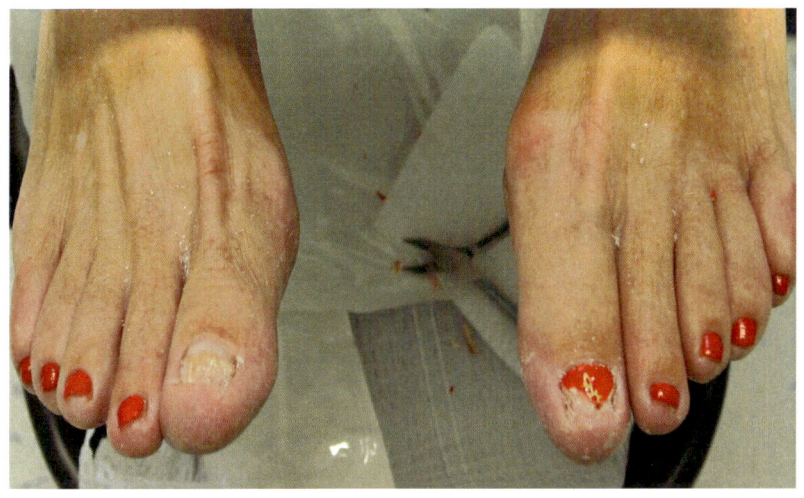

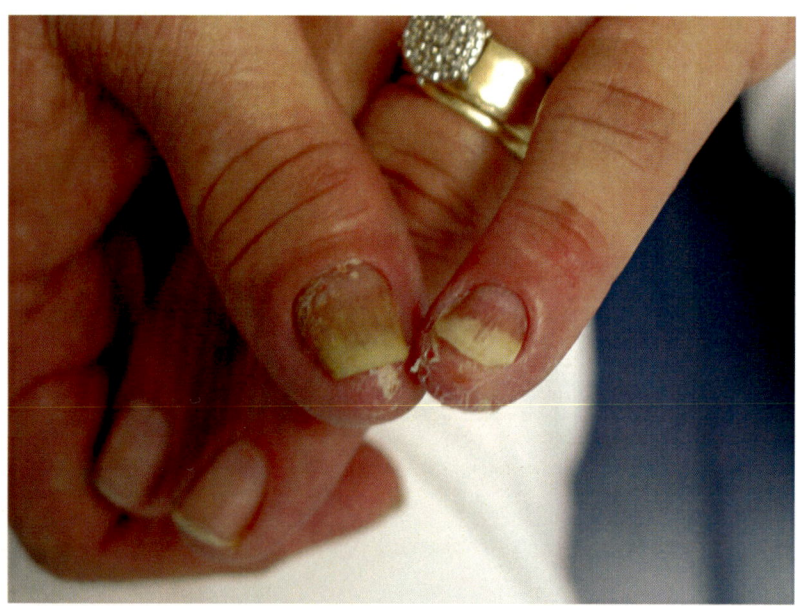

Dermatitis and onycholysis from artificial nal "Homekit" self applied by patient.

Injury following artificial nail removal by prying.

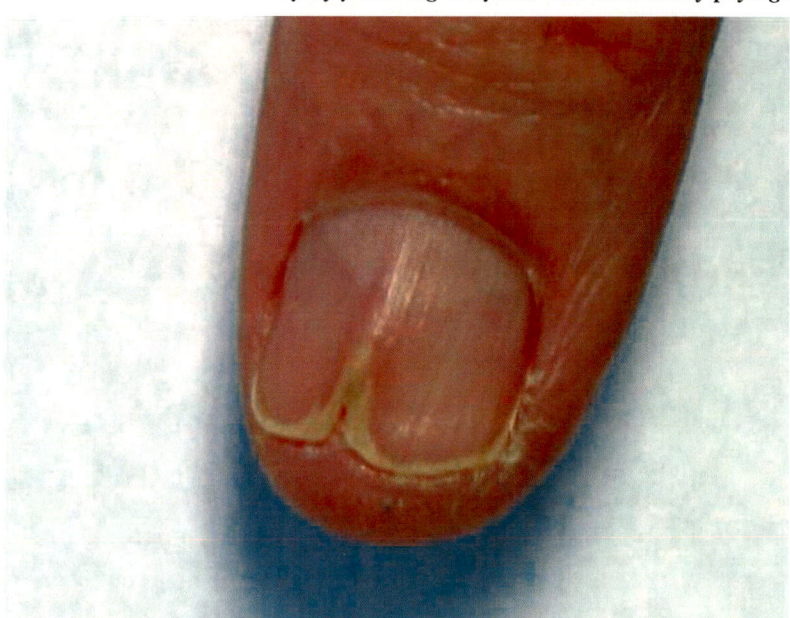

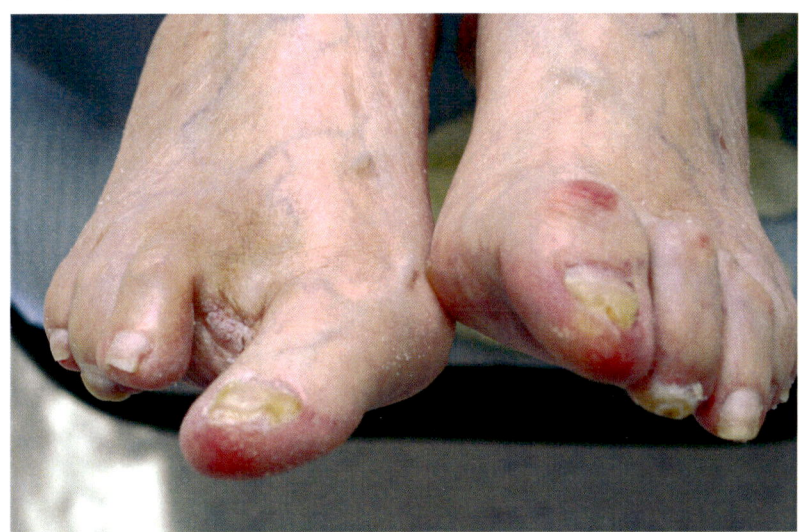

Patient who had amputation of right 2nd toe following a staph infection by a nail tech who provided a corn removal service with a Credo® blade in an assisted living home.

Viral infections (herpes) on toe confirmed by Tzanck test; family history of herpes and fever blisters on mouth.

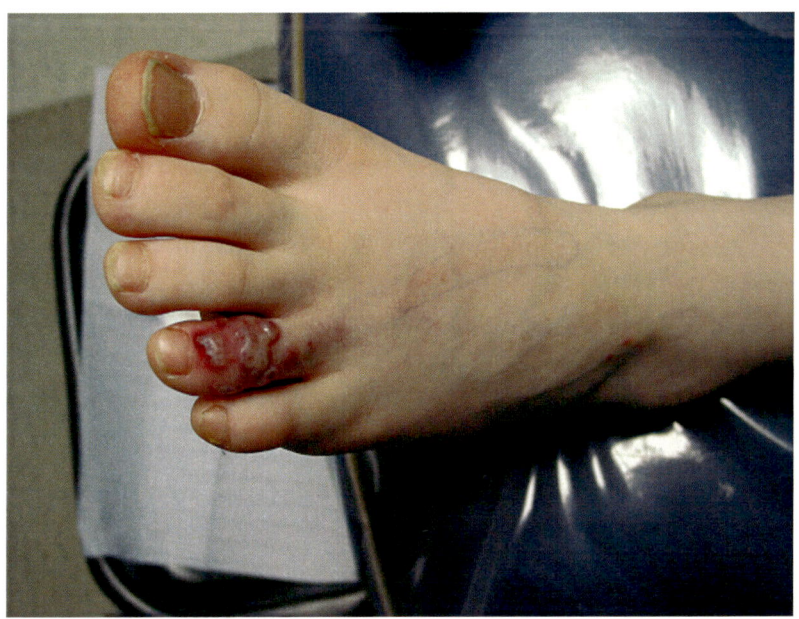

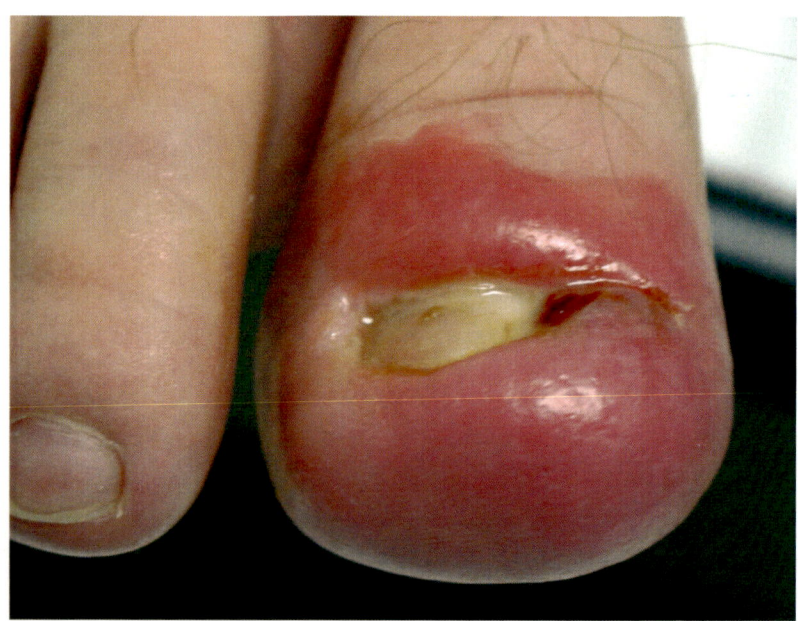

Severe ingrown nail above

Common ingrown nail below.

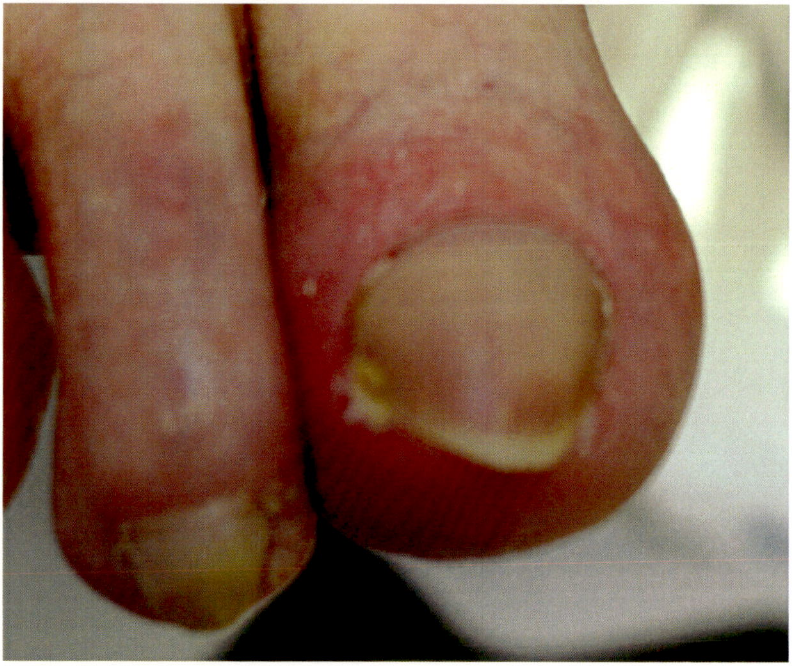

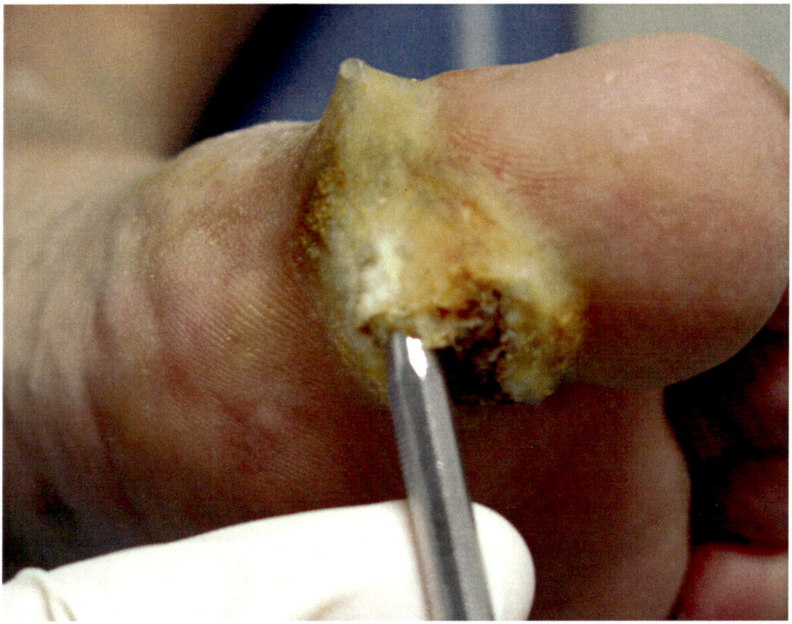

Patient with neuropathy (cannot feel probe)

Paraplegic with heel ulcer

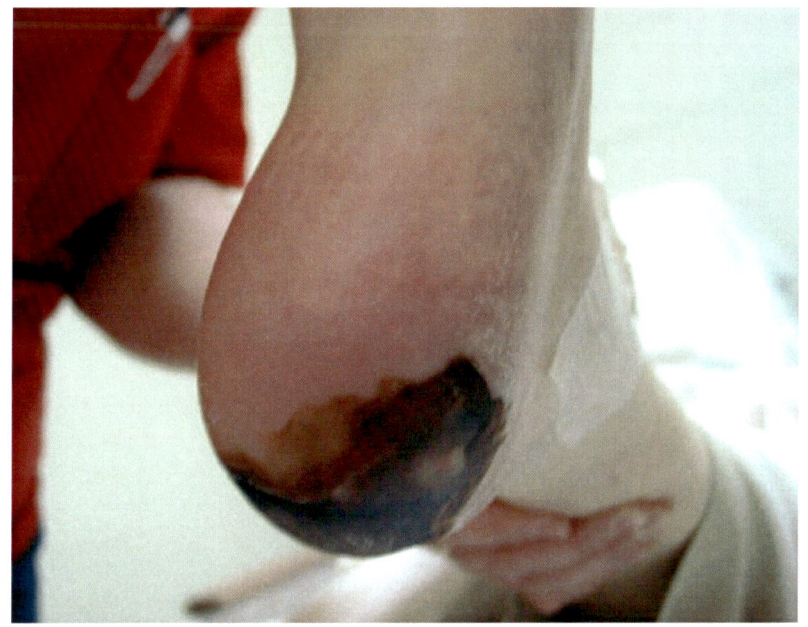

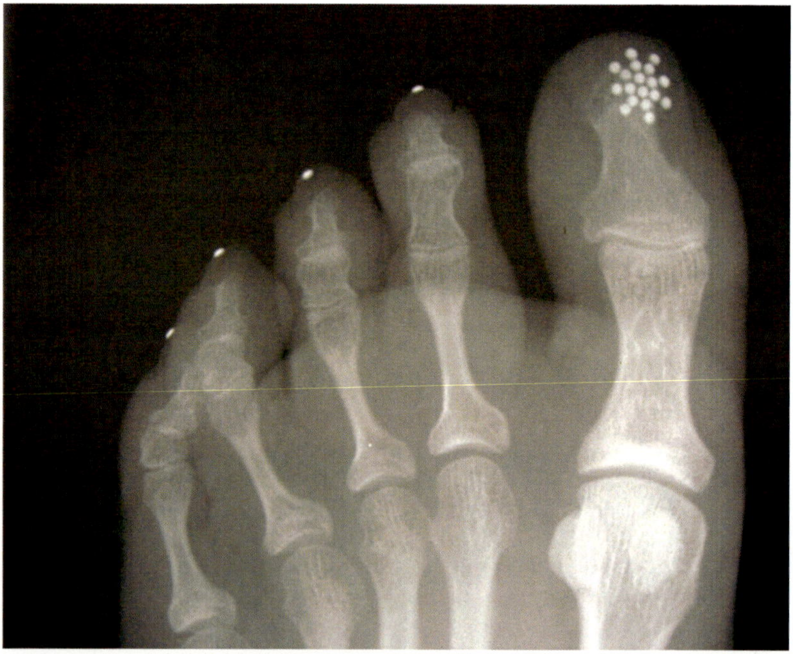

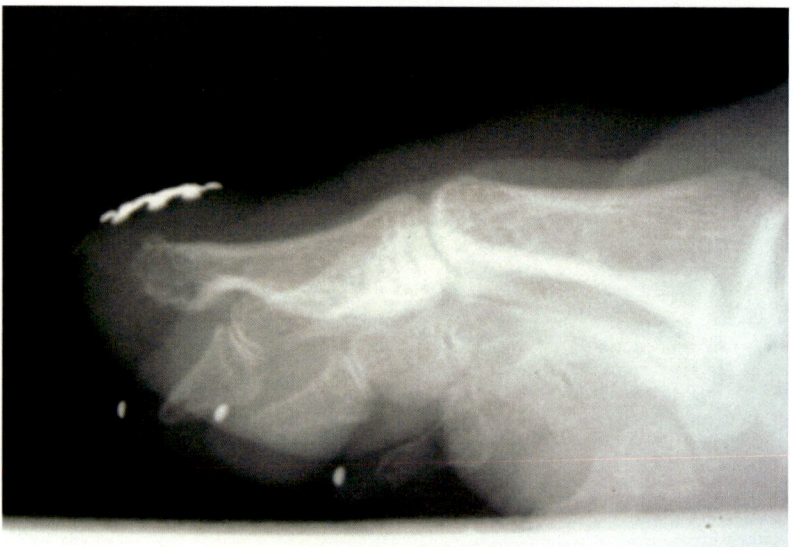

X-Ray showing nail art. Nail technician referred patient for painful big toe. Patient has bone spur directly under nail art.

X-Ray showing nail art and bone spur. Same patient as above with great toe pain.

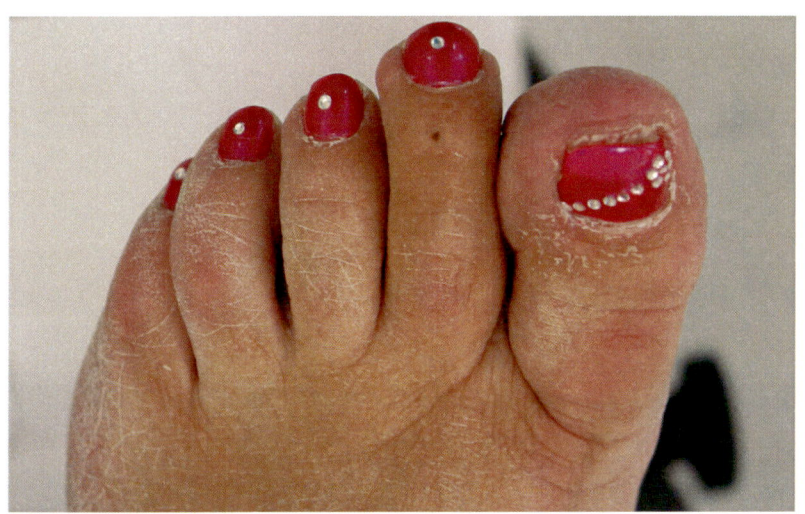

ABOVE:
Patient with
nail art who
had swelling
and pain in
forefoot.

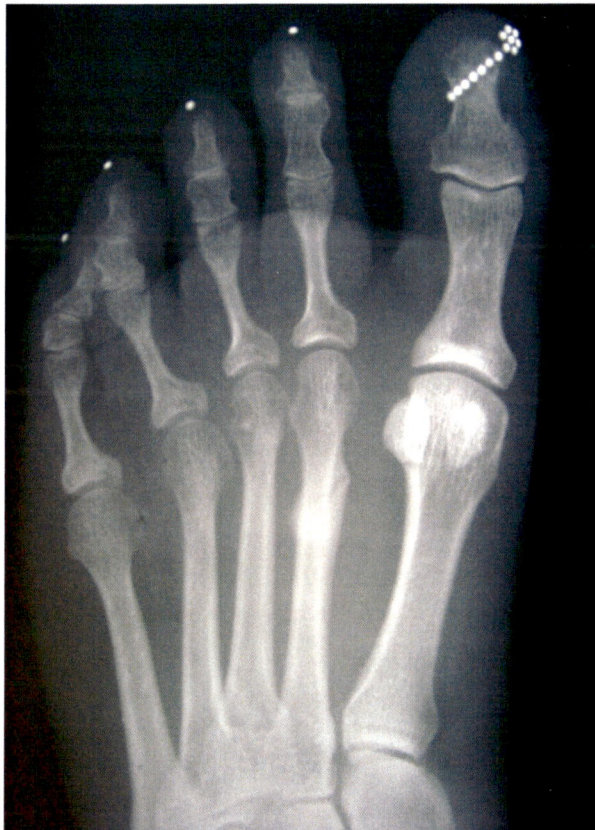

LEFT:
X-Ray of same
patient with
nail art who
has mid shaft
fracture of 2nd
metatarsal.

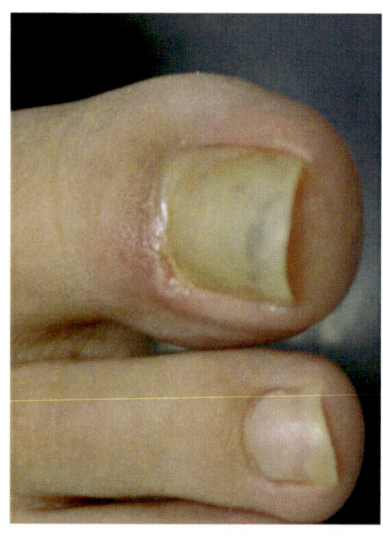

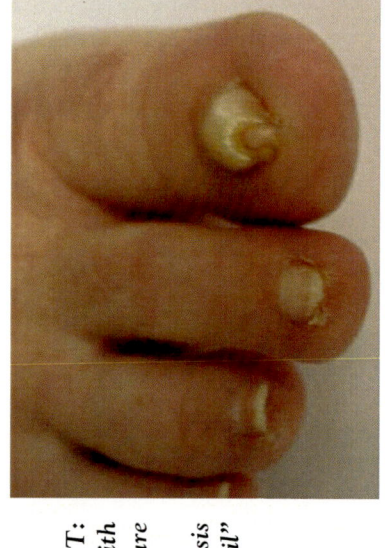

PHOTOS on LEFT:

Top: *Severe case of tinea pedis (athlete's foot) and ingrown nail*

Bottom: *Improvement after one month of oral antifungal and antibiotic treatment with additional nail surgery*

PHOTOS on RIGHT:

Top: *Onycholysis with infection from pedicure*

Bottom: *Onychocryptosis or "pincher nail"*

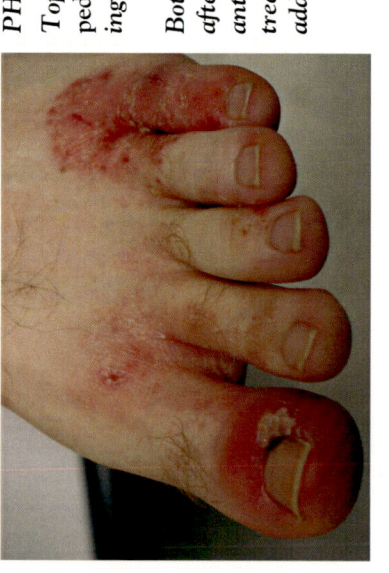

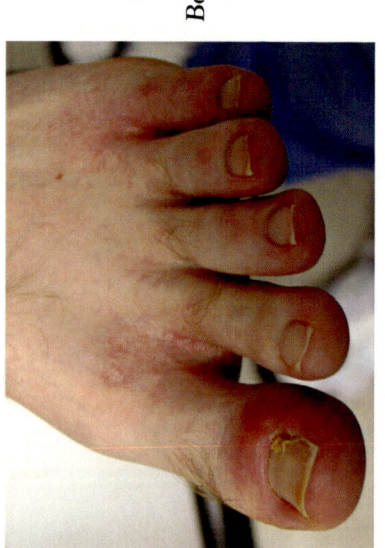

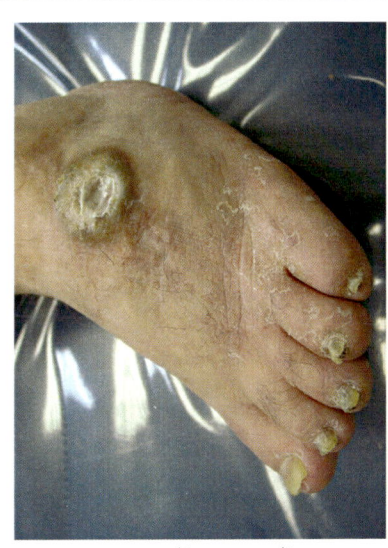

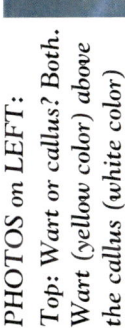

PHOTOS on LEFT:

Top: Wart or callus? Both. Wart (yellow color) above the callus (white color) underneath wart.

Bottom: Wart or callus? Wart

PHOTOS on RIGHT:

Top: Wart, cancer, or callus? Wart

Bottom: Wart, cancer, or callus? Wart

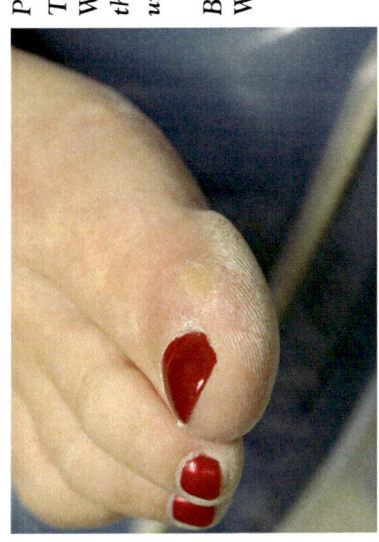

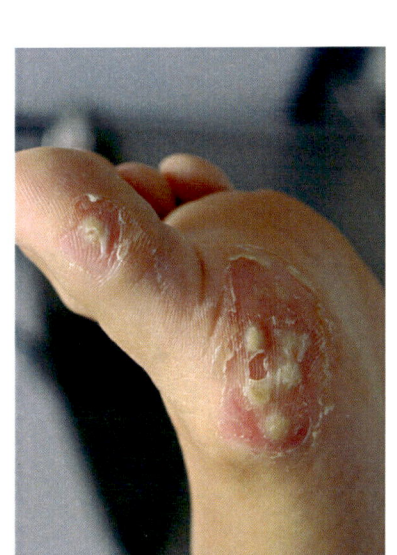

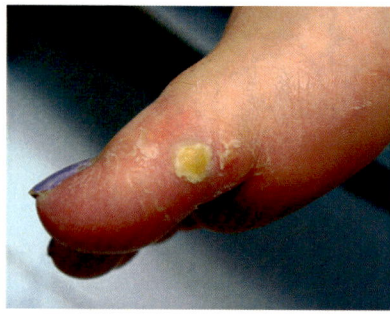

Wart or callus? Wart

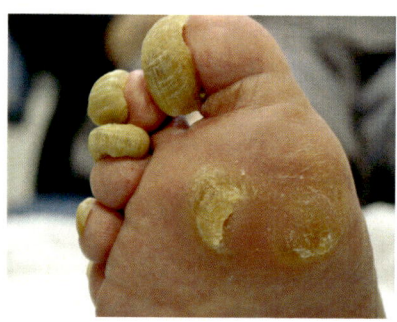

Wart or callus? Callus

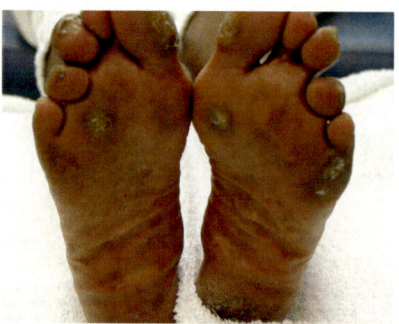

Wart or callus? Callus

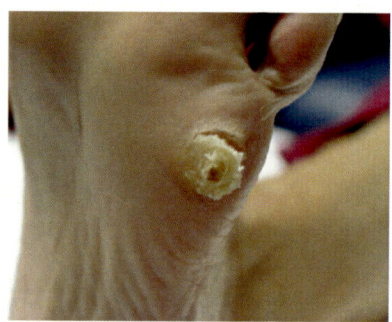

Wart or callus? Callus

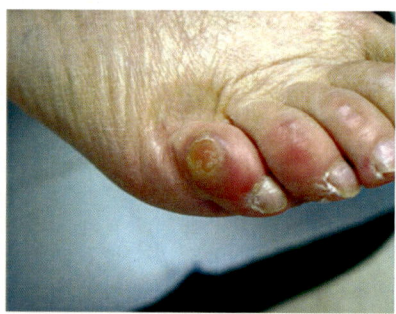

Infected and inflamed "corn"
Heloma durham

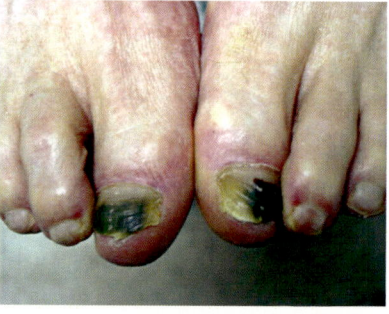

Nail fungus and Pseudomonas

1. Stainless steel basin in pedicure whirlpool chairs are best choice for cleaning surfaces

2. Fiberglass whirlpool basin

3. Pedicure whirlpool "Throne Chair" - Photo by Betty Davis

Premier Beauty Show, Orlando, Florida

Portable personal nail kits can provide a method to reduce health risks
at the nail salon. Photo furnished by
Dr. Siegal.

"Nail Bar" photo by Betty Davis.

challenged to improve nail enhancement products. After six months, he developed a product the beauty industry now recognizes and respects as SolarNail® Liquid, the first ever cross-linked monomer formulation that creates greater nail strength and flexibility. Initially, Dr. Nordstrom only gave SolarNail® to his patient, but when he tested his product at a nearby cosmetology school, Creative Nail Design was born. The entire family then went to work, filling their first orders in the dining room of their home.

During the company's first seven years in business, it doubled in size each year. Nail enhancements were a dominant focus for the company through the 1980s, with important product introductions that included Nail Fresh®, Formation® Nail Tips and GelBond® adhesive, in addition to the wildly popular SolarOil®.

In the 1990s, the company created Radical™ Liquid, the first multidimensional cross-linked monomer that was primer-optional, Ultra Powders that offered easy workability with a creamy flow, ScrubFresh®, now a standard in professional sanitation, and Retention+® Liquid, which created a covalent bond to keratin and was the answer to lifting.

In 1997, Creative entered the spa pedicure market. The entire industry was focused on the nail enhancement category, following the lead of Creative. With innovation and market share on their side, Creative began to look at diversifying and taking the lead in other categories of the business. At that time, the pedicure market represented around 2% of the total industry revenue. Pedicures were mostly done in the summer for sandal season, and there was only one company producing budget professional pedicure products that could be purchased in bulk. Technicians thought feet were smelly and clients were embarrassed to show their feet.

SpaPedicure®, a system known as state-of-the-art in the Spa category is a "facial for the feet". It takes the goodness of the sea to soothe and rejuvenate with marine alpha-hydroxy acid complex, hydrating sea extracts, mineral-rich seaweed, beach sand, and Dead Sea salts plus aromatherapeutic oils and soothing botanicals for a technique that takes pedicures to the next level. In the research and development of Spa-Pedicure®, Creative collaborated with Scripps Institute of Oceanography to identify replenishable ingredients from the sea that could live up to the

SpaManicure® was launched with the revolutionary idea of incorporating a systemic approach to manicure services. Formulated with ceramides, crystalline citric acid and vitamins, this line raised the bar and allowed nail technicians to redefine their menu offerings and pricing strategies.

In November 1999, Creative completely revamped its color line, mastering the professional nail enamel category.

In 2000, Creative launched Perfect Color Powder. This line of advanced sculpting powders offered easy workability in a variety of color shades.

In 2002, CreativeSpa® was born as a division dedicated to servicing the growing resort/hotel and destination spa industry. Again, Creative led the way with revolutionary ideas for reaching this market and inspiring a fresh approach to manicure and pedicure services.

In 2004, Creative celebrated its 25th year with 2 major product launches: Brisa™ Gels, which provide a natural-looking odorless approach to nail enhancements, and Raw Earth™ SpaPedicure®, a system of products that provide a vitamin-and-mineral-infused warming pedicure.

Today, Creative remains a family business, although it was acquired by Revlon in 1995, and in April 2000 by The Colomer Group based in Barcelona.

Located in a custom-built facility in Vista, California, Creative's headquarters is renowned for its multi-million-dollar research and development center. Products are created with the best ingredients; the R&D team is amongst the finest in the industry.

Creative has concentrated on educating the practitioners who use its portfolio of innovative products through formalized education workshops – The Creative Academy – and "master technician" programs. Today, Creative Nail Design is recognized as the education leader in the nail category, training professionals in all topics from medical emergencies to makeovers and massage.

OPI

The company history of OPI is taken from its Web site, http://opi.com/aboutmain.asp.

A family-owned company committed to the highest quality products and to our customers' well-being, OPI has long been a leader in the community and within the Professional Beauty Industry. Quite simply, we are dedicated to excellence.

OPI was founded in 1981 by President & CEO George Schaeffer, who immigrated to the U.S. as a child from post-World War II Eastern Europe. OPI continues to be family-owned, with Schaeffer at the helm, and has grown to become the world leader in professional nail care.

From its inception, OPI broke through nail industry barriers. Schaeffer was one of the first in the nail industry to focus on and limit sales of product to and through beauty professionals only, and who realized the importance of education in both the sale and use of the product. From the very beginning, OPI has shown its commitment to quality by putting batch numbers, instructions, and ingredients on all products it sells.

OPI also takes a lead within the Professional Beauty Industry, raising the standards by which the industry operates. OPI is active in numerous industry associations whose aim is to ensure that consumer safety is always preserved, through products and services that are developed to meet and exceed safety standards. The company works closely with federal, state, local, and international agencies and scientists for the same purpose.

Probably more than any other professional nail care product it produces, OPI is renowned globally for its Nail Lacquers – a brilliant, chip-resistant, professional formula available in over 200 fashion-forward colors. With clever names that customers look forward to with each new Collection, OPI Nail Lacquers are beloved around the world, and trusted by professionals. Neither OPI Nail Lacquers nor any other OPI product or service is subject to animal testing.

OPI continues to be unrelenting in the fight against diversion of Professional Beauty products, spending millions of dollars in an effort to protect consumers from unwittingly purchasing tainted, unsafe product, and to help the Professional Beauty Industry maintain its high standards of quality.

NSI

The company history of NSI is taken from its Web site, http://www.nsinails.com/about.html.

For more than 40 years, NSI has been at the forefront of researching, developing and manufacturing innovative products with cutting edge ideas for the professional nail care industry.

Since 1957, NSI has been a family-owned, family-operated manufacturer of high quality monomers, polymers, and other enhancement products for the professional nail industry.

As early developers, inventors, and chemists, NSI pioneered and developed the first non-yellowing, cross-linked formulations used in all traditional acrylic systems today.

As pioneers, NSI was the first to introduce fiberglass-reinforced polymers, light activated liquid and powder acrylics, UV cured gels, as well as air- and heat-activated polish sealants. Our chemists continually meet the demands for innovative products.

Fred Slack III, along with his sons Rick and Kirby, and an international team of field testers have been instrumental in the development of numerous NSI products. The company owns the patent on Elation and French Fin Tips, which use Poly Flex TM, a unique material that far exceeds the limits for tip performance.

In going the extra mile for quality control, NSI requires batch and tracking numbers on all products. When a nail technician does experience a problem, it can be quickly identified and solved.

Mandatory inspection of manufacturing procedures plus many levels of quality control ensure that all NSI products maintain consistency from batch to batch.

Chronological information was reprinted with permission from *NAILS* magazine, February 1993, "The History of Nails by Annie Gordon", and from the following links: http://www.thehistoryof.net/the-history-of-cosmetics.html, http://beauty.about.com/cs/nailpolish/a/nail_polish.htm, http://www.handson.originationinsite.com/nailarthistory, and http://www.digitalhistory.uh.edu/do_history/fashion/Cosmetics/cosmetics.html.

Chapter 21
Artificial nails: acrylic nails, UV gel nails, and nail wraps - What are they?

Artificial nails: Whether called acrylic nails, UV gel nails, or nail wraps – all are chemical compounds that nail techs apply to the natural nails with three results in mind: to strengthen and elongate the nails,

Problems with their application, as well as problems with the potential toxicity of some of the components, dictate that these products should be applied by properly trained professional nail technicians.

Acrylic nails are often singled out as the only artificial nails with problems. This is incorrect. Due to their composition and similar ingredients, acrylic nails, UV gel nails and nail wraps are equally likely to present challenges to the nail techs who apply them. When proper application techniques are not followed, problems result, such as overfilling of the natural nail, overheating of the nail bed, excessive filing of the nail plate, and contact with potentially toxic chemicals that may cause contact dermatitis. Nail techs are to keep polishes and artificial nail material a sixteenth-of-an-inch away from the nail borders to avoid contact hazards with skin.

Acrylic Nails: The term acrylic nails is actually shorthand for "normal nails that have been enhanced by artificial overlay." To create a traditional acrylic overlay, a nail tech mixes a liquid (monomer) and a powder (polymer), starting a reaction in which their molecules combine to form larger molecules in a chain reaction that ends only when all the molecules are used up. That's what happens chemically.

What the nail tech sees is a semi-liquid bead of thickening artificial product that needs to be spread evenly over the client's nail plate before it hardens. For clients who want longer nails, a plastic nail extension is glued onto the tip of the nail plate, and an artificial nail product is filled in and spread over it as well. When the nail product hardens, the nail tech files and shapes it to look like a natural nail, then adds a layer of polish.

UV Gel nails: The term gel nails is industry shorthand for "normal nails that have been enhanced by an artificial overlay of acrylic that has a different molecular structure, appearance, application procedure, and curing methods than do traditional acrylic nails." UV gel nail products come as a pre-mixed thick viscous adhesive (cyanoacrylate.) The nail tech applies this gel directly to the nail plate. It is hardened or cured by exposure to ultraviolet (UV) light. The UV light activates chemicals called photo-initiators that cure the gel by heat. When not used correctly, the light-energy-induced heat can burn the nail bed, causing pain.

Nail wraps. Sometimes called "no light gels", they are not really UV gel nail compounds. Nail wraps begin when the nail tech applies a fabric, such as fiberglass or silk, to the nail with a thickened mixture of cyanoacrylate adhesive. The tech may add a filler material, and then sand and shape it to achieve the desired effect. Nail wraps cure by exposure to air. Some wraps are called dips when nails are dipped into a common container of acrylic powder – which is unsanitary and technically illegal due to contamination issues. Nail wraps expose both tech and client to chemical contact hazards, as do all artificial nails.

Acrylic nails are often singled out as the only problem artificial nails. UV gel nails and nail wraps present just as many issues when proper application techniques are not followed. Excessive over-filing of the natural nail and improper chemical contact both happen with UV gel nails and nail wraps, and the UV light curing process can burn the nail bed if improper light wattage strength or light exposure time is incorrect.

Some artificial nails cure with different properties, depending on their formulation. All artificial nails harden and shrink. Improperly pinching the artificial nail product as it cures can pull up the artificial nail that it separates from the nail plate. Nail techs should not pinch in or overfill the sides of the nails while applying artificial nails. Separation of the artificial nail from the nail plate may allows water to enter when washing hands. This may allow pseudomonas or fungal organism enter to grow under the artificial nail.

Certain nail preparation chemicals need special attention to avoid injury. For example, acid nail primers are used to clean the surface of the nail so that acrylic products adhere better. Acid primers burn skin on contact. Newly-developed "non-acid primers" are a better choice for overall nail health. Find out which one your nail tech uses.

Both monomer liquids and vapors from potentially toxic solvents can cause extreme dermatitis from prolonged skin contact or vapor exposure. Other potential problems for both client and nail tech are inhaling toxic airborne artificial nail dust from electric filing or vigorous manual filing of acrylic-coated nails. Ventilation and vacuuming dust at the source with special vent hoods attached to electric filing tips can reduce this issue.

The longer a person "wears" improperly applied artificial nails, the more likely a problem will arise. Improper and repetitive application and removal of artificial nails weakens and dries out the nail plate, and affects the skin folds around the nails. Many become more sensitive to chemicals each time they get artificial nails. For them, the moment of reaching allergic sensitivity may come. (See picture of Dematitis page 148.)

Consumers should also take responsibility in the proper maintenance of artificial nails. There should be no pain involved when artificial nails being applied or removed. Nail techs should keep a 1/16 inch border of the skin around the nail from all nail polishes and artificial nails to avoid potential contact hazards..

Medical professionals have three different responses when their clients wear artificial nails:

One. Never use artificial nails.

Two. Artificial nails can be worn safely. Their safety depends on the proficiency of the nail technician and the quality of the artificial nail product.

Three. Don't wear nail enhancements, acrylic nails, UV gel nails, or nail wraps all the time. Give your nails a break – once a month, once every six months – to reduce allergic reactions and skin sensitivity.

Results really do hinge on the technique and experience of the nail tech and the health of the client's nails. Most dermatitis or skin contact allergies occur in the application process. Most nail plate damage occurs in the removal process.

Cheap artificial nail services, nail techs in too much of a hurry, and utilizing services from unsanitary salons are a recipe for infection. Inexpensive services are a huge price to pay in the long run. However, infections have occurred in expensive, well maintained salons as well.

In short, consumers need to know the correct application procedures and what the dangers are, and to trust their own assessment of the risks involved for them personally.

What to do when problems occur

When contact dermatitis, infection, or injury occurs with artificial nails, do not rush to remove the nails. Book an appointment with a doctor. He or she may elect to keep the nails on and topically or orally treat the surrounding tissue first. Soaking nails off with acetone in the presence of infection may not be the best approach.

Oral antibiotics, anti-fungals, topical anti-fungals, anti-inflammatories, antibacterial creams, or medicinal soaks may be used to treat dermatitis, infection, and injury. Drainage under or from the side of the nail usually results in surgical removal of part or all of the natural nail plate and/or incision and drainage of the nail border. Most contact dermatitis triggers a type IV delayed hyper-sensitivity allergic reaction unless the cause is a visible artificial nail product currently touching the skin-border of the nail.

Patients with lymphedema can wear artificial nails. Patients with the active infection lymphangitis should not. Nor should diabetics with circulation disorders that have resulted in ulcerations, nor diabetics with profound neuropathy or inability to feel sensation in their feet or hands.

Chapter 22
Damage to nails and other salon injuries

Damage, infections, or skin contact dermatitis/allergies to the nail plate and nail bed are caused by six principal factors:

1. Overfiling of the nail plate by electric file or manual filing

2. Improper application and misuse of artificial nail products, use of poor quality nail products, and improper use of nail hardeners

3. Improper cleaning and disinfection of nail instruments

4. Improper disinfection of the whirlpools or soaking tubs

5. Inhalation of artificial nail dust or product vapors

6. Accidental injury to the skin

1. Overfiling

Nail techs file the natural nail plate to ready it for artificial nail application. They also file it when removing acrylic nails. Overfiling with either manual or electric files can cause serious damage to the nail bed.

Notes on technique. Safe use of an electric file or manual file involves the removal or thinning of the artificial nail product by one-third and spare-filing the natural nail plate. Slightly bevel the artificial product to the natural nail, and then back fill or rebalance.

Avoid excessive filing or total removal of the artificial nail on a frequent basis. Artificial nail products will usually not disperse through the nail plate due to the fact the product is polymerizing immediately upon contact with the nail plate. Full length artificial nail products should not be applied to a damaged or thinning nail plate. Instead, one can elect to use a thin coat of an artificial nail product (acrylic, UV gel, or nail wrap) to keep thin but not damaged plates from over flexing or succumbing to the effects of brittle nails.

Proper rebalance techniques can protect the nail and result with a dependable high quality artificial nail product that should adhere well. For complete removal of artificial nail products, soak the artificial nail with warm acetone on cotton balls kept in close contact to the fingertips with aluminum foil for 15 to 30 minutes. Gel nails will require more electric file removal of the artificial nail before applying acetone soaks. Acetone is flammable and should be heated only by warm water bath in a separate plastic bottle.

2. Improper application.

Most nail plate damage occurs with improper removal technique. Most dermatitis or skin contact allergies occur with improper application techniques.

Artificial nail product chemicals and nail polymers can be caustic or potentially harmful when used improperly. For example, older acid nail primers clean the surface of the nail so that acrylic products can adhere to the nail plate by hydrogen bonding. Methacrylic acid primers burn skin on contact and are sometimes found in cheaper nail salons. Improper splashing of monomers on skin can lead to dermatitis.

More-recently-developed "non-acid primers" are better choices for overall nail health. They work by stronger covalent bonding, which may help prevent lifting of the acrylic product. This will prevent micro-leakage of water and help prevent nail infections. Ask your nail tech which primer she uses.

Monomer liquids or solvents with vapor inhalation and contact hazards can cause extreme dermatitis from a tiny amount of prolonged or repeat contact on skin. Other problems include airborne acrylic dust from electric files or vigorous manual filing, which affect both client and nail tech.

Some naturally thin nail plates do poorly with artificial nail extensions. However, sometimes a protective thin artificial nail coat overlay can be used on a thin nail plate to strengthen it. Do not extend or paint the overlay past the free nail to avoid catching the artificial nail on material which could potentially avulse, tear, or damage the natural nail plate.

Artificial nail products will shrink by an average of 12% during the curing process. Some off brands or improper mixtures of artificial nail products will shrink more than 12%. The hyponychium, the skin just under the tip of your nail, acts as a barrier and holds the free edge of the nail to the finger (see Chapter "Your nail anatomy"). Do not pinch in or over file the sides of the nails when applying artificial nails. Pinching will change the natural curvature ot the nail and can lead to damage to the nail bed as the artificial nail cures and shrinks.

Comments: Thinner nails may increase the rate of insensible water loss and trap moisture under even a thinly applied coat of protective artificial nails. This could increase the rate of pseudomonas "the greenies" infection. The thickness of the natural nail is one key issue whether you should use artificial nail enhancements or not. This need to be further documented.

Shrinkage in combination with improperly pinching the artificial nail product can lead to damage of a weakened nail or previously injured hyponichium. Doug Schoon confirms this fact in his book, *Nail Structure and Product Chemistry*.

I also base this upon application of an artificial nail to my own natural nail by an experienced nail tech to experience the attachment and eventual removal process. The artificial nail stayed on for 2 hours and then was removed. The process was not painful but pressure from lifting was noticeable and for a short while almost verging as uncomfortable. Occasional touching of the nail folds with the nail file during manual filing process were noticeable. The removal process took 15 minutes and there were residual minor signs of the application process for about 2 weeks.

Overall, I think artificial nails can be used if performed on a healthy natural nail plate by a well trained nail technician and proper product nail border distances are maintained. You will find other physicians and nail techs who will argue that the applications and removal of any artificial nail will result in some damage to the natural nail.

The principal reason for onycholysis or separation of the natural nail from the nail bed still remains overfiling of the natural nail plate and improper artificial nail removal techniques

Overuse of nail hardeners:

Remember, nail hardeners work to strengthen nails with formalin by cross-linking proteins that act as a cellular fixative. Nail hardeners per FDA regulations can legally have up to 5% formalin. Nail hardeners can sensitize your body much quicker than lower-formalin resin-containing nail polishes (.002%).

Most current US manufactures of nail hardeners do not use more than 2% formalin concentrations. 1% formalin is a very fast fixative. 1.25% is considered super strong and fast reacting. Under 0.25% loses efficacy. Average time is 10 days of use. Use only until the nail is hardened, then stop using it. Continued use of nail hardeners will cause the nail plate to become overly hardened and brittle. People tend to then use more hardener, which can result in sloppy technique that allows too much hardener to touch skin, which may sensitize the individual. Never apply nail hardener directly to skin. Nail-hardener formalin-sensitized individuals may then react to the lower formalin concentrations in nail polish.

Also, recall, from the nail polish section in Chapter 19, that modern nail polish formaldehyde concentrations are so low they are unlikely to become a sensitizer to skin. For formaldehyde to become an active inhalation or contact allergen it has to convert to the pure anhydrous gas form or free formaldehyde. Most current nail polish concentrations contain 0.002% pbb formalin in the form of methylene glycol (only a few parts per billion "ppb" may form free formaldehyde). Studies show that nail polish has actually much less free formadehyde concentrations than the carpets, wallboards, construction materials used in homes or offices.

3. Improper cleaning and disinfection of the nail implements

Improper cleaning and disinfection techniques are a major reason that nail fungus and bacterial infections occur from client to client. I urge nail technicians to not work on fungal nails or infected nails, but rather to refer these clients to a physician. (See Chapter 29 "Referrals to medical professionals") Removal of all visible debris with a brush, detergent, and water, and immersion with an EPA registered tuberculocidal agent such as 70% alcohol for a full 10 minutes or more, is usually sufficient to take care of most organisms.

TAKE SPECIAL NOTE: Personal clinical experience, statements from experienced nail techs and statistical information for the Nail Salon Infection survey website data estimate that nail techs in the US experience at least three (3) pseudomonas "greenies" nail plate infections per year. Pseudomonas nail plate infections are more prevalent with newer inexperienced nail techs than with experienced nail technicians who have improved their technique over time and training.

If you estimate that are 380,000 to 400,000 licensed nail techs or cosmetologists performing nail services a year, it could be extrapolated there are over 1,000,000 pseudomonas infections per year. If you multiply how many additional infections that are from are from improper home use of artificial nails or unlicensed individuals applying artificial nails the numbers could be even larger.

Failure to change alcohol or other EPA registered disinfectants on a daily basis, failure to soak and completely immerse the instruments for a full ten minutes, and failing to fully remove all visible debris from the instruments violate proper protocol and make effective disinfection protocols ineffective.

Proper sterilization with an autoclave (not dry heat) is a more effective way of insuring proper disinfection. Texas is the first state to mandate this form of disinfection, which it instituted in response to the recent death of Kimberly Jackson via pedicure near Houston.

4. Improper disinfection of the whirlpools or soaking tubs

New recommendations from the INTA (International Nail Technicians Association) and the NMC (Nail Manufacturers Council) appropriately address the issue of proper whirl-pool disinfection. Whirlpools have been a major source of contamination and infection due to poor design features that do not allow proper drainage and visualization of pipes and filters. New regulations require proper standing disinfectant contact time with proper EPA registered agents of pipes, basins, and filters.

The media has had a field day with stories where hundreds, of people have been contaminated by nail salon whirlpool outbreaks nationwide. Following simple but effective proper disinfection procedures from the INTA and NMC can remedy this problem. Again, almost all nail salon injuries are preventable.

NOTE: Do not shave your legs or arms 24 hours prior to getting a pedicure, manicure, or whirlpool service. Visible nicks or even imperceptible micro- cuts are portals of entry for bacteria to enter.

5. Inhalation of artificial nail dust or chemicals

Some people may never experience an artificial nail product chemical contact allergy, while others relate having such a rare or severe allergy to nail products that just walking into a salon can trigger an allergic reaction. It is, however, more likely that a person will have an unpleasant reaction to a fragrance than any other nail product. Fragrances top the list of vapor-induced irritants.

Salon inhalation work disorders (SIWD) are triggered by chemical vapors or dust from artificial nail filings and other dust allergens that are not properly ventilated from the work area. Nail techs can also get carpal tunnel syndrome and rotator cuff injuries from years of extensive manual filing and buffing of natural nail plates or manual shaping of artificial nails.

6. Accidental injury to the skin

Accidental injury during nail debridement, trimming, or providing pedicure and manicure services are facts of life in a nail salon. Most every nail tech has experienced an unintentional injury to a client with cuticle service, nail nippers, or manual and electric filing equipment. Nicks, cuts, lacerations from drill burns, cutting cuticles, trimming callus, and use of pumice stones can lead to infections that sometimes end up being seen by a medical professional in the Emergency Room. This means that proper disinfection and/or proper sterilization of instruments and electric nail files is a key prevention modality to avoid hazards from accidental skin trauma in salons.

Chapter 23
A baker's dozen of 12-Step Programs

1. How to have the best polished nails

2. How to have stronger, healthier nails

3. Supplements that may help with nail deficiencies

4. Sterilization: the 100% solution

5. How to choose a great salon

6. When to not use artificial nails

7. When to not get a manicure

8. How to prevent ingrown nails

9. Prevention and care of calluses

10. Care and prevention of cracked, dry feet

11. How to work with nail fungus and athlete's foot nail fungus

12. How to fit shoes, running shoes, and orthotics

13. Truths and myths about orthotics

Program One

How to have the best polished nails

1. Avoid water manicures (soaking hands prior to the manicure) when your nail plate is too thin or damaged from acrylic-nail overfilling; wait until the nail thickens and heals. When you notice chipped or cracked nail polish after a water manicure, it means the nail plate absorbed enough water to swell and dislodge, or chip, the polish. Avoid water manicures to prevent this.

2. The shelf life of polish is about two years if left unopened. Cap tightly. Store at room temperature or in the refrigerator, and away from direct light. Rapid temperature changes can cause moisture to condense in the bottle. Allow refrigerator-stored polish to come up to room temperature before you open the bottle.

3. Use high quality nail polish. It's made from higher quality dyes that stain less.

4. Paint over the front edge of the nail and slightly under the tip. This helps prevent chipping. Don't paint onto the skin under the nail (hyponychium), as it could lead to allergies or contact dermatitis.

5. Apply two thin coats of colored polish rather than one thick one. Thinner coats dry quickly and last longer. Need more than two coats of polish to cover the nail? The polish may be too thin or may be of poor quality or designed to be a sheer shade.

6. Don't mix nail polishes. Create your own colors by applying a coat of one shade, then a second coat of another.

7. Let nail polish dry slowly. Rapid drying will cause the polish to bubble and deform, and will decrease its luster.

Well-ventilated salon rooms may have fans or strong drafts. Protect the drying nail with a protective shield.

8. After your polish dries, add a clear topcoat for longer-lasting results and a beautiful shine.

9. Every day, paint a fresh layer of clear topcoat polish over the original pigmented color to help maintain luster.

10. Don't soak your polished nails in the bathtub or in dishwater. The nail plate will swell with water and cause chipping.

11. Use nail oil to keep the skin around the nails healthy. This will decrease chipping, and prevent skin breaks and cracks, which are potential sites for infection.

12. Don't bite nails. Look your best with smooth edges.

Program Two
How to have stronger, healthier nails

1. Protect your nail tips. Avoid tapping, strumming, and biting. Don't use nails as tools. Use a pencil to dial a phone, a letter opener to open envelopes, a cutter or scissors to open packages.

2. Use hands or finger pads – not nails – to do simple chores. Avoid picking up objects when your fingernails may strike a hard surface. Instead, slide the object sideways into your hand.

3. Wear rubber gloves when doing dishes or other "tough on the nails" jobs. Wear regular gloves during cold weather or when doing chores.

4. When gardening, use gloves, or dig your nails into a bar of soap to prevent dirt from getting under them.

5. Shape and file nails with a fine grit file. Round the tips in a gentle curve. File snags or irregularities to prevent further breakage or splitting.

6. File in the same direction the nail grows. Back and forth filing can cause the nail to split. File once a week with a soft or fine 240-grit disposable nail file.

7. Do your nails tend to split? File lightly. A smooth nail will tear and split less. Massage penetrating nail oil into the nails to moisturize and protect.

8. Don't push living skin around the nails. Metal instruments aggressively used to push dead skin on the nail plate can scrape away the protective cells of the nail surface protecting the eponychium.

9. See your doctor for severe breakage or tearing problems. In some cases, nail polish can protect the nail surface. Be careful of some nail hardeners as they may have higher levels of formalin, which can damage thinning nails by further splitting or breakage. Use nail hardeners only to reach the desired effect, then stop. Too much hardener can make brittle nails even more brittle.

10. Nail polish remover may dry and damage nails. Use it infrequently and according to instrucitons.

11. Don't expose nails to harsh chemicals and alkaline substances. Nails are strongest when slightly acidic.

12. Daily biotin (2.5 mg a day) may help some people with problem nails. When a person is in good overall health and has strong nails, supplements are unnecessary. Pregnant

women should not take biotin without a doctor's permission. Nail health is a reflection of general health.

Program Three
How to stop swelling or edema of the lower extremity and blisters from hiking

1. The calf acts as a pump to reduce fluid in your legs, so walking with doctor's permission and evaluation may reduce swelling of the lower extremity.

2. Support stocking found over the counter and compression stockings by prescription may compress distended veins or lymph channels to help reduce swelling or venous stasis ulcerations per your doctors advice.

3. If you are unable to wear stockings in the presence of peripheral venous disorders, keep your legs elevated 4 times a day for 30 minutes 6 inches higher than your heart to minimize swelling of you lower extremities.

4. Keep you legs elevated when you are sitting for long periods of time. Legs in a dependent or hanging position can add greatly to lower extremity edema or swelling.

5. Check to see if you have swelling in your legs by depressing the skin over the skin bone or tibia for a few seconds, and see if the skin remains visually indented. Check with your doctor if this condition persists, and you may need a prescription diuretic.

6. Swelling or edema of the lower extremity may be a sign of kidney disease, high blood pressure, cardiac heart failure, liver disease, blood clot, abdominal cancer or many other medical problems. Check with your doctor if swelling of your legs occurs.

Blister Prevention

7.   Blisters are caused by friction and sheering forces. If you can reduce friction, you can reduce blisters. Do not wear shoes or boots that are too tight or too loose.

8.   Moisture can be a great precursor of blisters from enhanced surface friction. Keep you feet dry and you will reduce the friction that is increased with moisture.

9.   If your feet do not sweat a great deal, heavy cotton socks are fine to hike or run with. For those whose feet do sweat a lot, polypropylene socks are best to wick away moisture from the skin and the polypropylene fabric also deflects sheering forces that cause blister formation.

10.   Moleskin, Second Skin®, and Band Aids® can also protect skin friction points such as the side or bottom of the feet prior to hiking or running.

11.   Orthotic custom insoles can reduce biomechanical friction by supporting the feet in a neutral position to reduce contact with shoes or boots

12.   Some absorbent powders can help absorb moisture and reduce sheering forces that cause blisters. Be aware some people are allergic to corn starch. In the absence of absorbent powders, petroleum jelly products or even Neosporin can make a good **temporary** anti-friction product. Use liberally on skin contact points while using socks.

Program Four

Sterilization: the 100% solution

Contaminated nail salon instruments – nippers, files, and the like – are a source of infection. Proper sanitation and disinfection procedures kill or inhibit microbes only when nail techs follow exacting protocols.

1. Proper sterilization kills 100% of all microscopic organisms.

2. With sterilization, there is no guesswork about which chemical to use to disinfect an instrument or how long to soak it.

3. Sterilization offers a 100 percent solution to the problems of improper sanitation.

4. Autoclaves are affordable and inexpensive to use. They cost about the same amount as ten sets of high quality nail instruments.

5. Instruments are sealed in a pack. Once autoclaved, they are protected in a sealed sterilized pack until use, an improvement over unsealed instruments sitting in a UV light box or dusty drawer.

6. Autoclave sterilization is the most effective form of disinfection and can be checked immediately by anyone, including the public. Color indicators on the sterilizing pack change color from pink to brown when the autoclave has reached the sterilizing temperature.

7. Clients can see the sterilized pack opened in front of them before pedicure services begin.

8. Nail salon use of sterilized instruments instills confidence in the public.

9. "We Sterilize!" is a great marketing statement for a nail salon.

10. The use of autoclave sterilization may protect the nail salon from implications of improperly disinfected contaminated instruments.

11. Salon use of autoclaves will instill confidence in medical professionals.

12. Sanitation and disinfection are safe and effective only when nail techs follow proper disinfection protocol. Not all have. Autoclave sterilization is the highest level of protection; the FDA agrees.

Program Five

How to choose a great salon

Nail techs who exhibit a genuine level of care for their clients will be able to give quick, correct information, explanations, and demonstrations – all in a non-defensive manner – in response to your questions. Carefully observe what goes on in the salon.

1. Does the nail tech examine you ask if you have medical problems, remove your old nail polish to check your toenails before the whirlpool, or ask you to fill out an information form?

2. Do you see nail techs shaving clients' legs? Do you hear them asking clients if they have shaved their legs in the 24 hours prior to whirlpool foot bath services?

3. Do you see someone cleaning and disinfecting the pedicure throne chair whirlpool equipment for a full ten minutes after each client?

4. Does the nail tech ask you to wash your hands and scrub under your fingernails prior to working with you?

5. Does the nail tech disinfect electric nail file bits between every client?

6. Does the nail tech get a new disposable nail file or properly disinfect the reusable manual nail file between every client?

7. Ask the nail tech how he or she cleans, disinfects, or sterilize their instruments.

8. Do you see dirty towels or dirty instruments lying around the work stations?

9. Do you see nail techs or staff eating in the salon?

10. Can the nail tech show and tell you how the salon ventilates noxious odors to the outside?

11. Can the nail tech name a doctor they refer their nail problem clients to?

12. Does the nail tech pry off artificial nails, or soak them off with warm acetone?

Program Six
When not to use artificial nails

1. When your nail is too thin or damaged. Use, instead, thin overlay products. Don't extend the length of the nail or use nail extensions. Extended nails can damage thin natural nails by over bending them.

2. When your nail is has been over filed by aggressive nail tech services. Nail techs should lightly roughen the surface of the natural nail with a 240-grit file to apply artificial

nail products. When you see a nail tech over file the nail—removing visible amounts of the nail plate—stop the treatment.

3. When you have active nail fungus.

4. When you have psoriasis or nail disease.

5. When you have open sores, lesions, or bleeding from split nails.

6. When you have active bacterial infections in the skinfold around the nail.

7. When you have candida/yeast infections of the cuticles or irritated skin around the nail plate.

8. When you have recurrent pseudomonas infections — the "greenies"—contracted from nail tech services. Find a different nail tech!

9. When you have immune diseases with visible lesions on hands or feet.

10. When you have pain upon application of artificial nails. Find a different nail tech.

11. When you are allergic to artificial nail products.

12. When you work with, treat, or visit patients in health-related critical care areas, burn wards, operating rooms, high-risk neonatal units, or surgical intensive care wards.

Program Seven

When not to get a manicure

Don't get a manicure service when, recently, you . . .

1. Cut your hands or fingers with paper cuts.

2. Trimmed the living skin near the cuticles too close.

3. Bit your hangnails, causing injury.

4. Have bleeding and tenderness from a hangnail.

5. Have an ingrown nail.

6. Injured your fingers or hands with housework.

7. Injured your hands gardening.

8. Developed cracked hands from dry weather.

9. Injured your hands from too much dish washing or use of strong cleaning chemicals.

10. Have a rash on your hands.

11. Have moles or skin lesions that are enlarging, changing colors, or chronically scabbed.

12. Cut your hands or fingers in any way.

Program Eight

How to prevent ingrown nails

1. Avoid all tight, narrow shoes. Look for wide toe box shoes to avoid pressure. Wear mesh running shoes, Crocs, or shoes manufactured with unusually wide toe boxes.

2. Trim nails straight across unless you are still having pain. See a podiatrist or dermatologist to help with trimming

when you have a problem with thick nails, painful nails, or ingrown nails. Rounding the nail corners with a 240 fine-grit nail file can help. Podiatrists may elect to cut out the ingrown nail, or round off the offending fragment, or round off a thick nail to reduce pressure on the nail corner.

3. Help prevent thick, ingrown toenails: keep your feet free of athlete's foot fungal infection.

4. Don't trim living skin near cuticles. Don't pull skin from nail borders.

5. Prevent severe pronation with orthotics. This will take pressure off the corners of the nails.

6. Avoid tight-fitting shoes constructed of leather or thick fabrics. Their hardness irritates toenails.

7. Avoid running up stairs barefoot. Walk! Tripping on steps barefoot is a quick way to rip off a nail or traumatically avulse the nail. When this type of injury occurs, see a podiatrist or medical professional to prevent infection.

8. Use night lights so you won't jam your toes into furniture legs.

9. Fit shoes with a thumb's-width distance between your toes and the front of the shoe.

10. Don't cut a V in the center of the nail to help an ingrown nail. This can promote fungal infections, or cause separation of the nail from the nail bed.

11. Chronic nail pain – in the absence of an ingrown nail or trauma – may be a symptom of a bony prominence or spur under the nail. See a podiatrist or orthopedist for an evaluation or x-ray.

12. Black pigmented lines or dark streaking from the base of the nail (when not caused by trauma) can be a sign of serious skin disease. See a podiatrist, dermatologist, or medical professional as soon as possible.

Program Nine

Prevention and care of calluses at home

1. The presence of a callus usually points to an underlying biomechanical or shoe-fitting problem. Get orthotics and shoe recommendations from a podiatrist or other competent medical professional to help with these problems.

2. When you have what looks to be calluses on the bottom of your feet, see a podiatrist. They could be warts or other problems that need medical or surgical attention. Sometimes a metatarsal bar can be added to orthotics to help take weight off the ball of the foot to relieve pressure during treatment.

3. Have a podiatrist surgically debride or trim your calluses with sterilized instruments. Podiatrists, experienced in this procedure, are the best choice for a safe and aseptic technique.

4. Credo blades or callus cutters are dangerous in anyone's hands, including your own. Do not allow nail techs to use these devices on you at any time.

5. When you purchase a Credo blade over the counter in a drug store, be very, very careful as it can cut your skin in a blink of an eye. Diabetics should never use or purchase one.

6. Diabetics should see a podiatrist every six months for callus care and overall foot maintenance.

7. A 40% to 50% urea cream/ointment with lactic acid cream (prescription only) should be used on severe calluses. It also helps to mildly exfoliate the calluses with a dininfected pumice stone, daily.

8. To control the buildup of calluses, use a pumice stone or file only when the feet are wet or in bath water. To prevent infection, properly disinfect the pumice stone or file with a 1:10 concentration of bleach. If you are a diabetic, have circulation disorders or have neuropathy or any physical limitations do not care for your calluses. See a podiatrist.

9. Do not go barefoot frequently when you have painful calluses on the bottom of your feet.

10. Use a cushioned-sole shoe when you have calluses. Running shoes or Crocs are a best first choice. Running shoes and Crocs absorb more impact than any other type of shoe.

11. Do not allow nail techs to use high-strength alkaline or acid cuticle remover chemicals on callused feet. When left on too long or not neutralized properly, they can dissolve more than callus.

12. Callus formation may be the result of excess friction, fat pad atrophy, boney prominences or other growths on the bottom or other areas of the feet, or a thinning, metabolic disease like diabetes. See a podiatrist or other medical professional when you experience these problems.

Program Ten
Care and prevention of cracked, dry feet

1. Persistent cracked feet may be a symptom of dry skin – or a symptom of an athlete's foot fungal infection. See a doctor for a correct diagnosis.

2. Chronic cracked feet may be a sign of dehydration. Drink plenty of fluids and see if the condition improves.

3. Cracked feet may be a sign of psoriasis, eczema, or other skin disorder.

4. See a doctor for skin problems. Use a prescription 40 to 50% urea cream/ointment with lactic acid cream at night and an antifungal cream during the day and note whether or not the skin improves. Do not use urea/lactic acid creams between toes.

5. Soak feet for 10 to 15 minutes in a foot bath, shower, or tub, and use a pumice stone while foot is still soaking to reduce the depth of the cracks. Those who are unable to reach their feet, and those who have diabetes, a circulation disorder, open sores, or neuropathy will be well served to see a podiatrist—and they should not get pedicures without written permission from a physician.

6. To avoid infection, those with deep fissures or bleeding, cracked feet will find the necessary treatment at a podiatrist's office. The dead, damaged tissue must be surgically removed with sterilized scalpels to help heal the deep crevices. Do not get pedicures or whirlpool bath services when your feet are in this condition: infections can result.

7. Do not walk barefoot or get in concrete swimming pools without swimming shoes when you have dry cracked feet. Vinyl liner pools are softer and create less friction on the bottom of the feet.

8. Use protective shoes, like running shoes or Crocs, to absorb impact; they will help prevent cracks from getting deeper.

9. Wear socks. Bare shoes wick moisture away from your heels. The new Croc shoes appear to be an exception. Polypropylene socks are recommended.

10. Leather sandals worn without socks wick moisture away from your heels

11. Foot powders do not help dry cracked feet

12. Physicians treating cracked feet will prescribe creams or approved combination lotions or creams with high percentages of some or most of the following ingredients: 40 to 50% urea, lactic acid, fruit acids, alpha hydroxy acids, exfoliate particles, aloe, glycerin, dimethicone, antifungal agents, tea tree oil, emu oil, herbal products, and other helpful ingredients.

Program Eleven

How to work with nail fungus and athlete's foot fungus

1. Recognize that you have a problem and get professional medical help. Over the counter medications are not going to have a high rate of cure when not used properly.

2. When nail fungus has lifted the nail plate from its bed, trim and file it to the area of healthy nail when the nail stops lifting. Soften nails in bathtub water for 10 minutes first to make trimming and sanding easier This will prevent water from being trapped under the nail and slow the advance of the fungus. Dark color is a symptom of invading fungal organism – or an additional bacterial infection. Get professional help for a correct diagnosis.

3. Use antifungal cream often. When you are delayed getting to a doctor, use a good antifungal cream and continue using this even when you start using oral antifungal medication. This will keep the nails soft, making them easier to cut, and will prevent shedding of more fungal organisms to the skin of other nails.

4. Do not use the same nail clippers once a family member has been diagnosed with nail fungus. The fungus can spread to other family members. It's always best to have your own clippers and to not share them. Clean your nail clippers with a brush and soap and water to remove fungal nail debris, then immerse them in 70% isopropyl alcohol for 10 minutes. Boiling is not as effective as steaming them under pressure. To steam clippers to near-sterility, cook them in a small pressure cooker for 20 minutes.

5. Wear larger shoes with a bigger toe box, like mesh running shoes or Crocs, to prevent rubbing the nails and nail tenderness. This means wearing wider, longer shoes. Use your thumb to make sure you have a thumb's width of room between your toes and the end of the shoes, and no pressure from the side of shoes. Make sure your socks are not tight. Tight socks can damage nails over time.

6. Once a week, clean your bathroom till it's squeaky clean on all tile surfaces. Use commercial bleach cleaner or mix your own from a ratio of 1 part bleach to 10 parts water. Soap scum film is made from fatty acids, and tile surfaces hold dirt, mold, bacteria, human body oils, and waste from showers. This is a media for fungal growth.

7. Check all family members for signs of athlete's foot or nail fungus and start treatment on them as soon as possible to prevent the spread of these fungal organisms

8. Always treat athlete's foot. The main cause of fungal nails is a previous exposure to athlete's foot and trauma. Treat your feet for two months to make sure the fungus is gone. For chronic cases, you may need additional oral medications while continuing to treat your feet prophylactic ally for a few days every other month to prevent outbreaks.

9. Never wear other people's shoes. They are always a potential source of fungal organisms.

10. Don't go barefoot. Wear slippers, Crocs, or flip flops on all surfaces in your home, gyms, showers, especially when you have animals that come in and out of the house.

11. Treat your shoes when you are prone to fungal infections. Treat all your shoes with a spray disinfectant. Take out the insoles, spray with aerosol disinfectant, and leave out to dry for 12 hours.

12. Genetics count. Some people and families are more genetically predisposed to fungal infections and will need longer treatment times and multiple medications.

Program Twelve

How to fit shoes, running shoes, and orthotics

1. Forget sizes. Use size as a means to estimate the proper shoe size and let your thumb do the rest.

2. There should be a thumb-width space between the end of the shoe and the end of your toe. And make sure the sides of both left and right shoes do not rub the first and fifth toes when you sit or walk.

3. Remember, you, not someone else, are the final decision-maker on the fit of your new shoes.

4. Too big is better than too small, in most circumstances.

5. Foot doctors know that improper shoe style and shoe size aggravate most foot problems.

6. Running shoes with a mesh toe box, not tennis shoes or walking shoes, are the best shoe for almost all foot problems. They absorb the most impact, even for those who are not runners. In many cases, Crocs are also a good choice.

7. Running shoes should have a nylon mesh toe box over all bony parts of the forefoot to reduce friction on the top or sides of all toes. Crocs are made with abundant extra room.

8. Slip-on shoes or flats can cause foot problems such as corns, ingrown nails or calluses. This is due to pinching of the forefoot by tightly holding the shoe onto the foot.

9. In general, any shoe that does not lace up tight around the top of the foot or ankle should be second choice for foot comfort.

10. Toss out shoes every six months. Think of shoes as having an expiration date. The foam in running shoes breaks down by exposure to oxygen even when they are not in use.

11. Shoes with removable insoles are generally of better quality.

12. When you wear orthotics and are buying shoes, tell the shoe store you want a pair of neutral-posted shoes, that is, shoes that are not self-corrected for pronation or supination. Your orthotics are usually already posted.

Program Thirteen

Truths and myths about orthotics

Quiz: *Orthotics – custom inserts that reduce pressure on the foot and keep the foot in a biomechanically neutral position – can help improve or relieve pain in the following foot problems: True or False?*

QUESTION	TRUE OR FALSE?
1. Hammer toes	*True, will reduce pressure with metatarsal bars embedded in the orthotics*
2. Bunions	*True, will reduce pressure by putting pressure in arch*
3. Calluses	*True*
4. Neuromas	*True*
5. Stress fractures	*True*
6. Heel pain	*True*
7. Warts	*False, will relieve pressure on warts, but will not cure or treat them*
8. Ingrown nails	*True, will relieve pressure and help prevent ingrown nails, but will not cure or treat them*
9. Flat feet	*True, will provide relief, but will not correct the underlying cause of flat feet*
10. Feet with high arches	*True, will help support the arches and relieve pressure on the ball of the foot and heel, but will not correct the high arch itself*
11. Diabetic feet, tender feet, fatigued feet, pain on the ball of foot, or muscle spasms	*True, will help with pain relief*
12. Ankle, knee, hip, back pain	*True, will sometimes be helpful as foot problems can be a source of these problems*

Chapter 24

The top 10 things state boards needs to do

1.   Ban the use of Credo blade (callus shavers)

2.   Require sterilization of instruments training in all states

3.   Posted prohibition of shaving legs 24 hours prior to whirlpool services

4.   Log times of proper disinfection of whirlpools and nail implements

5.   Correct improper application and removal of artificial nails with CEU training

6.   Correct improper use of electric files with CEU training

7.   Correct improper ventilation of salon workplace vapors or electric file dust and avoidance chemical contact with CEU training

8.   Require all 50 states to ban nail techs from treating and working on nail pathology without written permission of a physician and require a medical interview

9.   50 state written ban of the use of chemical 100% MMAs and acid nail primers

10.   Require all 50 states to institute CEUs,

The top 10 things the Nail industry needs to address

1. All states need to ban the use of Credo blade callus shavers

FACT: *The Credo blade is the most dangerous item in a nail salon*

"Credo" is actually the brand name of a callus-shaver in-strument made by a company in Germany. Credo blades are the industry standard. The instrument holds a small, double-edged razor blade that functions exactly like grandpa's old-fashioned safety razor. Instead of cutting whiskers, Credo blades shave a layer of skin from calluses or corns. Indeed, one version of Credo's blades is called a "Credo Corn Cutter Callus Shaver", and includes a fit-on rasp. Credo blades cost between 9 and 20 dollars, and a pack of 10 blades sells for about 5 dollars. Use of these blades has been banned in 22 states. (See picture of Credo blade at http://www.cachebeauty.com/pedicure1.htm)

Callus cutters or Credo blades tend to produce avulsion (flap) and laceration injuries, depending on how rough, cracked, dry, or elevated the callused skin may be. Injuries occur with callus shavers when used by folks at home, and injuries occur when they are used by even the moist experienced of nail techs. The razor blades themselves are never sterile, so when injuries happen, and they do, they increase the rate of infection

Nail techs using callus shavers, nail nippers, files, elec-tric drills, and cuticle pushers accidentally cut skin every day in salons across the country. Several stories of blood-spilling with Credo blades have been printed in both Nailpro and *NAILS* magazines. Callus shavers cause more serious lacerations than any other nail salon device

Physicians and consumers should make sure this device is banned in their respective states.

2. Hair Removal by shaving with razors prior to salon services

And

3. Whirlpools and Pedicure Jet Spa Chairs

Fact: Several hundred nail clients in the United States alone have contracted serious infections from poor sanitation control in pedicure whirlpool chairs when microbes entered their bodies through the tiny cuts made by of shaving prior to nail salon services.

Freshly razor-shaved legs typically have many tiny nicks. Shaving your legs prior to any nail salon activity is unwise. Nail technicians are banned from the act of shaving the legs or arms of hair in most states. The use of razors may have been partially responsible for the *Mycobacterium fortuitum* outbreak in Watsonville, California in 2000. Shaving the legs of patrons of the Fancy Nail Salon in Watsonville may have created portals of entry for bacteria. Beeswax removal is a safer alternative, or other epilating electrolysis devices may be employed by licensed aestheticians.

Breaks in the skin can be dangerous portals for infection.. The problem exists with poorly disinfected standing water in pedicure spa chairs. PVC and flexible plastic pipes that are internal to these units may also be unable to properly flush contaminated water after each client's use. Extensive contact time with disinfectants like bleach is necessary to disinfect the units.

In the Watsonville, California, outbreak in 2000, poor sanitation is one factor for the presence of mycobacterium in poorly maintained jet filters. A black tarry substance was discovered by Santa Cruz Health Department, inspectors in the pipe screens of the custom water spas at the Fancy Nail Salon. The spa owner admitted to never having cleaned the filters. *Mycobacterium fortuitum*, the principal bacterium found in the Watsonville outbreak, is primarily a soil and/or waterborne bacteria found sometimes in poorly chlorinated water supplies. Manufactures of fiberglass pedicure chairs state in their literature to not use strong abrasive cleaners or you will scratch you fiberglass surfaces. Fiberglass spas surfaces cannot be abrasively cleaned and drained. This is very different from stainless steel whirlpool tanks that can be rigorously cleaned and sanitized between patient visits. Panels to access ALL tubing and drain systems for maintenance must be designed for service.

4. Trauma to nail plates and acrylic nail removal

Fact: Most nail plate injuries occur with removal of artificial nails. Nail techs in discount salons have been known to pry artificial nails off the natural nail plate with serous resultant injury and damage.

Careful attention to removal and reapplication of artificial nails is the way nail technicians should handle this problem, but not all perform proper protocol to save time. Trauma from the leverage and forceful removal of artificial nails is a matter of concern to prevent damage to the nail.

There are proper ways to remove acrylic nails, which include a combination of mechanical debridement and warm acetone-soaked cotton wrapped in foil around the fingertips for 15 minutes. The acetone should be heated with a warm water bath. This produces the best and least traumatic removal, according to nail technicians familiar with this procedure.

UV cured nails are activated by UV light and must be ground off with careful electric file debridement to just before visible nail and then soaked with warm acetone since acetone by itself does not work as well on UV gel products. Nail wraps can be removed with warm acetone as well. Take the time to do this right.

5. Proper use of electric files

Fact: Electric files represent an instant way of damaging nail plates and require certified training.

Improper use of electric files can cut or burn skin. Electric files can gouge, dangerously thin, or damage the nail plate, and permanently damage the nail matrix.

The electric nail file industry has been more prominent in recent years and is training nail techs to prevent nail injuries from prying artificial nails from the natural nail plate.

Electric file courses are taught through Association of Electric File Manufactures (AEFM) AEFM.org

6. Proper ventilation of salon workplace vapors and electric file dust and avoidance of chemical contact must be routine in every spa.

FACT: Some nail techs prematurely retire from salon service work due to improper nail chemical-handling protocol and inhalation of dust particles and vapors causing salon inhalation work disorder (SIWD).

The use of proper ventilation, face masks, and disposable gloves help avoid chemical contact by isolation of the nail tech from these agents. It is your duty as a nail tech to take responsibility to protect yourself from these chemical that in time can cause you to be come sensitized. It is your duty to protect your client from direct exposure to these agents. Chemical vapor ventilation in salons, nail polish and improper artificial nail applications concerns should be discussed with clients

Vacuum systems directly attached to the electric nail file can help capture the dust generated by filing artificial nails. Quiet vacuum system can also discharge this dust to collection or vent systems outside the salon work area.

All volatile chemical vapors should be ventilated to the outside air in all nail salons. This is rarely done correctly. Noxious vapors from acetone, ethyl methacrylates, primers, monomers and other products will cause neurological symptoms like headaches or blurred vision.

The applications of artificial nails – acrylic nails, nail wraps, or gel nails cured with UV light – should require the use of gloves to prevent chemical contact with the nail tech's skin to prevent long term allergic dermatitis.

Older methacrylic acid nail primers are organic acids used to clean the surface of the nail plate before acrylic application layers. The product may cause skin burns and irritation if it comes in contact with any skin. Non acid primers should be used and requested on nail service. Gloves should be worn.

Watch out for chemical cuticle removers, some cuticle treatments and callus removers. Some of these products use caustic potash, a powerful and dangerous alkali, or a base called sodium or potassium hydroxide, to dissolve the dried skin fold on the base of the nail plate (sometimes referred to as cuticle) near the eponychium that accumulates at the beginning of the nail or proximal nail plate.

Nail technicians find this easier than forcing the dried skin away with probes or cuticle sticks, which should not be preformed anyway due to the destruction of the protective nail-skin surface. These strong alkali agents should be used with caution and have been used to dissolve calluses by nail techs, which is not the intent of the manufacturer.

7. Require all 50 states to ban nail techs from treating and working on nail pathology without written permission of a physician

FACT: Nail tech have no specific training on how to refer or follow up with physicians to help clients with medical problems.

Tennessee is one of a few states that have rules that require nail techs to get written permission from a medical professional to perform services on clients with medical problems or skin pathology. The Tennessee regulation reads as follows:

0440-2-.12. Communicable Diseases

No patron with definite open sores, exhibiting symptoms of infectious or contagious disease or disorders of the skin, or parasitic infestations, will be served in a shop or school unless written permission from a physician has been secured.

In all salons, a clearly-documented system to refer should be in place so that when a person with medical problems (such as nail fungus, an ingrown nail, or skin disease such as advanced psoriasis) wants beauty services on their hands or feet, all salon personnel— owners, managers, nail technicians, receptionists – know how to handle the situation correctly and legally. Moving forward with this level of clarity is a great way to work.

Referral to a physician will prevent all sorts of problems. The Tech-to-Doc and Doc-to-Tech referral forms show how easy it is.

8. Ban MMA and acid nail primers through all 50 states.

Fact: MMA has caused more damage or dermatological allergic reactions from artificial nails than any other nail product

The monomer methyl methacrylate (MMA) is the bonding agent formerly used by many nail technicians to apply acrylic nails. This product has been deemed a hazardous substance by the FDA and has been the agent responsible for a large number of cases of nail infections, skin allergies and dermatitis of the nail plate.

MMA has been replaced by ethyl methacrylate (EMA) for reduced incidents of nail dermatitis. However, some salons still use the illegal MMA agent for tighter bonding to the nail plate at the risk of the client. There is a widespread effort by nail technicians to ban the use of this agent. The federal government (FDA) bans MMA (see link) http://vm.cfsan.fda.gov/%7Edms/cos-210.html but it needs the support of the physician-based community to help achieve this ban by contacting state cosmetology boards and make sure your boards have written enforceable bans on MMAs and specified in your state cosmetology regulations. Most states already do.

Acid nail primers are too caustic to be used in salons. Acid nail primers do not promote bonding as well as the new non acid nail primers and should be also banned from salon use.

9. Require sterilization training of instruments in all states

FACT: *As a result of a recent death in Fort Worth, Texas from an MRSA Staph infection in a nail salon, Texas is now the first state to implement autoclaving of nail salon instrumentation.*

The biggest concern in nail salons is proper equipment sanitation and disinfection. Since nail technicians are not supposed to be working in a blood field or sterile environment, the standards for keeping their instrumentation clean from bacteria, fungal, and viral organisms historically have been more relaxed than those in the health care profession.

However, with the advent of mutating HIV strains; Hepatitis A, B, and C; bacterial and bacterial spore infections;

and fungal and other viral organisms, the stakes have increased. If liquid disinfection of instrumentation was done properly, steam sterilization would not be necessary. However, not all nail techs take the time to properly sanitize and disinfect their instrumentation. For this reason, sterilization training should now be implemented in addition to proper disinfection. Hepatitis B can live on most surfaces for 7 days.

Sterilization is the destruction of all microorganisms. You can sterilize instruments but you cannot sterilize skin. You can use antiseptics on skin but you cannot kill all the bacteria on skin. That is why in some surgeries even with multiple applications of Betadine® (povidone iodine) is used to reduce the maximum number of bacteria but infections can still occur. When a nail tech accidentally cuts the skin, she can take action if the cut is identified that would include cleaning the area with soap and water, applying a topical antibiotic and referring to a physician.

Many HIV or hepatitis clients who scratch lesions like mosquito bites or scabs contaminate their distal nail plate with infectious fluid or debris that can cross-contaminate nail tech instrumentation. Use of improperly cleaned nail nippers can transfer fungal and bacterial spore debris. A viral particle transmission called herpetic whitlow has been confirmed.

Hepatitis C transmissions has been alluded to but not confirmed. No instance of HIV transmission has been documented in a nail salon to date.

State boards consider alcohol, phenols, and quaternary compounds i.e. detergents adequate. But many health professionals and even nail technicians agree that current methods of sanitation and disinfection using alcohol need to be replaced by sterilization protocols – autoclaving.

Clients deserve peace of mind when they come into any salon that the instrumentation is completely safe. The heat activated color indicator and sealed/unopened freshly sterilized bag will attest to each client they are getting safe instrument. No other method gives such complete assurance.

Currently, nail technicians practice their respective state-mandated sanitation protocols for cleaning their instrumentation. These regulations are basically similar form state to state and include:

• Brushing the instruments with soapy water;

• 10 minute soaking in a 70 percent alcohol based sanitation fluid or suitable agent; and

• Storing the instruments in a plastic container with lid, or in some states, keeping any clean instrument under a UV sterilizer when not in use.

Alcohol and detergents used almost exclusively by nail technicians do not kill bacterial spores. Only liquid gluteraldehyde will do this after 30 minutes to one hour of soaking. But imperfections (see picture) in instrumentation or the collection of excessive debris from debridement can render even these longer soaks inadequate. The UV sterilizer is almost useless as a true sterilizer in nail salon applications and is at best, nothing more than a temporary light storage box. The only other safe and faster bacterial spore elimination is provided by autoclaves.

Autoclaves should be an integral part of all salons to give the patrons complete assurance that they are receiving the best infection control. This sterilization move in the industry is being resisted at many levels until recently in Texas. Some upscale salons across the country are already autoclaving, but this represents a very small percentage of salons. Disposable nail files or instrumentation and clients bringing their own nail nippers are possible alternatives to states who are not autoclaving.

Also, remember that most all state cosmetology laws use sanitation for care of only normal, non-infected nails. For those nail techs that treat fungal nails without doctors' permission, they risk contamination by the nail nippers and unsterile instruments.

Additional disinfection fact: Physical therapists protect their patients from contaminated paraffin baths with plastic sleeves

Paraffin was traditionally used as a physical therapy modality for arthritic extremity conditions. The nail industry adapted wax paraffin to their pedicure routines for the soothing and softening effects of hot wax.

Physical therapists have protected their patients from direct contact with the wax to prevent contamination of the wax and to prevent possible dermatitis. They accomplished this with a protective plastic bag over the extremity before the dipping and layering process. Some salons do not protect their clients from direct contact with wax, and some reuse the wax against certain state protocols. Bacteria combined with exfoliated skin and moisturizers can collect in wax used improperly in this manner. Herpes viral transmission has been confirmed by a contaminated waxing procedure in a nail salon.

Last disinfection reminder: Gloves *Fact: Disposable surgical gloves stop many infections*

Medical professionals use gloves to protect patients and clinicians from contamination. Medical facilities use universal precaution in all medical settings. Phoebe Rich, MD, a dermatologist and contributing writer to *NAILS* magazine, says that "toenail fungus is contagious, but whether you contract it depends on your genetics. Some families have a genetic susceptibility to fungal infections due to an inherited blind spot in the immune system that doesn't recognize fungus and fight it off properly".

If you have this fungal susceptibility then you are at high risk of developing fungus not only from clients but also from gyms, health clubs and even hotel rooms. Someone with this propensity who comes in the salon, the nail tech should always wear gloves. Repetitive application of strong chemicals with hands such as the exfoliating AHA products and the sodium and potassium hydroxide cuticle and callus remover for calluses require gloves.

Your doctor should treat the nail fungus for a minimum of 3 months and you wait a minimum of an additional 6-9 months before you are allowed to get pedicures with written permission only. The nail tech should be alerted you have fungus and take extra precautions with their instrumentation if they are not using long enough disinfection times.

10. Require all 50 states to institute CEUs

Fact: CEUs are mandated in almost professional service industries

Finally, yearly mandatory CEUs (continuing education credits) are definitely needed to maintain their certification (just as many professionals maintain their licenses) are necessary to introduce new approaches to better nail care. The nail industry wants to consider their nail techs "professional". All the textbooks in the world are not going to get the information disseminated and practiced regarding new whirlpool disinfection protocols or new techniques in sterilization without mandatory continuing education requirements.

Additional CEU facts regarding Artificial Nails and the natural nail plate.

Fact: Millions of women in the US have contacted a bacterial infection from artificial nails in the past decade from poor artificial nail application technique.

Nail salons have caused many medical nail problems during the evolution of nail enhancements. They can be summed up as nail infections from improper application technique. Yearly CEU training is necessary to help all nail technicians achieve proficiency in artificial nail application and electric file technique

Artificial nails are the application of layers of bonding agents or chemical polymers to build up an aesthetic construction lattice on top of the nail plate with several different chemical polymers and powder acrylic mixtures. The lack of proficient application of these bonding agents sometimes allows water to build up under the nail and cause what is termed in the nail industry as "the greenies" i.e., bacterial Pseudomonas infections.

The beauty industry has become so cavalier about this problem they diagnose and treat these problems with medications, disinfectants and bleaching agents sold directly to clients with claims of curing these problems.

What are the results of implementing "cures" for these top ten problems?

ANSWER: Preventing infections!

If these 10 corrections to the nail salon industry were adopted by all states there would be a multi-million dollar cost savings to the health care system. Unconfirmed estimates predict the average podiatrist sees about one pedicure related fungal or bacterial infection every other month. That is 6 per year. There are about 14,000 practicing podiatrists, which tallies the number of foot/nail infections a year to about 84,000 individuals seeking services for nail or skin related pedicure infections from podiatrists only.

When you add the number of dermatologists, internists, private physicians, emergency room doctors (estimated 250,000) and nurse practitioners (estimated 115,000) treating bacterial and fungal infections from manicures and pedicures it could total over one million patient visits. That does not include infections that don't get reported and are handled by clients treating themselves at home with over the counter treatments.

If you accept the estimate that 1,000,000 people per year may obtain a fungal nail infection, dermatitis or bacterial infection from a pedicure or manicure and with the single average new patient/doctor visit costing over $100, you could reason the partial burden to the health care system could be $100 million dollars.

When you add the average cost of antibiotic therapy, steroid therapy or a $1000 antifungal therapy, you could see these medical services cost over $200 million to the health care market per year. This does not include injuries that are self-inflicted by improper personal nail care or application of artificial nail services at home

This total does not include individuals that have to have multiple rounds of antifungal medicines, multiple surgeries or amputations that could well drive this annual cost well over the $200 million amount. One foot or leg amputation can easily exceed $50,000-$100,000 when considering follow up costs associated with physical therapy, prosthetic services and follow up physician services or hospitalizations.

The sad fact is that once a diabetic gets an amputation they have an average 5 year life span after the first amputation. Nail Techs should always ask about their client's medical history to avoid potential medical problems and refer the client to physicians when a problem is noted. Nail techs should not accept high risk patients without knowing more about the client's history.

My patients, even when faced with the fact they know that a pedicurist or manicurist has caused their nail disorder are reluctant to take matters further or confront the shop that caused the problem. Many times there is a rapport established and the patient does not want to take action until the bills start coming from the doctor's office.

I have been consulted on several lawsuits. All have been settled out of court. It has been such a common problem to get "the greenies" or a pseudomonas infection that many nail techs diagnose, treat, and defend their application technique for artificial nails. This may be because traditionally the industry has perpetuated that pseudomonas is not really much of a problem. It can be a big problem to a client with a poorly functioning immune system.

Council of Nail Disorders
www.nailcouncil.org/

The Council for Nail Disorders (CND) is the first organized group of health care professionals formed to advance education for physicians and the general public regarding the diagnosis and management of nail disorders. CND has been chartered to assist health care professionals in proper diagnosis and treatment in an effort to reduce the incidence and persistence of nail disorders.

The Cosmetic Ingredient Review Panel
www.cir-safety.org/

The Cosmetic Ingredient Review (CIR) was established in 1976 by the Cosmetic, Toiletry & Fragrance Association (CTFA) with support of the U.S. Food & Drug Administration and the Consumer Federation of America. Although funded by CTFA, CIR and the review process are independent from CTFA and the cosmetics industry. The Cosmetic Ingredient Review thoroughly reviews and assesses the safety of ingredients used in cosmetics in an open, unbiased, and expert manner, and publishes the results in the open, peer-reviewed scientific literature.

Chapter 25
Case studies
Bacterial Infections and Infection control Medline link articles

An outbreak of mycobacterial furunculosis associated with foot baths at a nail salon.

http://www.ncbi.nlm.nih.gov/entrez/query.fcgi?db=pubmed&cmd=Retrieve&
dopt=Abstract&list_uids=14679446&query_hl=46&itool=pubmed_docsum
New England Journal of Medicine 2002 May 2;346(18):1366-71

Winthrop KL, Abrams M, Yakrus M, Schwartz I, Ely J, Gillies D, Vugia DJ.
Epidemic Intelligence Service, Epidemiology Program Office, Centers for
Disease Control and Prevention, Atlanta, USA. kwinthro@dhs.ca.gov

BACKGROUND: In September 2000, a physician in
northern California described four patients with persistent, cul-
ture-negative boils on the lower extremities. The patients had
received pedicures at the same nail salon. We identified and
investigated an outbreak of *Mycobacterium fortuitum furunculosis*
among customers of this nail salon. METHODS: Patients were
defined as salon customers with persistent skin infections below
the knee. A case-control study was conducted that included the
first 48 patients identified, and 56 unaffected friends and family
members who had had a pedicure at the same salon served as

controls. Selected M. *fortuitum* isolates, cultured from patients and the salon environment, were compared by pulsed-field gel electrophoresis. RESULTS: We identified 110 customers of the nail salon who had furunculosis. Cultures from 34 were positive for rapidly growing mycobacteria (32 M. *fortuitum* and 2 unidentified). Most of the affected patients had more than 1 boil (median, 2; range, 1 to 37). All patients and controls had had whirlpool footbaths. Shaving the legs with a razor before pedicure was a risk factor for infection (70 percent of patients vs. 31 percent of controls; adjusted odds ratio, 4.8; 95 percent confidence interval, 2.1 to 11.1). Cultures from all 10 footbaths at the salon yielded M. fortuitum. The M. *fortuitum* isolates from three footbaths and 14 patients were indistinguishable by electrophoresis. CONCLUSIONS: We identified a large outbreak of rapidly growing mycobacterial infections among persons who had had footbaths and pedicures at one nail salon. Physicians should suspect this cause in patients with persistent furunculosis after exposure to whirlpool footbaths.

PMID: 11986410 [PubMed - indexed for MEDLINE]

Outbreak of extended-spectrum beta-lactamase-producing Klebsiella pneumoniae in a neonatal intensive care unit linked to artificial nails.

http://www.ncbi.nlm.nih.gov/entrez/query.fcgi?cmd=Retrieve&db=PubMed
&list_uids=15061412&dopt=Abstract
Infection Control Hospital Epidemiology 2004 Mar;25(3):210-5

Gupta A, Della-Latta P, Todd B, San Gabriel P, Haas J, Wu F, Rubenstein D, Saiman L.
Department of Pediatrics, Columbia University, New York-Presbyterian Hospital, New York, New York 10032, USA.

BACKGROUND: From April to June 2001, an outbreak of extended-spectrum beta-lactamase (ESBL)-producing *Klebsiella pneumoniae* infections was investigated in our neonatal intensive care unit. METHODS: Cultures of the gastrointestinal tracts of patients, the hands of healthcare workers (HCWs), and the environment were performed to detect potential reservoirs for ESBL-producing *K. pneumoniae*. Strains of *K. pneumoniae* were typed by pulsed-field gel electrophoresis using XbaI. A case-control study was performed to determine risk factors for acquisition of the outbreak clone (clone A); cases were infants infected or colonized with clone A and controls (3 per case) were infants with negative surveillance cultures. RESULTS: During the study period, 19 case-infants, of whom 13 were detected by surveillance cultures, harbored clone A. The overall attack rate for the outbreak strain was 45%; 9 of 19 infants presented with invasive disease (n = 6) or developed invasive disease (n = 3) after colonization was detected. Clone A was found on the hands of 2 HCWs, 1 of whom wore artificial nails, and on the designated stethoscope of a case-infant. Multiple logistic regression analysis revealed that length of stay per day (odds ratio [OR], 1.05; 95% confidence interval [CI95], 1.02 to 1.09) and exposure to the HCW wearing artificial fingernails (OR, 7.87; CI95, 1.75 to 35.36) were associated with infection or colonization with clone A. CONCLUSION: Short, well-groomed, natural nails should be mandatory for HCWs with direct patient contact

PMID: 15061412 [PubMed - indexed for MEDLINE]

Survey of infection control procedures at manicure and pedicure establishments in North York.

Johnson IL, Dwyer JJ, Rusen ID, Shahin R, Yaffe B.
Department of Public Health Sciences, University of Toronto, Toronto, ON. ian.johnson@utoronto.ca
Canadian Journal of Public Health 2001 Mar-Apr;92(2):134-7 Related Articles, Books, LinkOut

OBJECTIVE: To describe infection control practices used by technicians doing manicures and pedicures in an urban setting in Ontario. METHODS: A random sample of 120 establishments was selected from a sampling frame. A survey was designed and administered to technicians through face-to-face interviews. RESULTS: Technicians in 72 establishments were interviewed, representing a 60% response rate. Twenty-nine (40%) of these technicians indicated that they had been immunized against hepatitis B. Technicians re-used almost all instruments even if this was not the intent of the manufacturer. Isopropyl alcohol was the most commonly used disinfectant. Many technicians did not wear gloves while performing procedures. Most did not follow universal precautions when asked how they would react to incidental cuts on either the client or themselves. CONCLUSION: There is a need for the development of infection control protocols for manicure and pedicure establishments since the potential for transmission of infectious diseases does exist.

PMID: 11338152 [PubMed - indexed for MEDLINE]

Neurological Symptoms From Nail Salons

Neuropsychological symptoms associated with low-level exposure to solvents and (meth)acrylates among nail technicians.

Neuropsychiatry Neuropsychological Behavior or Neurology 2001 Jul-Sep;14(3):183-9 and Neuropsychiatry Neuropsychol Behav Neurol. 2002; 15(1):44-55 (ISSN: 0894-878X)
LoSasso GL, Rapport LJ, Axelrod BN.
Department of Psychology, Wayne State University, Detroit, MI 48202, USA.

OBJECTIVE: To evaluate reports of neuropsychological symptoms among women occupationally exposed to products commonly used in nail studios. BACKGROUND: Typical preparations found in nail studios contain a variety of organic solvents (e.g., toluene, acetone, formaldehyde) and (meth)acrylates with known neurotoxic properties. Little research has focused on the neuropsychological sequelae of exposure to these substances occurring in the cosmetics industry. METHOD: Participants included nail salon technicians (n = 150) and controls (n = 148). Nail technicians were compared with demographically similar controls using the Neuropsychological Impairment Scale, a self-reported measure of neuropsychological and psychological symptoms. Aspects of the workplace environment (e.g., square footage of the salon, adequacy of ventilation, hours worked) also were assessed. RESULTS: A MANOVA revealed small but significant differences in the overall level of symptoms as well as in individual scales measuring neurologic complaints, cognitive efficiency, memory, verbal learning, and academic skills (p < 0.001). Moreover, nail technicians were significantly more likely to score above the clinical cutoffs than were controls on four of the seven clinical scales and two of the three summary indices. Multiple regression analysis indicated that the severity of symptoms was associated with level of occupational exposure (p < 0.01). The cumulative impact of workplace size and ventilation were most strongly associated with symptom severity. CONCLUSIONS: Exposure to low-level neurotoxins common to nail studios results in the self-reported experience of cognitive and neurologic symptoms similar to other types of solvent and (meth)acrylate exposure. The profile of reported symptoms is consistent with deficits typically observed in this type of neurotoxic exposure: neurologic complaints as well as perceived problems with cognitive efficiency, memory, and learning. Additionally, the nail technicians reported a higher overall level of complaints and greater severity of symptoms than did the controls.

PMID: 11513102 [PubMed - indexed for MEDLINE]
PMID: 11877551 [PubMed - indexed for MEDLINE]

Pathogenic organisms associated with artificial fingernails worn by healthcare workers.

Hedderwick SA, McNeil SA, Lyons MJ, Kauffman CA.

Infection Control Hospital of Epidemiology 2000 Aug;21(8):505-9

Department of Internal Medicine, Department of Veterans' Affairs Healthcare System, and University of Michigan Medical School, Ann Arbor, Michigan 48105, USA.

OBJECTIVE: To determine differences in the identity and quantity of microbial flora from healthcare workers (HCWs) wearing artificial nails compared with control HCWs with native nails. DESIGN: Two separate studies were undertaken. In study 1, 12 HCWs who did not normally wear artificial nails wore polished artificial nails on their nondominant hand for 15 days. Identity and quantity of microflora were compared between the artificial nails and the polished native nails of the other hand. In study 2, the microbial flora of the nails of 30 HCWs who wore permanent acrylic artificial nails were compared with that of control HCWs who had native nails. In both studies, nail surfaces were swabbed and subungual debris was collected to obtain material for culture. *Staphylococcus aureus*, gram-negative bacilli, enterococci, and yeasts were considered to be potential pathogens. All organisms were identified and quantified. RESULTS: In study 1, potential pathogens were isolated from more samples obtained from artificial nails than native nails (92% vs. 62%; P<.001). Colonization of artificial nails increased over time; by day 15, 71% of cultures yielded a pathogen compared with 21% on day 1 (P=.004). A significantly greater quantity of organisms (expressed as mean log10 colony-forming units +/- standard deviation) was isolated from the subungual area than the nail surface; this was noted for both artificial (5.0+/-1.4 vs. 4.1+/-1.0; P<.001) and native nails (4.9+/-1.3 vs. 3.7+/-0.8; P<.001). More organisms were found on the surface of artificial nails than native nails (P=.008), but there were no differences noted in the quantities of organisms isolated from the subungual areas. In study 2, HCWs wearing artificial

nails were more likely to have a pathogen isolated than controls (87% vs. 43%; P=.001). More HCWs with artificial nails had gram-negative bacilli (47% vs. 17%; P=.03) and yeasts (50% vs. 13%; P=.006) than control HCWs. However, the quantities of organisms isolated from HCWs wearing artificial nails and controls did not differ. CONCLUSIONS: Artificial fingernails were more likely to harbor pathogens, especially gram-negative bacilli and yeasts, than native nails. The longer artificial nails were worn, the more likely that a pathogen was isolated. Current recommendations restricting artificial fingernails in certain healthcare settings appear justified.
PMID: 10968715 [PubMed - indexed for MEDLINE]

Permanent loss of finger nails from sensitization and reaction to acrylic in a preparation designed to make artificial nails.

Fisher AA.
Journal of Dermatological Surgical Oncology 1980 Jan;6(1):70-1

Six years ago a patient suffered a severe allergic reaction from sensitization to methyl methacrylate in a mixture of materials designed to make artificial nails. There was marked erythema, edema, and pain of the eponychial and paronychial tissues with persistent paresthesia of the finger tips. Gradual destruction of the nail plates developed and since no regrowth of the nails resumed in six years, the loss of the finger nails is found to be permanent.
PMID: 7356701 [PubMed - indexed for MEDLINE]

Chapter 26
Letters from physicians and professional nail technicians

Shelley Sekula-Gibbs, M. D.
Bay Oaks Dermatology
17300 El Camino Real, Suite 103
Houston, Texas 77058
(281)480-7546 Fax (281)480-5324 www.bayoaksdermatology.com

Dear Dr. Spalding,

The nail care industry is in serious need of a makeover. When a client visits a nail salon she may not realize that she could be exposing herself to a host of germs. Although some salon's owners are making strides to improve their disinfection practices, many are still woefully ignorant about disease transmission and the need to treat nail instruments more like surgical tools. Anytime the skin is cut or filed with dirty instruments germs can be introduced. Today's beauty conscious clients should insist that nail technicians adhere to disinfection practices in keeping with the high standards established in hospitals and clinics.

Across the nation, unfortunate nail clients continue to develop progressive ulcers on their legs after receiving in contaminated whirlpool tubs. Even in this relatively up-scale salon, cleaning and disinfecting were superficial. In 2005, a disabled woman from Dallas, Texas, died after developing an infection allegedly from a pedicure. Higher prices may not translate into high disinfection standards. The buyer should beware.

The solution for providing safe services in salons is within our reach.

1.   States must require nail salons to hire licensed technicians who are well versed in disinfection practices.

2.   Existing laws should be enforced. Currently, when prohibited instruments, like Credo blades, are discovered in salons, authorities are not allowed to confiscate the dangerous "paring knives". A small fine issued and little else is done. Incentives should be in place for salon owners and technicians to conform to higher disinfection standards.

3.   Clients must be aware of potential dangers in nail salons. Ask questions. Ask the technicians to demonstrate how instruments are disinfected, and ask to see the cleaning solutions that are used. If the technician can not explain the process, find another salon. Verify that the cleaning solutions have the following statements written on their label - " bactericidal, fungicidal, virucidal, and tuberculocidal".

4.   Check filters on whirlpool tubs before getting a pedicure. Frequently, these filters have not been washed or disinfected. Hair and skin particles build up and contaminate the whirlpool footbaths.

5.   Metal instruments should be sterilized. An autoclave works best, but high and intermediate level disinfectants can also be used. Hospital grade, low level disinfectants, are not strong enough to be effective on instruments that can cut or abrade skin.

6.   If an autoclave is not available, the next best thing for the clients to do is purchase her own instruments and bring them with her to the salon.

The nail industry stands at a crossroads. With hard work, adherence to scientific principles, and continuing education, salon owners and technicians can advance nail services in both profit and safety and clients will be well served.

Sincerely,
Shelley Sekula-Gibbs, M. D.
Diplomate of the American Board Of Dermatology
Fellow American Society for Dermatologic Surgery
Assistant Clinical Professor Baylor College of Med.

Dr. Spalding comments

Dr. Shelley Sekula-Gibbs is one of the most influential dermatologists in the United States and has been on the front battle lines with nail salon safety as a physician and a serving Texas politician. She is a tremendous consumer advocate who understands bacterial contamination and has exposed nail salon concerns nationwide. Dr. Sekula-Gibbs has been interviewed by every major national news station regarding nail salon safety. She has served as a consultant and a reviewing investigator in several salon incidents nationwide.

Carolyn L Siegal, D.P.M
Podiatric Medicine & Surgery, Beverly Hills

Dear Dr. Spalding, Colleagues, and Friends,

As a podiatrist in private practice, I witnessed an increase in the number of patients with infections developing after repeated nail salon visits. These patients had no other risk factors for these infections (which included nail fungus, plantar warts, and digital bacterial nail fold infections) besides attending a nail salon on a weekly or monthly basis. After medical treatment for these infections, I found that many of these patients were not willing to forego their routine professional nail appointments at the salon. To many, routine nail treatments are not only perceived as a form of basic grooming, but also a form of self-nurturing.

After researching the medical data and reports regarding infectious outbreaks in the nail salon industry, I realized that there was a need to create a method for my patients to reduce their risk of contracting diseases in the nail salon should they continue to participate in this popular form of personal care. I developed a small collection of stylish nail kits designed to carry to the salon so that a client's personal set of tools is used during each professional nail treatment. My research showed that reputable national organizations and publications such as the Food and Drug Administration, The American Academy of Dermatology, the California Department of Health, and the New England Journal of Medicine have published reports regarding the risks of nail salons. I decided to create a method for my patients to reduce these well documented nail salon risks by not only providing a complete, organized, compact kit for patients to use at each appointment, but by also developing a way that would motivate my patients to use this protection.

By placing the full set of professional nail tools in stylish cases, I found that my patients were not only motivated to carry their own tools to the nail salon, but that they were anxious to help their family and friends do the same. Since the initiation of this project, I have been able to accommodate the high demand of this portable nail kit on a national level. This surprising national consumer demand for this portable carry-along nail kit confirmed that there was a dire need for a simple and realistic method to reduce health risks at professional nail appointments. An effective method to fully prevent infections in the nail salon setting is to abstain from these cosmetic establishments. For some, this is a realistic approach. However, should one choose to continue to have professional nail treatments, carrying one's own tools and using a disposable tub liner on the small portable foot tub at each appointment, can simply reduce the risk of contracting the infections that medical professionals see daily in their offices, as well as the more severe infections documented in medical literature.

The following information explains why these risks are present. Nail salons across the country are not monitored by the stringent federal agencies that are used to strictly monitor medical offices and hospitals; yet both the cosmetic and medical industries use sharp implements which can puncture skin and spread disease.

Autoclaving, or heat pressure sterilization, is the method required by federal organizations such as the Occupational Safety and Health Administration (OSHA) to effectively sterilize implements in medical offices, surgery centers, and hospitals. According to a Food and Drug Administration commentary, autoclaving is the most effective way to sterilize tools in order to eradicate all forms of bacteria and blood borne diseases (such as hepatitis). The medical doctors quoted in this report state, "If in doubt, bring your own implements". This report also states that the Center for Disease Control recommends that regulated forms of hospital sterilization and technician practices are necessary to prevent the transmission of blood born diseases in the nail salon setting. Hospitals are required to dispose of tools after each use and to autoclave the tools which are used on multiple patients. This technical and expensive form of medical sterilization is not required in the cosmetic industry even though sharp tools, which can puncture skin and spread disease, are used on multiple clients at the salon. Hence, the health risks are not only present due to the lack of sanitation in certain nail salons, but simply because sharp tools are commonly used on multiple people without hospital grade autoclave sterilization.

It is exciting to hear about the state which passed legislation for nail salons to use autoclaves. However, the consumer may commonly be uncertain as to whether the nail technician is following the time consuming manufacturing guidelines for these machines. This is important when considering very busy salons which must see many clients in short periods in order to meet competitive business demands. In addition, we can only hope that the state will strictly monitor each salon in a consistent fashion. To ensure an effective system, the improved regulations must be partnered with stringent monitoring guidelines. The documented case reports of nail salons "cutting corners" in regard to sanitation regulations confirm that strict and consistent monitoring of safety practices will be essential as the laws improve. A client can simply remove the uncertainty regarding these issues through a method which provides complete knowledge about where one's tools have been. By using a personal set of tools, there will be no question regarding who the tools have been used upon and if they have been cleaned properly.

It is important to note that an autoclave is not the same apparatus as the blue ultra violet light machine that is seen in many salons. I commonly ask my patients, "Would you feel comfortable being operated on with tools which were cleaned in this 'toaster oven' type cleaner?" According to the Hepatitis C Project, a nationally recognized organization developed by experts in the field of liver disease, chemical disinfectants, "disinfect rather than sterilize." In addition, "research suggests that commercial solutions may not kill the hepatitis virus." This organization also states, "To be as safe as possible, customers prefer to bring their own equipment with them to the nail salon." This suggestion makes sense when evaluating the fact stated by these medical experts that, "In at least 1 in 10 cases of hepatitis, people have no identifiable risk factors for infection; in other words, it is not known how they got hepatitis C."

The risks in the nail salon setting also include the foot baths. The Northern California case of over 100 pedicure customers developing ulcerative mycobacterial boils on their lower legs confirms that the whirlpool foot baths present a severe health risk. Research on this serious breach in sanitation codes was published in both a 2005 article in Emerging Infectious Disease and in a 2002 article published in The New England Journal of Medicine. Although there are some state regulations now in place to help prevent bacteria from colonizing in the pipes of these chairs, chairs which re-filter the water between each client, there is still very little being done to regularly monitor these regulations in order to ensure that they are being followed by the salons. In California and Texas, "inspectors visit the salons every 4-5 years," according to an expert in the field. In addition, the California Department of Health's Board of Barbering and Cosmetology reports that there are approximately 14 inspectors for the entire state of California. These inspectors only evaluate severe cases where formal complaints are made and when many individuals are affected. The funds and man power are simply not available for this cause at the present time. One can appreciate the significance of this lack of monitoring through another notable outbreak of mycobacterial infections published by the San Diego Emergency Medical Alert Network in 2003. There are also isolated reports of this infectious process documented in medical journals (for example, the 2004 Georgia cases of M. mageritense furunculosis documented in Emerging Infectious Disease, April 2005); hence, the risks are valid and supported by medical documentation. I therefore recommend that should you choose to receive a professional pedicure, either bring your own small tub, or use a disposable liner on the small portable foot soaking tub. I am commonly told by nail salon patrons that they feel "safe" when they witness their nail technicians "cleaning the tubs after each use." I must remind them that it is not only the cleanliness of the tub that one must be concerned about, but rather the cleanliness of the pipes within these whirlpool chairs. The consumer is not privy to how often the salon cleans the pipes after the salon has closed. The consumers are also not able to see the methods by which salons clean these pipes. Hence, unless you are able to witness the salon's compliancy with their maintenance requirements after business hours, the serious health risk remains present.

The risks however, do not only include the dangerous and severe infections noted above, but also chronic non-fatal infections. The chronic infections, such as fungal nails and plantar warts, are commonly not reported to state boards or to media publications. These less severe infections, which also include digital bacterial nail fold infections, are simply treated in medical offices across the country with no further recourse. These infections, however, are not always easy to treat. Nail fungus, for example, typically requires a three month oral medication treatment during which the patient's liver must be monitored each month. Bacterial nail fold infections typically require an office procedure and oral antibiotics. According to a report from the American Academy of Dermatology, "the health risks in nail salons include viral infections such as HIV, hepatitis, and warts; bacterial infections such as staphylococcus and strep, and fungal infections such as yeast, nail fungus, and athlete's foot." The California Department of Health's Board of Barbering and Cosmetology also reports that nail salon risks include not only HIV and hepatitis, but also bacteria and fungus. An argument that "considering the millions of manicures and pedicures performed each year, the relative number of infections is low and likely not to occur," does not take into consideration the 36 million Americans who have nail fungus (Podiatry Today, 2003), or the millions of individuals who contract painful plantar warts or athlete's foot each year. In addition, this statement does not take into account the thousands of dollars spent by patients and insurance companies for medical office visits and medications for treatment. Although not as severe as hepatitis or sepsis, these less severe infections are the cause of physical stress and financial strain on millions of nail salon patrons across the country.

Although I receive an abundance of support from medical experts across the country for promoting that each person use their personal set of tools at the salon, there are a few who have not shown such support. I would like to take a moment to comment on the concerns brought to my attention.

1. In response to the concern that carrying your own tools is dangerous since the tools are likely to be "un-professional, low budget, or unfamiliar to nail techs", I recommend that you make sure that you carry tools which you have discussed with your nail tech and that he or she feels comfortable using. Some clients ask their nail techs to sell them the tools of their choice. When developing my kits, my team designed professional nail tools which were given to focus groups of nail technicians across the country. After approximately one year of tending to the details requested by nail techs, we forged our unique molds of high quality tools with which our focus groups were satisfied. However, I commonly recommend that should your nail tech prefer a certain brand of tool, please buy it and keep it in one of the organizational compartments within a portable kit.

2. In regard to the comment, "unfamiliar tools are more likely to cause injury," it is important to note that injuries are simply caused by aggressive manicuring techniques. This statement is confirmed by the case of the Colorado woman who contracted herpes on her cuticle regions (ABC news, 1998), the woman in Fort Worth who died of sepsis after a cut on her heel during a pedicure (MSN/NBC/Associated Press, 2006), and the 2006 publication by the San Mateo County Disease Control and Prevention Unit which reports an acute hepatitis C case associated with a pedicure. This San Mateo report also states, "Anecdotal reports from patrons of pedicure salons indicate that the practice of trimming tissue… using a variety of cutting instruments is not uncommon and that

bleeding can result." The risk of cutting skin has clearly been a well documented result of aggressive manicuring techniques and has proven to be present even when the nail salon's "familiar" tools are used. However, should your nail tech verbalize that she is "uncomfortable" with the brand of tools that you bring for her to use, do not hesitate to simply ask her which brand she prefers and add this tool to an organized kit.

3. In response to the comment that "buffers and abrasives can create more work for the nail techs and cause cumulative trauma", there is no scientific medical evidence of this claim. All buffers can present a risk to the surrounding skin of the nail or to the nail plate itself if used aggressively. According to the California Board of Cosmetology and Barbering, "If an item cannot be disinfected (such as a nail buffer or emery board), it must be thrown away after each use." Those who attend nail salons regularly report that buffers and files are used repetitively for many weeks. The safety risk is higher if a buffer causes skin damage on one person and is then used on many other clients. An educated nail salon consumer and nail tech would know to throw the tool away should trauma occur. The product information in my kits advises that if an implement comes into contact with blood, then it should be discarded immediately. Should your nail tech use their "common" buffer on a client and cause nail or skin trauma to that client, we can only hope that they discard it. If you prefer to not base your safety on a hope, carry your own tools so that you know exactly where your tools have been. As stated by the FDA report, "If in doubt, carry your own" professional buffer.

4. In response to the comment that "Kit instructions incorrectly suggest that proper cleaning is not required between services," the instructions inside of my kit list the steps to clean the tools through methods used in medical offices for basic medical procedures. The instructions advise that each tool be wiped down with betadine solution, alcohol, or hydrogen peroxide after each use. It also instructs one on how to remove any fibrous and nail remnants from the tools, and that should a tool come into contact with blood, it should be discarded immediately. When tools are used on multiple parties, they need to be sterilized (free of all micro-organisms). If the tools are used on only one person, they need to be disinfected

(free of basic pathogenic organisms which may not include resistant bacterial spores or the hepatitis virus). I commonly inform my patients that "you will not catch a disease from yourself and therefore disinfection of your personal set of tools is safe". If you buy a kit that states otherwise, please be advised that you should perform the cleaning steps mentioned above after each nail treatment.

5. "Customers often use these kits on family members and pets, making them more likely to cause infection". The health conscious consumers who are going out of their way to stay safe are unlikely to use their personal set of nail tools on other people, or on their cat or dog. My kits repetitively promote the use of a personal kit on only one person: the kit owner. This instructional message is highlighted in the product literature, the product box, magazine and newspaper interviews, and the product insert. I am not certain about what type of unhygienic, uneducated person would use their personal care items (hair brush, toothbrush, nail tools, etc...) on their animals, but I think that this type of person is not one who is taking care of themselves through basic forms of routine grooming. I would also imagine that an individual who is grossly lacking in hygiene to this extent, would typically not be one who would try to decrease their health risks in nail salons through the use of their own personal portable nail kit. I was not able to find medical or scientific data to support this claim and wonder if this comment is simply a fabrication used to promote unfounded biased opinions. If professionals are genuinely concerned that this sharing of personal care items between people and animals is a reality, then a more effective approach would be to simply advise the public that the nail care tools that one purchases as a personal set of tools should only be used on the kit owner. The kit, which you are buying in order to decrease health risks associated with sharing of nail salon tools, should not be used on anyone, or anything, else.

6. "Existing regulations regarding proper cleaning and disinfection are more than enough to protect the consumer." By the mere fact that Dr. Spalding has written this well documented book, that he has included the input of several reputable professionals who are working to create safety in the cosmetic industry, as well as by the multiple reports of medical evidence referenced in this letter, this is obviously a false statement.

In reference to an instruction that nail salon consumers should avoid "factory nail shops," I would like to contribute the following. The case reports of infections occur in both lower end salons, as well as upscale salons. One can therefore assess that the risks are not related to the amount of money charged for services. With that said, over 6.2 billion dollars are spent on professional nail care annually. This growing number confirms that professional nail treatments have become a basic form of grooming available to many levels of socioeconomic populations. Many consumers do not have the expendable income to pay for the more expensive salons. A consumer can attend a local nail shop and receive a manicure for 7-10 dollars; while in the upscale salons the manicures range from 25-60 dollars. The fact that the "factory nail shops" are inexpensive, as well as the fact that they do not require an appointment, will contribute to their consistent public demand.

I believe that it is our duty as experts to warn consumers of the risks involved and to provide realistic methods to reduce these risks. The most effective methods to reduce risks include fully abstaining from salons, visualizing your nail tech sterilize tools in a medical quality autoclave for the forty five minute time period prior to your appointment, or carrying your own tools and disposable tub liner to each nail treatment. I have found that the former two options are not realistic options for many nail salon patrons. In addition, simply waiting for the laws to change while aimlessly asking about "where the money is going and why there aren't enough inspectors to uphold the law and protect the consumer" is not a pro-active, effective, or safe option either. Although it is exciting to witness significant improvements made in the sanitation regulations of the nail salon industry, the goal of having federal agencies mandate that all nail salons (in every state) follow the sterilization techniques required in hospitals may not take place within the near future.

In the interim, it is the responsibility of the professionals in the medical and cosmetic industry to educate consumers and nail technicians through scientific data, medical reports, sanitary guideline training, education of universal precautions, and team work amongst the professionals involved. I am proud to be in association with the other professional contributors of this book who share a similar vision of education, prevention, reduction of risks, and improved sanitary regulations. Through each of our unique methods, it is clear that we are all striving to make a difference as a team. With that said, I also commend Dr. Spalding for publishing this incredibly useful educational tool which will only bring us closer to our common goal.

Very Truly Yours,
Carolyn Siegal, D.P.M.

References:
1. Winthrop KL, et al. An Outbreak of mycobacterial furunculosis associated with footbaths at a nail salon. New England Journal of Medicine.2002;346:1366-71
2. Kurtzweil, P. Fingernails: Looking good while playing it safe. U.S Food and Drug Administration
3. AAD. Hair and Nail Salons Linked to Infectious Diseases. American Academy of Dermatology. March 1999
4. Vugia, D. Mycobacteria in nail salon whirlpool footbaths, California. Emerging Infectious Diseases. www.cdc.gov/eid.2005;11:4
5. An acute case of hepatitis C associated with a pedicure. San Mateo County Disease Control and Prevention. 2006
6. California Department of Consumer Affairs; Consumer information sheet. Manicure and Nail Salon Services Fact Sheet. California Board of Barbering & Cosmetology, www.BarberCosmo.ca.gov. August 2004
7. Highleyman, L. Preventing HCV transmission in personal care settings. The Hepatitis C Support Project, San Francisco (UCSF). Sept 2002, Version 1.0.
8. San Diego Medical Emergency Medical Alert Network. Mycobacterium Infections and Foot Spas. County of San Diego, Health & Human Services Agency; community Epidemiology Division. www.emansandiego.com
9. The Associated Press. Family sues salon over death after pedicure. May 2006. www.MSNBC.com.

Dr. Spalding comments:

Dr. Siegal is one of many physicians in the country who in their practices see nail infection problems stemming from poor disinfection protocols in the nail salon industry. Dr. Siegal responded in a novel way to the disinfection issue by developing a product line of personal nail instruments which must be properly disinfected by the consumer. Many nail patrons have been helped by her approach to the disinfection problem in nail salons.

Tina Marie Chieco, DPM
FOOTCARE ASSOCIATES
2320 Main Street
Bridgeport, CT 06473

Dear Bob,

It is with great anticipation, that I await your new book. Practicing as a podiatrist in Connecticut, my office deals with nail salon mishaps every day. Unlike some states, Connecticut has no regulations in place to protect the consumer. It is troublesome to know that getting your toenails done can put a person at risk for illness. Would you like a side of hepatitis or pseudomonas or herpes with that red nail color? If people don't believe this they are making a grave mistake. Maybe they should ask the woman who lost her leg from a nail salon bacterial infection!

In our state salons are on every corner. I strongly advise my patients to stay away or at least bring their own instruments or not use the whirlpool. I have to say they have been listening because now they send their friends in with infections. I'm getting a reputation as the doctor who yells about the perils of nail salons and I'm just fine with that. I have to admit it is distressing to know that some podiatrists do send patients to salons for routine care. I think our profession forgets the basics at times. My patients know they come not just for C&C but for my knowledge of the foot. Because no one knows the foot better than a podiatrist. Amen.

Bob, having gone through podiatry school with you it does not surprise me that you wrote this book. You have always been one step ahead of everyone and always in the right direction. I want your readers to know how well thought out and researched this book is. It is with great pleasure to have you as my colleague and the future of podiatry is certain with a doctor as yourself.

Your Esteemed Colleague,
Tina Marie Chieco, DPM

Dr. Spalding comments:
Dr. Tina Chieco and her husband, Dr. Bob Schwartz are graduates from my class of 1997 at the New York College of Podiatric Medicine. We were best friends in medical school and

spent long study hours together. They both practice in Connecticut where that state has failed to institute nail technician safety guidelines with reported precipitous results. I can safely reiterate Connecticut is an antithesis of Texas. Drs. Chieco and Schwartz are very conscientious podiatric practitioners. If these doctors say the citizens of Connecticut are suffering from poor disinfection practices and inappropriate medical treatments by nail techs, then the state legislature should step in quickly to create the now absent nail salon regulations.

Tracey C. Vlahovic, DPM
Temple University School of Podiatric Medicine
8th at Race Streets
Philadelphia, PA 19107

Dear Dr. Spalding,

I am so thrilled that you were brave and willing to bring this book to life. This book comprises my concerns with the nail industry. You have provided cautious, yet balanced information that will benefit physicians, nail technicians, and patients alike. I am so proud that you are a member of our profession.

As someone who treats patients who have developed mainly fungal nail infections from pedicures on a daily basis and teaches Dermatology to third year medical students, I have gotten on my soapbox about the dangers of pedicures with patients and students. Now there is finally a book filled with enough information for the consumer to make an educated decision and for future physicians to have a different way of educating their patients.

The main points we all need to take from this book are:

1. The nail industry desperately needs to have laws---but these laws need the manpower to be enforced.

2. Instruments need to be autoclaved and this needs to be clearly marked in the salon with sterile packaging with indicator strips.

3. Clients need to be aware of the risks of pedicures and be able to purchase their own equipment if they feel the need.

Overall, there needs to be a dialogue between physicians and the nail care industry. Measures, such as a client interview, need to be made, especially concerning patients who are at risk (Hepatitis B and C, HIV, Diabetes, PVD). The nail technician should be able to contact a local physician for any concerns with these clients or if any blood is shed.

Hopefully this book will be a wake up call to everyone involved in the nail care field. This book can serve as a dialogue between patient and physician, state board and nail technician, and most importantly, nail technician and client.

Sincerely,
Tracey C. Vlahovic, DPM

Dr. Spalding comments:

DR. Valhovic is one of the few medical school professors in the country who has taken the time to understand and study the crux of the ubiquitous nail salon disinfection dilemma. She has treated many nail salon infections in her practice and seen the ravages that can occur. DR Valhovic has also been outspoken about the changes necessary to protect the public from nail technicians who are not following prescribed protocols for proper sanitation. I sincerely appreciate her efforts to carry the torch and spread the word regarding this very important subject matter.

Dr. Dennis Arnold, Podiatrist
Founder of the International Pedicure Association

As a Podiatrist "working" on the feet over the last 25 years, I became more aware of and concerned about the practices of another group of professionals also "working" on the feet – the multitude of pedicurists. Having a pedicure has become very popular. Concurrent with this popularity, numerous safety issues have been reported, in terms of infections, contamination, etc. As a podiatrist, I felt I could help lend my years of experience to work together with the pedicure industry to help solve many of these concerns. I felt it was imperative that both the medical and pedicure professions work together.

Therefore, I formed an association named the International Pedicure Association (IPA) where the pedicurist can turn to for help with educational information and support. This was also developed as a resource center for the consumer to become more knowledgeable regarding salon and pedicure safety.

When a pedicurist joins our association, their name and salon location is listed in a directory on our Web site. In addition, they receive a certificate and decal to show the consumer that they are a member of an association that promotes safety. The pedicurist also has access to a member-only section with up-to-date educational materials, along with interaction with other members of IPA and podiatrists to share their knowledge.

A major goal of the International Pedicure Association is to link the medical and pedicure industry more closely together through a mutual referral network. By law, the pedicurist is not allowed to diagnosis or treat a health condition. However, the pedicurist can be better trained to recognize foot conditions that need referral to a medical professional such as a podiatrist. The podiatrist can in turn recommend a pedicurist that is a member of our association for a pedicure or maintenance of their feet.

Currently there are only a handful of states that require mandatory continuing education for the cosmetology industry. By being a part of the continuing education process whether state required or not, the International Pedicure Association is hoping to fulfill a need within the pedicure industry to elevate the standards for safer pedicures.

For more information regarding the International Pedicure Association please visit: www.pedicureassociation.org

Dennis Arnold, D. P. M.

Dr. Spalding comments:

Dr. Arnold is the first podiatrist to develop an association of well trained nail technicians and cosmetologists with extended professional training to protect the public and increase awareness in the nail profession. Every nail tech who has completed his course has been impressed with what they have learned. His website identifies the names and locations in the US of these exceptionally well trained nail techs.

Mr. Charlie Ton
Regal Nails Salon and Spa
11488 S. Choctaw Dr., Baton Rouge, LA
888-414-6245

Our company has been in the nail industry for over 10 years. Throughout the years, we have conducted extensive research into the business and proper sanitation practices, and educated our franchisees to understand the importance of their work as it relates to sanitation and safety. We stay up to date with all the latest guidelines dictated by the various State Boards and continually take measures to ensure consistency and compliance in our salons. In recognizing that sanitation is imperative, we have created many procedures that deal not only with day-to-day compliance issues but also with procedures focused on continuous prevention methods. We've always been and continue to be committed to sanitary conditions in our franchisees' salons.

We continually stress the significance of the following topics.

1. Using Consent Forms
2. Comprehending the Inspection Report
3. Emphasizing Sanitization Process
4. Emphasizing Sterilization of implements using Autoclave or Barbicide Plus
5. Emphasizing Spa Sanitization and Disinfectant Process
   a. Understanding the Components of Spa Pedicure Thrones
   b. Review the CNN and Local Channels videos about Spa Bacteria Outbreaks in California and Local Issues
6. Recommending the use Spa Cleaning Logs
7. Use of signs notifying the public that if they have autoimmune disorders, pedicures may be hazardous to their health.
8. Issuing of Material Safety Data Sheets [MSDS] for all products
9. Quarterly Newsletter
   a. Updates on State Board Reviews
   b. Reiteration of Sanitization Process
   c. Recommendation of Sanitation Products that are EPA approved and hospital grade, such as Pediclear, Sanitex Wipes, and Sanitex Spray
10. Regional Meetings
11. Emphasizing the prohibited the use of MMA
    a. Review the CNN video about MMA case in VA

The above mentioned items are an on-going part of our daily operations to avoid any negative incidents, to ensure consistent quality and above all, to protect our customers.

Before we turn over the space to our prospective franchisee, it is mandatory for the franchisee to attend a two day orientation and training session at the corporate offices in Baton Rouge. At this time, we inform the franchisee of our operations and recommend products pertaining to new guidelines decreed by the various states and emphasize the hygiene and disinfecting of utensils and equipment in their salon. After completing the course, the franchisee will receive a training certificate.

We employ full time inspectors whose duty is to travel to each salon to help regulate the guidelines set forth by Regal Nails, our Leaser, as well as the State Board. Our Regal Nails Inspectors are our eyes and ears in the field. They are an essential component in our system. They monitor, check, and regulate the salons according to our inspection checklist which includes items ranging from dusting to specific points such as wiring corrections. They check all pedicure thrones to make sure that they are up to date and that they are cleaned properly. They also monitor the performance of our high end exhaust systems installed in each salon to remove dust and fumes from the salon. They send their reports to us, we review every detail, and follow up to make certain that any problems are corrected immediately. If an item is not corrected, our inspectors impose fines on the franchisee that will continue to recur until the problem or situation is taken care of. If those fines are not paid, and if the situation is not corrected, we have the right to revoke the franchisee's lease.

To completely understand the pedicure spa sanitization process, we need to identify the function of the spa itself. There are two types of jets that are used by salons. The first type is the piped jet. In this system, the water runs from the basin, through pipes, to the pump, then through pipes back to the basin. In order to properly disinfect these piped spas, we require the technician to use an EPA approved cleaning solution to flush the entire system between every customer. We also require the franchisees to remove and clean the suction cover daily, and to use a Spa Cleaner solution to sanitize the spas weekly. Alfalfa Nail Supply and T4 Spa Engineering & Design are no longer manufacturing the traditional piped jet systems. Regal Nails has not provided piped spas to any new or remodeled salons since June of 2005. All of the spas that we recommend are now pipe-less. This system has no pipes to clean. The water is sucked in and pushed out of the jet, and travels through no pipes, resulting in no standing water. There is less maintenance with a pipe-less jet. The technicians are required to remove the jet cover and to clean it and the pedicure basin with an EPA approved cleaner between each customer. Each night they are required to sterilize the system with Pediclear and must allow the spa to soak overnight. We designed our spas for ease of cleaning and safety for the customers. We install a dual check valve on each spa. This valve is used to stop any bacteria from entering the water system, thereby, eliminating contamination of the next spa. We require the final step of any pedicure to be cleaning the spa, so the spa is always prepared and readily available for the next customer.

Franchisees are required to have only licensed technicians in the salon; therefore, all technicians have been trained by their states to sanitize all products. We, still reemphasize the entire process at our orientations, meetings and in each printing of our newsletter. Sanitation and safety for the customer is the foundation of our business. For that reason, we continually stress the importance of this. Our recommendations on spa cleaning are as follows:

PEDICURE SPA SANITIZATION

Please follow these instructions for cleaning your pedicure spas. It is very important that you sanitize your pedicure spa prior to use by each customer to prevent the spread of bacterial infections.

For Each Customer for Traditional Piped System
a. A regular pedicure is usually achieved during the first 20-30 minutes.
b. While the technician is polishing and/or massaging for the next 10 minutes, use this time to disinfect the spa and tools.
Disinfecting the spa
    1. Drain dirty water. Fill tub with fresh water.
    2. Place all pedicure tools that need to be sterilized in the spa.
    3. Add 1 level scoop (2 grams) of Pedi-Clear Disinfectant crystals to spa. Turn on jets, and circulate for 10 minutes. Pedi-Clear is EPA approved and kills 99.999% of bacteria and viruses.
c. Drain all water, wipe surface with disinfecting wipes (We recommend Sanitex wipes, from Crosstex)
d. Place all pedicure tools in Autoclave

e. For next customer, Continue back to step a

For Each Customer for Pipe-less Jet System
a. Drain dirty water, and rinse the tub with shower head
b. Remove suction screen. Spray with Crosstex Sani-Spray on both impeller and suction screen.
c. Wipe all surfaces with Crosstex Sani-Wipes
d. For next customer, continue back to step a

B. Disinfect Each Night (all systems)
a. Remove the screen and clean all debris trapped behind the screen for each spa.
b. Fill the tub and add 1 level scoop (2 grams) of Pedi-Clear Disinfectant Crystals. Circulate for 15 minutes, and let it soak overnight.
c. The next morning, drain water and wipe surface with disinfectant wipes. The spa will now be ready for the first customer.

C. Sanitize Weekly for Traditional Piped Systems
a. Use Lexi Spa Cleaner to sanitize the entire system, including pipes, jets, and pumps. Spa Cleaner removes soap scum, mold & mildew.
b. Fill tub with warm water. Add 4 tsp of Lexi Spa Cleaner.
c. Circulate for 15 minutes. Drain. Rinse spa with clean water.

ADDITIONAL SANITIZATION PROCESS

Nail Stations - Clean with disinfectant wipes after each customer.

Wet Sanitation for Non-electrical equipment – Wash all utensils with soap and water, dry them with clean towels, then soak them in Hospital Grade Barbicide Plus (wet disinfectant) for at least 15 minutes then rinse with clean water. After rinsing and drying with a clean towel, utensils are then placed in UV Sterilizer.

Use of Autoclave: All utensils are washed with water and soap, dry them with clean towels. Insert them in Crosstex Pouches and seal. Set correct timer and temperature recommended from the manual. After sterilization process, arrow on pouches will turn to dark brown from red color.

Electrical equipment – Unplug. Clean and wipe with a disinfectant, specifically made for electrical equipment. Pat dry

Utensils - All tools, instruments, or supplies that come into direct contact with a client and cannot be disinfected must be disposed of in a waste receptacle immediately after use.

Linens - Disinfect all linens by using detergent and bleach

Liquids - Pour a small amount of liquid to a container for each service. Dispose of the leftover liquid in an empty container and follow correct disposal procedure.

Personal Cleanliness - Thoroughly wash hands and the exposed portions of arms with anti-bacterial soap before providing services to each client and after smoking, drinking, eating, and using the restroom.

Prohibited tools and instruments - Razor edged tools designed to remove calluses (such as Credo tool) are prohibited. Nippers are to be used only for removal of loose cuticles.

We also supply each salon with Material Safety Data Sheets (MSDS). This gives the ingredients of every product that we provide and is required to be present in all salons at all times. To guard our franchises even more, we send out newsletters quarterly which include important information about the sanitation process, development of our company, and new rules and regulations regarding our company, the Leaser, and the State.

Everyday is a new learning experience for us and our franchisees. Therefore from time to time, we feel if a franchisee needs additional training, we arrange for them to re-attend our Orientation course. We also have random regional meetings in different areas at least once a year to ensure continuing education and proper implementation of new guidelines.

We are constantly trying to learn about new ideas and concepts that will help us to not only maintain, but also to improve our operation. With the help of our Regal Nails inspectors we are assured that our franchisees are adhering to our standards. Our mission is to adapt to all changes, educate our franchisees, and always improve upon our existing operation. We strive to be the industry leader for excellent sanitary conditions for nail salons.

Charlie Ton, President and CEO

Dr. Spalding comments:

I found Charlie Ton to be very accessible for a busy CEO. I had a very interesting conversation with Mr. Ton who has a background in chemical engineering and understands the chemical disinfection requirements of the nail salon industry as well as artificial nail MMA versus EMA issues. His sister, Belle Ton, who is an RN, is in charge of overseeing salon operations, producing their quarterly nail salon safety newsletter and additionally promotes all Regal Nail's disinfection standards. Staci, his marketing manager, also strives for increasing public safety in the Regal salons. Regal Nails have their own internal corporate inspectors and any substandard disinfection issue or public safety issue can ultimately result in a revocation of a franchise. To date, only two franchises have been revoked. Regal Nails is also taking the lead in the industry by requiring autoclave sterilizers in new franchises even in states that do not yet require sterilizers. Mr Ton's new T4 Spa whirlpool designs have pipe less impeller systems that are a great improvement over former whirlpool designs. I am convinced that Mr. Ton and his staff are setting precedent to attempt to operate the largest network of franchised safe salons in America's Wal Marts. He also encourages the public to report any infractions as soon as possible.

Doug Schoon
VP of science and Technology, Creative Nail Design Inc.
Top Ten Reasons Why It's Not a Good Idea to "Bring Your Own Implements"

Recently some companies have begun capitalizing on media reports of salon skin and nail infections. They are selling kits containing supposed "salon quality" implements/tools, files etc. and these companies are telling customers that it is safer and smarter to take their own implements to the salon. These kits are sold using fearsome pictures that suggest developing a serious infection is likely, unless they buy a kit now. That's pure nonsense!

Considering the many millions and millions of manicures and pedicures performed each year, the relative number of infections is actually quite low. Of course no one wants to be the next case, no matter how remote the possibility, but these kits won't really prevent infections and can actually make matters worse. Here's why:

1.   These kits contain cheap low-quality "budget" implements that tend to break, rust or quickly become dull.

2.   These kits can't compare in safety to properly cleaned, disinfected and stored "professional quality" implements and tools.

3.   These kits contain tools that are unfamiliar to the nail professional and may be more difficult for the tech to use due to low quality design.

4.   The nail tech's use of familiar tools, rather than the unfamiliar tools brought in by a client, results in much less likelihood of accidental cuts, damage or other similar injury.

5.   These kits often contain sharp metal pushers, which are more likely to cause cuts, injury and infection.

6.   Professional tools perform in a much safer fashion and do a better job overall.

7.   These kits contain poorly made, ineffective abrasives and buffers that create far more work for the nail professional and can

increase the risk of the nail tech developing cumulative trauma disorder.

8.   These kits contain incorrect and improper information/instructions regarding proper cleaning and disinfection.

9.   Kit instructions incorrectly suggest that proper cleaning and disinfecting isn't needed between services.

10. Customers often use these kits on family members and pets without proper cleaning and disinfection, making them much more likely to cause infections.

11. Existing regulations requiring proper cleaning, disinfection and storage are more than enough to protect the consumer.

Don't be fooled by fear-based marketing tactics. Save your money! Here's the best way to prevent nail infections. It's simple! Make sure that your nail professional follows the rules and regulations required by for your state or local regulatory authority.

BUT, you won't find someone like that if you're looking for the cheapest services in town. Go looking for cheap and you'll get it. As consumers you must accept responsibility for paying attention to the sanitation practices of the salons you visit. Be smart, choose salons that play by the rules and do things right, especially when it comes to properly cleaning and disinfecting. Don't look for "factory nails", but instead a nail professional trained and skilled in the latest and best practices of the industry. Also, look for salons that care about taking the time to ensure your health and safety.

But, most important of all- find out who the responsible government agency is for ensuring that salons follow the rules and regulations- then hold that agency accountable! It's their job and they should be doing it, but unfortunately too many have become lax and are not properly enforcing the very regulations they are paid to uphold. This is one of the biggest problems, in my opinion!

For example, in the USA most State Boards or their equivalent do not have enough inspectors to ensure that salons are practicing proper cleaning and disinfection. In California and Texas most salons are visited once every four or five years. That's ridiculous! Is this what taxpaying consumers expect? Too many state governments are siphoning away money collected from professional fees and licenses and use it for other unrelated purposes. Instead, they should be doing the responsible thing and using more of this money to ensure consumer safety in salons. Consumers should be asking where the money is going and why there aren't enough inspectors to uphold the law and protect the consumer.

Some states have addressed these issues by writing more stringent, costly and difficult to follow regulations that don't address the real problems.

Here is what these states should actually do:

1.   Hire enough inspectors to properly inspect all salons on a yearly basis and closely monitor every salon that is not in compliance with existing rules and regulations.

2.   Enforce existing cleaning and disinfection standards already adopted by most states. These regulations are based on hospital standards of cleanliness. These practices are far more than enough to protect salon clients when properly and consistently performed.

3.   Properly train inspectors so they understand what to look for and what to do about it. A frighteningly large number of inspectors are improperly trained and do not have a sufficient understanding of salon practices or products.

4.   Always make rules and regulations based on scientific fact and expert opinion, not fear, paranoia or special interests.

Hospitals regularly use proper cleaning and disinfection to control disease and prevent the spread of infection. When properly performed, "cleaning and disinfection" is more than enough to protect clients and ensure their well-being.

In short, the best advice I could give the consumer is to not patronize a salon or nail professional that can't convince you their services are always performed in a sanitary fashion and that they religiously practice proper cleaning and disinfection. That's the only way you can be sure you're protected.

Doug Schoon

Dr. Spalding Comments:
Doug Schoon has been an asset to this book and to the nail industry in general. Doug and I don't agree on every issue regarding personal nail kits and sterilization, but we have immediately found common ground that we feel will get this

industry back on track. I look forward to everything Doug contributes to the world of nail technicians and nail salons.

Diana Bonn - Indiana
Nail Technician
State Board Member - Indiana State Board of Cosmetologists

The razor type callous cutter has been banned in almost 25 states as of this time. Indiana is working on the new rule as I write.

For the past five years I have been warning Indiana nail techs that these razor-type instruments are dangerous. One wrong move and the razor blade could send the client to the hospital with a serious wound with an open portal for infection. There is no reason to cut hard, dry skin off of a foot. Proper exfoliants and pumice stones will work for the client, along with home maintenance.

Nail technicians are not taught in school how to use this razor blade or any harmful, dangerous implement. In my personal opinion, only licensed medical personnel should be allowed to use this type of tool. Just because a nail technician is licensed does not mean that he or she was trained to use a medical instrument.

Also, the consumer has to be aware of blood-borne pathogens. When a nail technician cuts a client with a razor, did the technician clean the pedicure chair and implements following strict OSHA guidelines to remove/clean the blood spill? Probably not.

I will continue to warn the consumer and the technician of this very dangerous instrument. But it is up to consumers to protect themselves.

Diana Bonn

Dr. Spalding comments:
Diana has been a champion of nail salon safety. Her continuous efforts protect the general public and she continues to fight to improve the nail salon industry. Her efforts to ban MMA's and Credo blades are legendary. I first met Diana in 2000 in Orlando and was immediately impressed with the dedication to her profession. She is an active state board member who truly is an advocate for the consumer of nail salon services.

Athena Elliott, Salon Consultant
www.yournailtech.com
Houston Texas

Dear Bob,

A few weeks ago, a new client to the salon hands over her personal nail goody bag. She wanted me to use her tools, because she felt safe from infection. It had everything I needed to do a pedicure on her. A pair of nippers with dried (cuticle) tissue still stuck to them. A metal pusher with more dried tissue. A foot paddle with callus dust embedded in the grit and a Credo blade. What more could I need?

I pointed out that her implements were dirty and could be breeding bacteria. Professionally I explained why there was need to sanitize and disinfect her implements before we started. She said, "At least it's my germs." By the time I was finished with my graphic descriptions she allowed me to use my sterilized nipper and pusher. I think I really scared her.

I started to think about my early days as a tech. I want your readers to understand that the horrible stories we hear about infection in the nail salon didn't happen over night. In fact, it has been an involving process.

In the early '80's being a good nail tech meant little more than applying a pretty set of fake nails that lasted 2 weeks or nail polish that could last at least 3 days.

I have to say I loved this time because the salon atmosphere was so relaxed that I often ate and smoked at my station while working on clients.

Using the same nail file on everyone was just as commonplace as using a Credo blade on calluses. It was also common to remove so much skin that clients would not be able to walk for a week. Many got infections because the blades became rusty being used over and over again.

By the early 90's, the steady increase of immigrants began to change the face of the dominantly Caucasian owned, salon industry. New salons started to appear on every corner and a price war began that still goes on today.

With less use of the illegal product MMA and increased use of electric files new problems began to appear.

New Clients would come in with drill damage resulting in bright red "rings of fire" shining thru the acrylic. I have been told many times that the painful experience caused them to seek out another tech.

Electric file manufactures saw a need for a national standard. They began to offer courses on the safe use of an electric file.

Improper application technique of acrylics meant your nails would "pop" up and moisture would breed underneath the acrylic resulting in bacterial infections with various shades of green.

The average day in a salon would include skin being sliced, holes being drilled into the nail beds and bacterial infections being spread from nail to nail. Most techs just didn't receive education from their products manufacturer.

I became annoyed with the industry. I wanted to do something different, so I went to school to train as an EMT.

While receiving intense training on infection control, I began to realize just how much the nail industry was lacking in this area. A short time later I decided to return to doing nails with a new attitude, and a new direction I would take my career.

1996: I was offered a position with a start up salon that pioneered autoclaving in the nail industry. My responsibilities as a nail technician were starting to take on a whole new approach. My next endeavor was to forge an alliance with a podiatrist. Through www.beautytech.com I met a Podiatrist named Dr. Robert Spalding. While I was impressed with the fact that he wasn't afraid of nail techs, Dr. Spalding realized that many of us were more educated for assisting in his practice than the people he hired and trained.

Getting as much continued education and receiving certification on everything I could get my hands on became the most important thing I could do to set myself apart.

Educating my customers on a "superior sanitation protocol" and keeping them up to date on my continuing education equated to the clients increased value of service. Not only would this more clearly help the client define to what they should be looking for in their nail tech/salon. It would prove to be the driving force in my success.

Changing mentality 2000: Several industry awards later and a new focus on teaching others the need for education I took a management position in 2000 at one of the largest day spas in town.

Mission: To write a progressive sanitation protocol that included autoclaving to 22 nail techs that were still doing "Madge manicures". Little did I know just how hard this would be.

The introduction of hand sanitizers, single use files, and fresh towels for every client was a concept that I thought would be easy to accept. Convincing these seasoned techs that there was need for thorough disinfecting of the spa pedicure chairs was like teaching a foreign language! Not even the Watsonville outbreak http://www.almadentimes.com/082505/pedicure.htm seemed to convince them.

Day spa mimics sterilization: The staff was instructed to wash their nippers and pushers then seal them in bags followed by inserting them in the autoclave for a specified length of time.

One day I observed a nail tech stuffing over 100 autoclave bags into the unit so the arrows would indicate the sterile process had been completed. Later she took dirty implements and stuck them into a bag that had been sterilized. This should have been grounds for termination, but I was told a 30-year employee should be given a second chance.

Where I live discount salons rank highest on the offender list simply because they are the majority. But I had to take a step back and realize that discount salons were not the sole offenders when it came to lack of education on sanitation in the salon.

2002: Several industry articles later and an industry recognition by trade magazine NailPro, top 50 Most Influential Nail Tech in Professional Nail Industry allowed me to begin a new avenue in salon consulting.

The evolution of nails salons have gone from safe to dangerously deadly. It has taken serious infections like MRSA , Watsonville outbreak and the death of Kimberly Jackson to make changes in our laws.

No matter how dangerously cheap or expensive services become, there will always be people who will fall into both categories.

With Texas leading the US in sterilization I am confidant the future of the salon industry will make a safe and positive impact forward for all salons.

> Athena Elliott, Houston Texas
> 2000 "Top 50 Most Influential Nail Tech NailPro
> Cover Artist - NAILS magazine, NailPro
> 1998 "Nail Tech of The year" NAILS magazine

Dr. Spalding Comments:

Athena Elliott was the first nail tech I ever corresponded with online. Her product knowledge and technique is impressive. Athena immediately introduced me to Karol Singleton and Beautytech.com. I am indebted to Athena for her help with my first article for *Podiatry Today* and her assistance with providing additional information with this book. Athena is a very conscientious nail tech who has seen the full spectrum of this industry. Any client lucky enough to experience her salon services in Houston, Texas will be in excellent hands. She is engaging, helpful, a very talented technician, and an incredible example of a top flight salon professional.

Debbie Doerrlamm

Roll back in time to 1994. I was just moving up from part-time nail technician to full time, and like most, I had questions. The problem was who to ask. The logical answer was my instructor, but she took ill after my 36-hour class 3 years earlier. The next option was the local supply house, but we all know how that goes—the nail stuff is over there in the corner. Now, grasping at straws, I reached out to the online community on America Online. What started out as a quest for information, grew to be the largest and now longest established portal Web site for beauty professionals, www.beautytech.com

Online forums as a continuing education resource are as close as your mouse. In 2006, BeautyTech continues to give the professional a place to hang out, complain, brag, and ask the obvious and not so obvious questions to a wide array of their peers; the seasoned technician, the educator, the student, as well as the manufacturers. Help arrives in your IN box almost immediately or on your Web browser from all different age brackets, geographical locations, and expertise levels. Along with the networking, you can find class and show calendars, articles galore, a mentoring program, quizzes to help students, and over 1,800 links to professional beauty Web sites.

I could go on and on about why every beauty professional should get involved in networking, but I will let Alice Wallace, Edison, NJ, a 12-year tech, 10-year networking veteran, share her thoughts.

"The networking here gives us the courage to try new things, or gather up that little bit of information we may be missing. We can get feedback, or just make sure that we aren't the only ones that are getting it or NOT getting it. I have learned, with my participation here at the beautytech.com message boards and mailing lists, how I wish to be perceived as a professional; by my peers, my clients and for my own well-being. Not a day goes by when I'm working that I don't think to myself, How would so-and-so handle this. I bring all of you to work with me, and with that I bring professionalism, ethics, and integrity. Stick around and read carefully, you will get an education like no other, and it's free. Never be afraid to ask a question."

It is not just nail technicians who benefit in a networking forum; owners get a better perspective of their workers, clients get better service from educated technicians, the trade magazines gain insight and article ideas, manufacturers receive instant firsthand feedback about their new products. Two side-bonuses are the friendships that blossom between techs the world over and the increase in income from the newfound knowledge. Over 50% of the participants of the BeautyTech forums say they have had a Measurable Increase in their income since they started networking.

Debbie Doerrlamm

Dr. Spalding comments:
Debbie saw a definite need for nail techs to exchange information and immediately acted on this void by creating

Beautytech.com. Debbie is a no-nonsense nail tech who can multi-task better than any other person I know. I met Debbie online and at the Premier Beauty show in Orlando. Her website service has been an excellent springboard for many nail techs pursuing continuing education information and for answering questions about the nail salon industry.

Karol Singleton

Early into my nail career I realized that there was more to doing nails than working in a salon. Education comes first and networking and learning from others a close second.

I saw the need for nail techs to gather and share information, and the world of cyberspace was just starting to put us in a position of gathering from all over the world.

I founded and instituted the most successful nail tech networking event in the world, called Nailtechs Networking the Internet. We met in Orlando Florida during the Premiere Show Each August. Nail techs from China, Japan, USA, Australia, England, Canada, Middle East, Germany attended as well as the who's who in the world of nails.

Manufacturers as well as distributors graciously donated gifts of nail products, and many of the major manufacturers used the Nailtech Networking Event in Orlando to introduce new product lines, getting them into the hands of the technicians.

I also was able to network with local podiatrist Dr. Robert Levine, successfully and we often referred patients /clients to each other over a period of 11 years, until he sold his practice. Often Dr. Levine was a guest speaker when I needed him to talk to nail techs in our local area. We encouraged doctors as well as nail techs to network.

I actively sought help outside of my area, and that is how I met Dr. Robert Spalding, through the Internet we often networked and came to possible suggestions for clients.

Dr. Spalding often was guest speaker at my Nailtech Networking events, attended by over 200 nail techs throughout the world. He gave informative slide shows on diseases, causes, and possible cures, when to seek medical help, and what the nail techs responsibilities are to the world of nail care.

Dr. Spalding, Dr. Levine and I were often found in magazine articles, networking gatherings, offering advice and structuring events to help the nail techs and their clients. In becoming comfortable with their expertise and working within this circle, I became a better nail tech and mentor for other nail techs and our clients.

Karol Singleton

Dr. Spalding Comments:

Karol Singleton has been a leader in the nail salon profession for many years. A seasoned nail technician herself, she organized one of the best attended annual nail technician conferences in many years. There were nail techs from the Middle East, Europe, Australia and almost every state in the US. She provided this service with the good will and passion to benefit this industry. She is a good resource for any nail tech coming into this business.

Betty Davis

I began my career in beauty industry in 2002. Upon entering beauty industry I had no idea what I would embark upon. My approach is somewhat different from that of other educators. Consumer's safety and protection is my first concern, beauty follows after. In the beauty industry workers place beauty first and sanitation falls somewhere after.

I have spent countless hours researching gathering and organizing information in which I can share with other beauty industry professionals in order to raise beauty industry standards. I have spoken out before our State officials regarding consumer protection. It has made a difference. Our State has now mandated (CE hours) .Along with banning the use of MMA. (a substance that was deemed poisonous and deleterious to consumers as well as nail tech performing services. This information was released by the FDA back in 1974. However, has taken over 30 years to enforce this much-needed rule.

Our industry is lacking in so many ways not until recently has Legislature, Senators, Physicians, consumers and others have began to take notice of the large number of consumers which are being affected by the industries lack of knowledge in regards to consumer protection.

I have gone undercover into salons/spas and watched how they knowingly or unknowingly break rule after rule—with no regard for the consumer.

I believe some professionals are truly not aware of hazards and dangers associated in our industry. It is also their responsibility to seek out updated information: not to be afraid of change, but to welcome it.

It's really a sad situation when you can walk up to anyone in the beauty industry and ask a simple question like "How do you disinfect your tools?" Most will respond with "I sanitize." Majority do not know the difference between sanitation, disinfection, & sterilization. Would you want someone working on you not knowing how to properly disinfect tools which are used on client after client? (Something to think about)

There are very few Cosmetologist, nail technicians, Barbers which are aware of proper sanitation /sterilization procedures. Yet we have over 200,000 licensees in the State of Texas alone. I have been Lecturer for over 2 years now and the numbers are astonishing. The number of beauty industry professionals which lack the knowledge of proper sanitation/disinfection/sterilization practices. Yet, they are allowed to work on consumers every day, client after client without ever disinfected implements or tools effectively. This is an outrage! I have been approached by so many consumers regarding their bad experience with salons/spas. Some have developed nail fungus, bacteria infections, plantar warts etc. Consumers are not aware of their potential dangers when visiting salons/spas. However, they are becoming more aware from advocates and media attention on our industry.

This is very common in our industry. Just look around. You ask 2-3 people have they ever had a bad experience with nail fungus or bacteria infection. 1 out of 3 will say yes or know someone who has. This is very serious!

I have spent time researching, developing relationships with physicians who are willing to offer their professional opinions in order to help raise the bar in our industry. I have spoken with over

12 physicians and all can agree on one thing – there is a real need for concern for consumer protection.

Consumers are not aware of the risk they are facing upon entering salons/spas. They are thinking they're protected, that their nail tech has their best interest in mind. Consumers assume that implements and tools are properly cared for. They assume that the State has control over sanitation issues and they are being protected. Reality is actually the opposite. Consumers are not protected. They are at risk every time they have nail services or pedicure services performed.

Let me give some examples: When sitting at a manicure table, how often do you see a dust-free table. (rarely ever) Look at acrylic brushes, containers which are filled with contaminated products. Porous finger nail files, which I believe to be a primary source in spreading infections. Porous files can not be disinfected/sterilized properly .Porous fingernail files should be used on one client only! Then disposed of or given to that client. If you are having a service performed and a nail tech pulls out a porous nail file, buffing block with visible white scratches from previous clients (think about this): How many clients has this tool been used on?

I have also lectured in different beauty schools. This is where it all starts. Schools are not properly educating students concerning health and sanitation issues. This should be priority, yet it is the most overlooked subject! Somehow at the beginning students are taught to focus on beauty and not proper sanitation/disinfection practices in order to protect the consumer's health while performing services. These two things go hand in hand.

My mission and goal is to help transfer important information to beauty industry professionals in order that they may gain the necessary knowledge to help protect their clients as well as themselves against infections.

A client's best resource is a well educated professional. The difference between a nail tech and a nail professional is Education. I have found that nail tech don't really care about safety, health only the bottom dollar. However, a Nail Professional makes investments in their education, implements and tools, quality products and respects educators and physicians which are contributing to helping increase consumer awareness in our industry. This is only the beginning of many much needed changes in our industry. Many businesses will fall to the wayside to lack of concern for consumers. Others will thrive because they have chosen to embrace education and change in our industry. For beauty industry professionals there are a lot of much needed changes being made in our industry make sure you make the right decisions. I am one with other professionals which are speaking up and out concerning health, safety of our consumers. So don't get caught on the wrong end .Raise your standards! Focus on how can I better educate myself? How can I better protect my clients? Do you know the difference in sanitation/disinfection/sterilization? Do you know when to refer clients out to physicians? When in doubt refer out. Can you recognize infections, nail abuse, bacteria infections, warts etc… Have you ever had clients come to you with damaged nails? If so , did you do a cover up or where you able to educate client on how to better protect their themselves against this type of nail abuse.

This is the only industry I know where licensed nail techs can nip, cut, scrap, rip off consumer's skin and not be penalized. Although, Credo blade has been banned years ago, this rule has not been followed many salons use this dangerous blade freely. We are not physicians we cannot and should not cut clients skin (including cuticles). Until about 2 years ago the Milady's book which is taught in schools encouraged the cutting of cuticles. Now the update version discourages cuticle cutting. Interesting… most of the same people wrote both books.

I do not apologize for my bluntness regarding our industry. My thoughts are not contaminated by industry products and years of doing the wrong thing. I speak from my heart. I share what others need to know from a consumer as well professional point of view. Let's began to focus more on client protection. Think beyond the box.

Embrace changes, build relationships with local physicians, educate consumers, make an investment in your business. Then step back and watch things happen!

This is the one thing consumers and professionals appreciate about me. I stand for what I believe to be right!

Dr. Spalding, my passion is to bring awareness and assist in making much needed changes in our industry. I believe one person can make a big difference so imagine if we have thousands.

This is why I am writing this insert for your book. Hopefully, this information in some way will help you. It is time consumers know that their incidents with salons/spas are not isolated. There are many others who have suffered at the hands of beauty industry workers.

Betty Davis

Dr. Spalding comments:

Betty Davis is the most proactive nail tech and passionate nail tech I have met in this business period. In 2006, with the help of a TV station, she independently launched her own undercover investigation in Beaumont, Texas. At her own personal health risk, she covertly videotaped and notified Texas state investigators to stop illegal activity in 8 nails salons resulting in tens of thousands of dollars in fines collectively. She has been personally been thanked by the Governor of Texas for her work. She has a new DVD video for sale of the actual footage called NAIL SALONS EXPOSED. I personally recommend this video for anyone who wants to see this TV station footage on the nail salon industry as a real problem nationwide. This video vindicates everything in this book and exposes all the "false prophets" of this industry who say this problem is "overblown". She also has suggested a web cast station devoted to this issue.

Chapter 27
What to look out for in a nail salon

Reprinted with permission from the NMC

When you see any of the following, leave the salon and find another place for service:

- If you see a nail tech shave the arms or legs of any client in the salon
- A salon that does not look clean in general, with hair, nail clippings, dust or debris on the floor, in drawers, on tables or furniture
- A salon that uses dusty or dirty nail files and other tools
- Products in unlabeled or unmarked containers
- Nail files and other tools stored in a dirty drawer or container
- Nail files or other tools stored in dirty or contaminated-looking solutions
- No lid or cover on disinfection containers
- Dirty or unkempt restrooms that lack liquid soap and clean towels

- Nail technicians using razors on your feet to remove a callus
- Nail technicians providing services to clients who have infected fingers, nails, toenails, or feet

Be wary of any nail technician or salon who:

- Fails to ask you if you have shaved your legs 24 hours prior to getting pedicure services or whirlpool soaking services
- Does not wash your hands or feet before performing any nail or pedicure service
- Does not wash their own hands before performing a nail or pedicure service
- Provides services that are painful or that damage your skin or nails
- Cannot demonstrate how they clean and disinfect their nail files, clippers, bits, and tools
- Cannot demonstrate how they clean and disinfect foot spas
- Does not have a logbook indicating when pedicure foot spas were cleaned and disinfected
- Uses something to "pry off" artificial nails
- Does not provide each client with a clean, disinfected nailbrush for scrubbing underneath nails
- Does not use a clean, freshly laundered or disposable towel
- Will not show you a current license when you ask to see it
- Says they are too busy to properly clean and disinfect their tools
- Sticks their fingers directly into jars or containers
- Does not ask questions about your health (conduct a client consultation) before performing services

Chapter 28

Five questions that the consumer should have to answer

Are you a diabetic?

People who have diabetes are three times more likely to have fungal nails and athlete's foot fungal infections between their toes. Disease-related damage to nerves, referred to as neuropathy, may result in numbness. Clients with diabetes-related poor eyesight are unable to see their feet clearly. Those with nerve damage may have injuries they cannot feel or see, especially on their feet. Such clients, who cannot feel pain, won't be able to signal discomfort during a pedicure.

Were a nail tech to accidentally nick or begin to nick the toe of a healthy client, that person would likely say "Ouch!" A diabetic client with neuropathy will not feel the nick – the nerve pathways that normally take the danger signal to the brain no longer work. Unless visible blood is drawn, neither the client nor the nail tech may notice the injury, and infection-prevention measures won't cross anyone's mind. Accidental injuries from nail services can result in major medical events for diabetics, including hospitalizations and amputations. (See picture on page 149.)

Nail techs who take on diabetic clients must treat them gently and be attentive to what is going on with their feet. Diabetic conditions develop, and symptoms progress over time: clients may not know that they cannot feel. The technician should explore this with them and assist them to become clear about what's going on with their feet. Referral to a medical professional may be appropriate.

Do you have poor circulation?

Poor circulation can create swelling and cold extremities. Skin stretched thin and tight by swollen tissue is more susceptible to injury. Nail techs should avoid vigorous massage, and pay attention when filing nails and providing other services so as to not disturb this vulnerable skin.

Swelling can result from arterial or venous medical conditions, or from lymph system problems. Poor venous circulation can cause swelling of the legs, a common side effect of heart bypass surgery, dialysis, stasis ulcers, high blood pressure, or diabetes. Knee replacements can also interrupt the flow of lymph, resulting in swelling. A person with poor arterial blood flow is more prone to ulcer formation and lesions between toes or on the bottom of the feet. A nail salon professional can be the first to see these abnormal changes in normal tissue, and the first to make a referral to a medical professional.

People with poor circulation need to be self-protective, to ask those doing body work or nail salon services to be attentive to their condition.

Do you have any loss of sensation, burning, tingling, numbness, or neuropathy?

Data that comes into our brains via the sense of touch, the ability to feel, is used, among other things, to protect our bodies from injury. People who have lost this input can be oblivious to pain. They may be unable to feel injury to their body when it happens, and may not notice wounds, ulcers, or infections, particularly on their feet.

Certain drug therapy for immune problems, cancer therapy, dialysis, chronic alcohol use, diabetes, back injuries, and nerve damage can cause neuropathy. Clients may also experience burning or tingling, precursors to numbness or neuropathy. Nail techs must identify this problem and focus intently on their work to avoid injury via massage, electric filing, or nail instrumentation.

Injuries – both those noticed by the salon professional upon first examination of the client, and those injuries, like nicks, generated by the nail tech – must be followed up properly, preferably with a referral to a medical professional.

A client with loss of sensation who is protectively attentive to his or her compromised body, will need to assess the value of nail salon services and the experience level and quality of their nail tech's work before booking nail salon services.

Do you have any kind of dermatitis or skin problem?
Have you shaved your skin recently?

People with medical skin problems like psoriasis, eczema, seborrhea, chronic athlete's foot, fungal infection between the toes, nail fungus, skin inflammation, or contact allergies to chemicals, nail polish, lotions, or artificial nails – none with these conditions should have manicure/pedicure services without a physician's approval.

Minor skin irritations can become a portal for serious bacterial infections and can be made worse by vigorous massage or trimming of affected skin surfaces.

People who have shaved their legs or arms within twenty-four hours of a pedicure appointment need to avoid both foot soaks and whirlpool services.

Do you have a blood-borne virus?

Blood-borne viruses include herpes or herpetic whitlow (viral blisters around the fingers or nails), HIV, and hepatitis B or C. This also includes viral plantar warts spread by direct contact or contaminated instruments.

Identification of these conditions would help avoid potential re-infection or injury with certain instruments. The tech could also avoid techniques or vigorous massage more likely to break or injure skin surfaces.

Many HIV and hepatitis clients take great care not to become stigmatized or ostracized because of their medical problem, and may not reveal their disorders. Asking the above question documents that you made the effort to avoid aggravating a potential problem. It's also increasingly the case that many people who have a blood-borne viral infection are completely unaware of it.

Clients with these conditions will be well served to know how their chosen service is properly done, to choose an experienced nail tech, and to make certain the salon of their choice autoclaves their instruments. Another option is to bring ones own instruments – nail nippers, files, and the like. Self-protection is always in style.

Chapter 29

Referrals to medical professionals
and medical referral forms

"Doctors have patients; nail techs have clients."
Dr. Robert Spalding

Nail techs are in an extraordinary position. They are not medical professionals, yet deal with medical issues on a daily basis.

They are not licensed to diagnose, prescribe, or treat, yet they see *bona fide* medical conditions – nail fungus, infections, neuropathies – and, unintentionally, create some of their own – draw blood, transmit infection – and, all day long, they deal with sanitization, disinfection, and sterilization.

A nail tech can, in one hour, go from having fun with a regular client by decorating her nails with rhinestones, to dealing with a new client who has a nail fungus condition remindful of "Digger® the Dermatophyte" ads – which requires the tech to do triage: Do I work with this lady? – or do I refer her to a medical doctor?

In yet another setting, a nail tech may be the first to recognize a potential or full-blown medical problem. For example, neuropathies rarely happen overnight. They develop over time. A nail tech may be the first to see a sore or infection on the bottom of a client's foot. How often do people, especially older, disabled, overweight, or simply unlimber people, see the bottoms of their feet? Add to this a condition where the nerves no longer send pain signals to the brain – people may literally not know they have injuries, sores, or infections on the bottoms of their feet. Here, nail techs find themselves on the front lines once again, referring to medical professionals for proper treatment.

The Tennessee Board of Cosmetology and other state boards requires nail technicians to get written permission from physicians before performing services for clients with skin/nail disease. However these licensing agencies do not provide forms for these referrals. Physicians may be very reluctant to provide this permission without first developing a relationship with a professional nail technician at an approved and qualified salon.

It's a huge responsibility to make decisions regarding client care. The articles and resources throughout this book document that there is more than meets the eye going on in nail salons. Who knew? The Tech-to-Doc and Doc-to-Tech referral forms may assist.

Dr. Spalding Speaks to Nail Techs about Referrals

Doctors will be impressed with your intention to protect your clients. And even though you cannot diagnose, you can identify symptoms on the referral form. This is genuinely helpful to physicians. It demonstrates conscientiousness, ethical decision-making, and a caring attitude towards clients. Providing a paper trail that documents that you did the right thing will protect you, the client, and the salon in the event medical problems arise. In addition, referrals are a great way to market ones services.

Personally, I appreciate referrals. When a nail tech is wise enough to refer, I will refer back a more educated person, and the tech and I will have a better understanding of how we can learn from one another to prevent problems and improve our services.

Physician's Concerns

One question I am always asked by my patients is, "I am a diabetic. Can I get pedicures?"

My answer is, "It depends on your doctor."

If you are a controlled diabetic, your doctor may give you permission with the below referral slip. If you are an uncontrolled diabetic, I personally would not suggest pedicures for my uncontrolled diabetic patient unless the nail tech was medically trained and working closely in constant communication with the client's personal diabetic physician or podiatrist.

The rule of thumb is, do not get pedicures if your doctor does not advise it or will not give permission to get pedicures. It is usually for good reason.

Examples of referral forms

Some typical sample forms are on the following pages. Feel free to copy them or to show them to your nail technician or your physician.

These sample forms can be downloaded at my website www.justfortoenails.com.

SAMPLE permission slips for physicians

PHYSICIAN MEDICAL ALERT FOR NAIL TECHNICIAN PERFORMING NAIL SALON SERVICES ON MY PATIENt

Patient's name and phone#_____

Patients Salon name and phone # _____

Patient's nail technician or cosmetologist name _____

I grant permission to provide services to my patient who is under my monitored health care with the following medical problem. Circled or otherwise written.

Minimal Neuropathy (Decreased sensation or distorted sensation in their hands or feet)

Minimal Circulation deficits or Vascular compromise

Controlled Diabetes

Ingrown nails without infection

Fungal nails

Cosmetic allergies or other allergies

Blood Borne illness contact hazard

Other medical problem or special instructions _____

VERY IMPORTANT

If any injury or new medical problem is noticed or suspected injury occurs while performing your services on my patient you must immediately contact this office at _____ by phone or_____ by fax to report the nature of the problem and have the patient set up an immediate appointment. If you cannot reach my office immediately, direct the patient to the emergency room or clinic and notify our office what medical facility you referred them to. You must notify our office in either case either by phone or fax.

If an injury occurs, clean the wound with soap and water, swap with 70% alcohol, Betadine or an approved antiseptic by your State Board of Cosmetology and bandage the area with a sterile dressing.

DR _____ Date:_____

Physician's Signature Authorization

SAMPLE: Nail Technician Client Referral to Dr.

Date_____

Salon name _____

Address:_____

City, State, Zip_____

Salon Phone_____

Nail Tech/Cosmetologist (Please print) _____

Client's name _____

I am referring my client for possible medical attention for one or more of the following.

___ Redness around the nail, foot, hand, fingers, face

___Accidental injury with nail/foot/hand care instrument

___Skin problem or rash

___Skin reaction to beauty product

___Nail discoloration

___Nail Thickness

___Nail pain

___Thin or brittle nails

___Foot pain

___Problem from acrylic, gel nails, nail wraps

___Painful thick skin or corns

___Other problem _____

Dear Doctor_____

I greatly appreciate you seeing my client and examining her for the above potential problem. If you determine she can continue my services, I have a form that you can authorize that allows her return with any restrictions or instructions.

Thank you for your assistance_____

Signature of Nail Technician
or Cosmetologist

Chapter 30
What is an accredited beauty school?

Per Clifford Culbreath, with the National Accrediting Commission of Cosmetology Arts & Sciences (www.naccas. org), there are approximately 1100 private or proprietary cosmetology schools that are accredited with the NACCAS organization exclusively. There are approximately an additional 1,500 cosmetology schools that are taught through junior colleges or vocational state schools. Finally, there are approximately 400 private or proprietary cosmetology schools that are accredited through the Council of Occupational Education (COOE) and the Accrediting Commission of Career Schools and Colleges of Technology (ACCSCT)

All states require these 3000 schools to be licensed to operate by the respective state boards of cosmetology in which the school educated students. Only two states, UT and PA, require the school be accredited through the Naccas.org. To be an accredited school with NACCAS, the cosmetology school must have been licensed with their state for two years before applying for consideration.

Pell grants are one of the largest grant programs available for students to have their education paid for by the US government. These grants do not have to be paid back but are issued to the school only if the student remains enrolled. If the student drops out, the Pell grant ceases.

For more information, contact NACCAS at 4401 Ford Avenue ~ Suite 1300, Alexandria, VA 22302 -- USA, Phone 703-600-7600 or Fax 703-379-2200. Visit the NACCAS website at www.naccas.org. Clifford Culbreath can be reached directly at 703-600-7600 Ext: 35 or via email atcculbreath@naccas.org.

New NACCAS Sponsorship Programs: Many professional beauty care product manufacturers, distributors and service companies want to attract more business from the NACCAS accredited cosmetology schools and their students. NACCAS is now expanding their Corporate Sponsorship Program. Opportunities are available at the four Annual NACCAS Workshop Conventions.

Affordable new advertising opportunities are also available within the NACCAS Review Newsletter. For more information contact Cliff Culbreath directly at 703-600-7600 Ext: 35 or via email atcculbreath@naccas.org.

Questions

What does it mean if a school is accredited?

Schools that are labeled "accredited" have met certain academic and institutional requirements established by the accrediting organizations. Some of the factors that accrediting organizations look for include a schools curriculum, quality of education, facilities, staff, and admission policies.

Are there benefits to attending an accredited school?

The primary advantage of a school being "accredited"

is their ability to offer financial aid to students. While NAC-CAS is not a government agency, they are recognized by the United States Department of Education. This being said, there are still a lot of good schools out there that choose not to be accredited.

Which schools are accredited?

You can find an extensive list of accredited schools in our featured schools section. For a complete list can contact your state's licensing board or the accrediting agency.

Who is the main accrediting agency for beauty and cosmetology schools?

The largest accrediting agency for beauty and cosmetology schools is NACCAS, which stands for the National Accrediting Commission for Cosmetology Arts & Sciences. NACCAS is recognized by the US. Department of Education and presently accredits approximately 1,000 institutions which serve over 100,000 students. These schools offer over twenty courses and programs of study which fall under NACCAS' scope of accreditation.

Who are some of the other accrediting agencies for beauty and cosmetology schools?

Other accrediting agencies recognized by the U.S Department of Education include ACCSCT (Accrediting Commission of Career Schools and Colleges of Technology), ACCET (Accrediting Council for Continued Education & Training), and SACS (Southern Association of Colleges and Schools).

The American Association of Cosmetology Schools (AACS), the Cosmetology Advancement Foundation (CAF), and the Beauty and Barber Supply Institute (BBSI), all sponsor ACE Grants which encourage highly motivated and qualified individuals to join the world of cosmetology.

What are the main associations within the cosmetol-

ogy industry?

One of the most widely recognized is the American Association of Cosmetology Schools, otherwise known as AACS. They are a national non-profit association open to all privately owned schools of Cosmetology Arts & Sciences. AACS specializes in updating its members with information about new teaching methods, current industry events, and Washington, DC updates. Most of this updating is done through a series of seminars, conferences and conventions held throughout the year.

Additional Contacts

American Association of Cosmetology Schools
15825 N. 71st St., Suite 100
Scottsdale, AZ 85254-1521
800-831-1086
480-281-0431
Fax: 480-905-0993

Jim Cox
Executive Director
800-831-1086, x 133
jim@beautyschools.org

Lisa Zarda
General Manager
(800) 831-1086 x 132
lisa@beautyschools.org

Jayne Morehouse
Morehouse Communications
Public Relations
16496 Falmouth Drive
Strongsville, OH 44136
Phone: (440) 846-6022

Fax: (440) 846-6024
jayne@morehousepr.com

Example of Advertisement or Information to attract students

A Career in cosmetology! The average income for cosmetologists is about $32,000 per year. Now there are over $3 million in scholarships available to help jump start your career and get you on your way to a great future!

The beauty industry wants you! ACE Grants are designed to help you begin your career in cosmetology. Sponsored by three major beauty industry associations: the American Association of Cosmetology Schools (AACS), the Cosmetology Advancement Foundation (CAF), and the Beauty and Barber Supply Institute (BBSI), ACE Grants are the first ever industry-wide effort to encourage highly motivated and qualified individuals to join the world of cosmetology.

Link for accredited beauty school directory:

http://www.beautyschoolsdirectory.com/faq/state_req.php

Chapter 31

The benefits of manicures and pedicures

What is the final verdict on pedicures and manicures? They are great services that benefit health and well-being when both nail professionals and clients follow the standard safety precautions detailed in this book.

Benefits of Manicures and Pedicures

- Very relaxing
- Relieves muscle tension in hands and feet
- Facilitates endorphin release
- Eases headache pain
- Eases back and neck pain
- Fosters increase in self-esteem
- Promotes positive thinking
- Contributes to a professional appearance

- Increases daily comfort level of feet and hands
- Fosters increased attention to self-care
- Improves health of skin on feet and hands
- Results in fewer hangnails
- Discourages nail biting
- Massage of hands/arms, neck/shoulders, feet/legs invigorates
- Decreases likelihood of cracked, dry skin and resultant portals of infection

These are but a few advantages to receiving a good pedicure or manicure service. I highly recommend that all clients find conscientious nail technicians to work with. The following associations and individuals can help you find well-trained nail techs who provide safe, high-quality nail services.

INTA (International Nail Technicians Association) http://www.chicagomidwestbeautyshow.com/MEMBERSHIP/InternationalNailTechniciansAssociation/tabid/93/Default.aspx

IPA International Pedicure Association
http://www.pedicureassociation.org

Dr. Robert Spalding, TN http://.www.justfortoenails.com

Betty Davis, TX   http://www.sparevolution.com/

Athena Elliot, TX http://www.yournailtech.com/

Viki Peters, CA http://www.kupainc.com/kb/

Nancy King, AZ http://www.nailcareconsulting.com/

Jaime Schrabeck, Ph.D, CA
http://www.precisionnails.com/consulting.htm

Creative Nail Design Master Pedicurist Log in
http://www.creativenaildesign.com/professional_login.asp

Chapter 32
Nail Salon Infection Survey and comments
www.nailsaloninfectionsurvey.com

Responses and comments as well as another national survey

Currently, I am unaware of any national data base that allows consumers, nail techs and physicians to log on and take separate surveys that will provide consumer and nail tech feedback and determine how prevalent infections are in the public domain. If you know of an infection acquired in a nail salon, or would like to anonymously report, or get information to report an infection, go to www.nailsaloninfectionsurvey.com – and leave a comment.

Here are some nail tech and consumer comments reprinted here with permission:

"Learn how to cut toe nails so people do not get ingrown toe nails."   TX

"I would like to se more salons using clean new implements, and filers each time they finish with a customer. Most places I have been use cuticle nippers on me then without washing it they put it some type of blue "sanitizer." Also, most places I go use an attachment to buff your nails (It's used with a pink lotion type substance these attachments are never cleaned. When I see them they are mostly satturated with that pink lotion substance. One time the attachment was so matted with lotion that it would not even turn or absorb any lotion. I was disguted and I made them change it out. I feel like these establishments are robbing women of a pampering experience. Most women go get manicures, pedicrues, artificial nales, etc. to make themselves feel better, but now we have to worry about infection insterad of enhoying the experience. It should also be easier for people to report salons that are not using proper sanitizing procedures." TN

"More regulation on this industry! A friend of mine has developed a skin infection on her ankle, which her doctor told her was community acquired MRSA. We both strongly feel like it came from this nail salon. I will not take the risk anymore and go to these places until I can trust that appropriate cleaning/sterilizing methods are in place. " TN

"Mystery shopping the spa or salon to make sure they are following all sanitation regulations at least twice per week." TX

"Education of professionals & Sterilization of implements and tools." TX

"In all honesty, the way we are treated (nail techs)" TX

"Sanitation monitored" WI

"Stop all the bogus product claims! Chronological aging takes place the moment of conception and no product prevents the ageing process. I do not believe what doctors have for sale as being the "product" that beats all beauty woes. If they did every one would look as if they are in the bloom of youth at all times.

Ageing is natural and just because you are young does not mean you are good looking and if you are old does not mean you are ugly! I better stop here. " FL

"I may have to undergo an amputation of my right index finger because of an aggressive infection from a nail salon" FL

"Texas recently updated making mandatory to use an auto-clave. I think this is ridiculous... I have been doing nails for 16 years and have taken great care of my clients with the regular sanitation... not one time have I ever had a client get an infec-tion from me, but I santized my implements, my clients hands etc. I think using an autoclave is something you use in a operat-ing room not a nail salon unless you are going to the NSS and they try to remove your toenail (a friend of mine went to have a pedicure at one of those places in the Wal Mart and they guy told her she needed to have her toenail removed so he did. I got really upset w/ my friend and told her that he should never have done that. He should have referred you to either your regular physician or to a podiatrist.) The NSS are the ones giving the nail industry a bad name.... quickee in and fast out MONEY MONEY MONEY is what they are after not quality and it burns me up they are the ones imposing on my money. Forcing our state to require thou-sand dollars autoclaves.. next I guess our salons will have to be white sterile operating rooms... see ya on Grey's Anatomy!!" TX

"I would like for the state boards to do their jobs. There are alot of nail techs who do things correct, follow the rules and regulations but the ones who do not the state board does noth-ing until something bad happens. The bad techs are making the ones who do things by the book look bad. The public shouldn't be afraid of us because of what some nasty salon did. there are a lot of discount salons that cut corners in order to give services at cheap prices and its putting a strain on the techs/salons who are trying to do things right. I'm just tired of the media and public clumping us all together. I agree that the public should be informed however if you gonna tell them the truth then tell them EVERYTHING. For instance its ok to bring your own tools for your manicure and pedicure however if someone is going to do that then they should expect for the tech to clean those tools before they start their services because the tech does not know what the client did with the implements, etc before they came to the salon. The media makes it seem that its ok for the tech to start your nail service right away if you bring your own items but if a tech does and the clients gets something then who is gonna get the blame? The nail tech does. The media needs to let the public know that its not ok and not to be surprised if the tech cleans disinfect sanitize sterilize the clients items before they begin services. We don't know what the client did to their items before they came into the salon. They might have let someone use their nail clippers who happens to have something contagious. Just because they bring their own items DOES NOT MEAN THAT IT IS CLEAN. Also I would like the public to know not only does the nail tech washes their hands thoroughly before services that the client also should wash their hands thoroughly. They should also tell that there are different types of whirlpools some do come pipeless and doesn't have filters for sanitation reasons. There are alot of things they public should be told but isn't and because of that its creating fear and also a false sense of security at the same time." TN

"I believe my state really needs to focus on nail salons using inferior services and products. I have so many clients who come into my shop with damage from these salons. It is frustrating for me to try to adhere to state board standards and other salons in my area can operate under such filthy conditions. I really feel that for a significant change to take place, we need closer supervision from our state boards." AL

"Education is hit-and-miss in this industry--I would like to see significant changes in the way students are taught. Too many classrooms don't even have a dedicated, licensed nail tech as an instructor, let alone any instructor at all. The students are often left to figure things out for themselves. Students are lucky to learn how to apply nail enhancements correctly and safely, let alone to get current information on how to sanitize and disinfect instruments and surfaces properly. They're taught just barely enough to pass state boards, and this is often outdated information. I, personally, was fortunate in my education--I had skilled, knowledgeable instructors who were with us for the entire class time, seven hours a day, five days a week until graduation. But after talking to other nail techs, I see that my experience was the exception, not the rule. Changes in the nail industry need to start from the ground up! I would also like to note that I do not use a pedicure/whirlpool chair, but I marked the questionaire according to my knowledge of what I would need to do if I used one. I actually do a 'waterless' pedicure--no footsoak at all, but a hot, wet towel wrap." WA

"Mandatory continuing education that is standardized across all 50 states and eventually internationally. More salon inspectors, better access to disinfectants with easy to understand instructions. Many of these chemicals require mixing and are very expensive. Less expensive, but equally effective alternative disinfectants should be available. Also, more local education. We currently have to drive 3 hours to get continuing education on disinfection and sanitation procedures as required by the state board. It would be much easier if each city had there own educator to teach these classes-more people would attend if they didn't have to travel so far." TN

"I would love to see ALL techs held accountable....especially the discount salons....Pictures with licenses, CEU's, Better educated nail techs and fines for techs, as well as owners " TN

"To start checking on salons and see what the practices are.. I know in Colorado that NO Board members are doing checks on salons with complaints.. I know of a lot of discount salons skipping on sanitation practices and I do not like being lumped in with them when dirty practices come up.. So I think a better system of enforcing the regulations would be a good start."   TN

"I would like to see state board inspectors start to enforce closing salons down, instead of just continuing to fine them over and over again or they can implement a suspension policy to suspend a salon owners license for a limited amount of time if they are fined more than five times or something to that effect. If they continue to be fined and suspended, then revoke their license for a certain amount of time. Just a thought. " TN

"…more education and better sanitation laws" MA

"Get rid of discount salons that use MMA in their acrylic. -Educate discount salons on the benefits of cleaning and sanitizing their implements. -Make discount salons stop using Credo blades. -Educate discount salons on the benefits of using salon quality products." TN

"if the state inspectors actually came and visited more salons more frequently, they could do a better job of enforcing the rules and regulations we already have. i am a clean freak and it drives me CRAZY to see so many in my industry NOT follow the rules that are out there in order to save time or money. my concern is for the safety of my clients, not the quickest way to get to the next client". HI

"Sterilization, not sanitation" FL

"I would like to see the number of state inspectors increased and non-compliant facilities not just fined, but shut down and their licenses revoked." CA

"Enforcement of existing laws applied to ALL salons before knee-jerk reactions such as insisting on sterilization of implements compared to proven DISINFECTION methods. Focus on salons which are unsanitary, use MMA, woodworking rotary tools and ENFORCE the rules for them before you go on a witch hunt with other STANDARD salons. TEST THE MONOMER THEY USE!!! Fine them for violations. Don't even get me started on the whirlpool spas. I DO NOT USE A WHIRLPOOL SPA AND I NEVER WILL. Clients don't care about the equipment. They care about the process. I DO NOT USE A Credo BLADE AND NEVER WILL. They are unnecessary. I could go on and on. The point is, there are two sides to every story. Your new Death By Pedicure book may very well sensationalize one side of this industry. I do hope you provide a BALANCED synopsis. PS I am not in the USA, I am in Canada, in a province where there is no licensing whatsoever for nail techs. Only local health regulations to abide by. You can bet that I EXCEED those regulations. I would welcome licensing in this province any time. One last point. Once you remove implements from an Autoclave, they are no longer sterilized. What then? Or are we going back to the days of dental acrylic? Thanks for your time."   Laura M. Canada

"Getting everyone to use the same sanitation procedures." TN

"To this realize that not all salons have pedi chairs, I use a bowl and massage rocks and I clean after each use. As well as sanitize and clean all implements. I think there could be the flip side of showing salons that are following the rules and that are trying to keep the client safe with all their procedures.

But the client has to take responsibility also, if they feel like something is not quite right they should remove the nail themselves or call their tech immediately so they can get it checked. Also if they don't follow guidelines that we share with them like wearing gloves etc, they have to take some responsibility for the longevity of their nails and the health of them. Most come every two weeks so a lot can happen in two weeks Specially if a nail lifts, if they know it is lifting they should remove it or come in for a repair. Most just keep it on their, and when they come at the end of two weeks the problem is already in force.

But i think they should not allow the pedi chairs in salons. If they want massage chairs they need to just make the chairs that are set high and with a base for the pedi bowl that can be carried off and emptied." OK

"Abolishing the rule for an autoclave, Nail salons are not sterile environments and will never be." TX

"I would make CEU classes more beneficial and not a waste of time." SC

"I just came across your web site, and I would like to tell you what happened to me. I am not the type to regularly get manicures & pedicures, but I decided to get a pedicure right before my daughter was born. That resulted in months of pain and it was one of the biggest mistakes of my life. Both of my big toes ended up being infected due to ingrown toe nails, and my doctors stated it was because of the way my toe nails were cut. (Which had to be from the salon because I have never caused myself to get one before). I wrote the salon asking for them to reimburse me for all of the medical expenses ($1700), and the owner called me up and argued with me for over 20 minutes stating she wouldn't pay me a penny – mainly because I am just going to her now with everything instead of first telling them right when it happened. (The reasons it took me awhile are: 1) it took awhile for the ingrown toe nails to become infected 2) I had to have one toe done in September, the other in October, and then one of the toes didn't heal properly so I had to go back this February to have it looked at 3) I met a woman who had the EXACT same thing happen to her from the same salon and had to have both of her toes done which 100% confirmed in my mind I had to do something about this).

"My question to you – do you know if I have a case to go to small claims court and try to get reimbursed for all of my medical expenses with all of the experience you have had with these types of issues? I don't know whether or not I should pursue this, and I would really like to hear your opinion. This has been a nightmare for me, and I think it's great you are writing a book on pedicures. It will save peoples lives!!

"Thank you for your time and your wonderful web site!!!!" TX

Article on another nail health survey

More than half of all Americans symptomatic of highly contagious nail fungus and infection, but unaware of it.

New Survey on Nail Health and Care Reports

Americans Sharing Nail Clippers, Files and Other Tools with Spouses, Kids, Pets & Others, But Unaware of Potential Health Risks

NILES, Ill., (April 19, 2004) -

More than half of all Americans are symptomatic of highly contagious, unsightly and often difficult to cure nail fungus and infections, and may potentially pass them along to others by sharing nail tools, according to a new survey on nail hygiene habits.

According to the *Fungicure* 2004 Nail Hygiene Survey of 830 Americans fielded by TNS/NFO Research Worldwide, more than 52 percent of respondents reported symptoms of highly contagious nail infections or fungus on fingernails, toenails or both. Yet, only 15 percent ever discussed nail care with their physician, and more than 77 percent of respondents believe that nail fungus is somewhat, not very, or not at all contagious.

According to the American Podiatric Medical Association, onychomycosis, a highly contagious nail infection, affects three percent to five percent of the population, or 12 million Americans. Many more may be unaware that they have the condition because it is typically not painful at the onset.

The study queried respondents on nail hygiene, the prevalence of nail and fungal problems, and attitudes about the prevention and treatment of nail fungus. The study confirms that Americans:

•   are promoting the spread of highly contagious nail infections through lax nail care,

•   are casually sharing nail care tools,

•   lack physician involvement,

•   are poorly educated about prevention practices beginning in childhood and continuing throughout adulthood.

"It's not surprising that the incidence of nail infection and fungus is so high," said Andrew Scheman, M.D., a dermatologist and specialist in nail fungus and infection. "Many people haven't been educated about the symptoms and don't believe they are contagious.

Consumers don't recognize that some of the most dangerous risks, such as improperly cleaned implements, are right in the home. Many people don't realize that these infections can be managed, but not easily cured, so prevention is a key."

Incidence and Diagnosis

52 percent of respondents reported nail fungus or infection symptoms. Women were more likely to report symptoms than men, with 56 percent of all female respondents reporting symptoms versus 46 percent of men.

By age, 69 percent of individuals age 24 and under reported problems, the most likely group to report symptoms, followed by those 25 to 34 years, and 52 percent of those 35 to 44 years.

Parents reporting on their children's nail health revealed an increase in nail problems as children age. Of those households with children under age 6, 28 percent reported problems,

41 percent of kids 7 to 12 years reported nail problems and 48 percent of kids 13 and older reported nail problems.

The vast majority of survey respondents (85 percent) report they have never discussed nail care with a physician. A physician had diagnosed only 19 percent of survey respondents as having a nail infection. It does not appear that physicians are gender biased when discussing nail health with patients as only 13 percent of both men and women say their doctor discusses nail health during their visits.

Sharing Tools to Groom Fingernails and Toenails

According to the survey, nearly half (49 percent) of all respondents share fingernail and toenail tools with others, including spouses, children, roommates, co-workers and even pets.

Highlights include:

• Of those who share, 88 percent of sharers do so with their spouses and 45 percent share with their children.

• Those who actually report nail problems share with others slightly more than those who are not symptomatic with 50 percent sharing files, scissors, clippers and other tools, potentially spreading fungus and infections.

• Spouses are the most likely candidates for sharing with 43 percent of the respondents sharing tools with their spouse, 23 percent with children and 5 percent with a sibling or parent. Two percent of respondents share with a roommate or friend.

• One individual reported sharing tools with a pet.

• Women, whether symptomatic or not, were more likely to share tools than men (51.8 percent vs. 47.7 percent) but men were more likely to use someone else's tools without their knowledge.

Lock Up The Clippers & Nail Files

Even a strict stance of not sharing tools with others isn't enough to keep nail fungus and infection from spreading, according to the survey.

Sixteen percent of respondents say they use others' manicure and pedicure tools, without their knowledge, to groom their fingernails and 8 percent say they use others' tools to groom finger and toenails. Men are twice as likely to use someone else's nail clippers without their knowledge.

Those "sneaks" most often use nail clippers, emery boards and nail files to groom their fingernails, and nail clippers and nail files to groom toenails.

The presence of fungus or infection symptoms won't deter some "sneaks," with 7 percent of symptomatic "sneaks" using others' clippers and 1 percent borrowing others' nail files or emery boards.

"There is no doubt that nail fungus and infection can be spread through the use of dirty grooming tools," Dr. Scheman said. "If we expect salons and spas to keep manicure and pedicure tools clean, we should consider it a priority to properly clean our own personal tools, before use and after use, at home."

Attitudes on Prevention

Less than half of respondents said they believed that sharing nail tools could lead to infection. However, they cited using a public shower (26 percent), using a public swimming pool (32 percent), going to a gym/fitness center (27 percent) and going to a nail salon (10 percent) as ways to contract an infection. Nearly 2 percent of respondents said they believe using public restrooms could lead to nail fungus or infection.

In terms of prevention, half of respondents cited better hygiene/cleanliness as the best means to combat nail fungus or infection. More than 32 percent of respondents reported never cleaning their nail grooming tools, saying they never thought about it. Twenty-two percent said their tools aren't dirty, and 18 percent said they don't share with anyone with an infection.

The Fungicure 2004 Nail Hygiene Survey was fielded by NFO Research Worldwide in late 2003. The firm surveyed 830 Americans, asking about nail care grooming habits, incidence of nail infection, attitudes toward the spread of nail infections and more. FungiCure® is a leader in manicure and pedicure health, and provides a full spectrum of products for finger and toe hygiene. For more information, visit www.alva-amco.com or call 847/884-0000.

Contact: Carson Stoga Communications
Susan Stoga - susan@carsonstoga.com
Donna Scherner - donna@carsonstoga.com
phone: 847/884-0000

Appendix A
State regulatory agencies for reporting violations

ALABAMA
Alabama Board of Cosmetology
Address: RSA Building, 100 N. Union #320, Montgomery, AL 36130
Phone: (334) 242-1918; (800) 815-7453
Web: www.aboc.state.al.us

ALASKA
Alaska Barbers & Hairdressers
Address: PO Box 110806, Juneau, AK 99811-0806
Phone: (907) 465-2547
Web: www.dced.state.ak.us/occ/pbah.htm

ARIZONA
Arizona Board of Cosmetology
Address: 1721 E. Broadway, Tempe, AZ 85282
Phone: (602) 784-4539 ext. 227
Web: www.cosmetology.state.az.us

ARKANSAS
Arkansas State Board of Cosmetology
Address: 101 E. Capitol Ave. #108, Little Rock, AR 72201
Phone: (501) 682-2168 Web: www.arkansas.gov/cos

CALIFORNIA
California Dept. of Consumer Affairs Board of Barbering & Cosmetology
Address: 400 "R" St. #5100, Sacramento, CA 95814
Phone: (916) 445-0916; (800) 952-5210
Web: www.barbercosmo.ca.gov

COLORADO
Colorado Barbers & Cosmetology Licensure
Address: 1560 Broadway #1340, Denver, CO 80202
Phone: (303) 894-7772
Web: www.dora.state.co.us/barbers_cosmetologists

CONNECTICUT
Connecticut Dept. of Public Health
Address: 410 Capitol Ave., MS12APPPO PO Box 340308, Hartford, CT
06134-0308
Phone: (860) 509-7569; (860) 509-8000
Web: www.dph.state.ct.us

DISTRICT OF COLUMBIA
District of Columbia Cosmetology & Barbering
Address: 941 N. Capital St. Room 7200, Washington, DC 20002
Phone: (202) 442-4320
Web: www.dcra.com, www.promissor.com

DELAWARE
Delaware State Board of Cosmetology & Barbering
Address: 861 Silver Lake Blvd. #203, Dover, DE 19904
Phone: (302) 744-4518
Web: www.professionallicensing.state.de.us

FLORIDA
Florida Board of Cosmetology
Address: 1940 N. Monroe St., Tallahassee, FL 32399-0790
Phone: (850) 488-5702
Web: www.myflorida.com

GEORGIA
Georgia State Board of Cosmetology
Address: 237 Coliseum Dr., Macon, GA 31217-3858
Phone: (478) 207-1300
Web: www.sos.state.ga.us

HAWAII
Hawaii Board of Barbering & Cosmetology
Address: PO Box 3469, Honolulu, HI 96801
Phone: (808) 586-2696
Web: www.hawaii.gov/dcca/pvl

IDAHO
Idaho State Board of Cosmetology
Address: 1109 Main St. #220, Boise, ID 83702
Phone: (208) 334-3233
Web: www.ibol.idaho.gov, www2.state.id.us/ibol

ILLINOIS
Illinois Dept. of Professional Regulation
Address: 320 W. Washington St., 3rd Floor, Springfield, IL 62786
Phone: (217) 782-0800
Web: www.dpr.state.il.us

INDIANA
Indiana State Board of Cosmetology Examiners
Address: 302 W. Washington, Room E034, Indianapolis, IN 46204
Phone: (317) 232-2980
Web: www.ai.org/pla/index.html

IOWA
Iowa Cosmetology Board of Examiners
Dept. of Public Health/Professional Licensure
Address: 321 E. 12th St. Lucas Bldg., 5th Floor, Des Moines, IA 50319
Phone: (515) 281-4416
Web: www.idph.state.ia.us/licensure

KANSAS
Kansas Board of Cosmetology
Address: 714 SW Jackson St. #100, Topeka, KS 66603
Phone: (785) 296-3155
Web: www.accesskansas.org/kboc

KENTUCKY
Kentucky State Board of Hairdressers & Cosmetologists
Address: 111 St. James Ct. Ste. A, Frankfort, KY 40601
Phone: (502) 584-4262
Web: http://lrc.ky.gov/

LOUISIANA
Louisiana State Board of Cosmetology
Address: 11622 Sunbelt Ct.., Baton Rouge, LA 70809
Phone: (225) 756-3404
Web: http://www.lsbc.louisiana.gov/

MAINE
Maine Board of Barbering & Cosmetology
Address: 35 State House Station, Augusta, ME 04333
Phone: (207) 624-8579
Web: www.maineprofessionalreg.org

MARYLAND
Maryland Board of Cosmetologists
Address: 500 N. Calvert St., Room 307, Baltimore, MD 21202
Phone: (410) 230-6193
Web: www.dllr.state.md.us/occprf/cos.html

MASSACHUSETTS
Massachusetts Board of Cosmetology
Address: 239 Causaway St., Ste. #500, Boston, MA 02114
Phone: (617) 727-3067
Web: www.state.ma.us/reg/boards/hd

MICHIGAN
Michigan Dept. of Consumer & Industry Svcs., Board of Cosmetology
Address: PO Box 30018, Lansing, MI 48909
Phone: (517) 241-9288
Web: www.michigan.gov/commerciallicensing

MINNESOTA
Minnesota Dept. of Commerce, License Division
Address: 85 7th Place East #500, St. Paul, MN 55101
Phone: (651) 296-6319; (800) 657-3602
Web: www.commerce.state.mn.us

MISSISSIPPI
Mississippi State Board of Cosmetology
Address: PO Box 55689, Jackson, MS 39296-5689
Phone: (601) 987-6837
Web: www.msbc.state.ms.us

MISSOURI
Missouri State Board of Cosmetology
Address: PO Box 1062, Jefferson City, MO 65102
Phone: (573) 751-1052
Web: www.pr.mo.gov

MONTANA
Montana Board of Cosmetologists
Address: PO Box 200513, Helena, MT 59620-0513
Phone: (406) 841-2335
Web: www.discoveringmontana.com/dli/cos

NEBRASKA
Nebraska State Board of Cosmetology Examiners/Credentialing Division
Address: PO Box 94986, Lincoln, NE 68509-4986
Phone: (402) 471-2117
Web: www.hhs.state.ne.us/crl/mhcs/cosindex.htm

NEVADA
Nevada State Board of Cosmetology
Address: 1785 E. Sahara Ave. #255, Las Vegas, NV 89104
Phone: (702) 486-6542
Web: www.cosmetology.nv.gov

NEW HAMPSHIRE
New Hampshire Board of Barbering, Cosmetology & Esthetics
Address: 2 Industrial Park Dr., Concord, NH 03301
Phone: (603) 271-3608
Web: www.state.nh.us/cosmet

NEW JERSEY
New Jersey Board of Cosmetology & Hairstyling
Address: PO Box 45003, Newark, NJ 07101
Phone: (973) 504-6400
Web: www.state.nj.us/lps/ca/nonmedical/coshair.htm

NEW MEXICO
New Mexico Board of Barbers & Cosmetologists
Address: 2550 Cerrillos Rd., PO Box 25101, Santa Fe, NM 87504
Phone: (505) 476-4690
Web: www.rld.state.nm.us

NEW YORK
New York Dept. of State, Licensing Svcs. Division
Address: 84 Holland Ave., Albany, NY 12208
Phone: (518) 474-4429
Web: www.dos.state.ny.us

NORTH CAROLINA
North Carolina Board of Cosmetology
Address: 1201 Front St. #110, Raleigh, NC 27609
Phone: (919) 733-4117
Web: www.cosmetology.state.nc.us

NORTH DAKOTA
North Dakota State Board of Cosmetology
Address: 1102 S. Washington St., PO Box 2177, Bismarck, ND 58504
Phone: (701) 224-9800
Web: www.governor.state.nd.us

OHIO
Ohio State Board of Cosmetology
Address: 3700 S. High St. #101, Columbus, OH 43207
Phone: (614) 466-3834
Web: www.state.oh.us/cos

OKLAHOMA
Oklahoma Board of Cosmetology
Address: 2401 NW 23rd St. #84, Oklahoma City, OK 73107
Phone: (405) 521-2441
Web: www.state.ok.us/~cosmo

OREGON
Oregon Health Licensing Office Board of Cosmetology
Address: 700 Summer St. NE #320, Salem, OR 97301-1287
Phone: (503) 378-8667; (503) 373-2114 (TDD)
Web: www.hlo.state.or.us

PENNSYLVANIA
Pennsylvania State Board of Cosmetology
Address: PO Box 2649, Harrisburg, PA 17105-2649
Phone: (717) 783-7130
Web: www.dos.state.pa.us

RHODE ISLAND
Rhode Island Board of Hairdressing & Barbering
Address: 3 Capitol Hill, Room 104, Providence, RI 02908
Phone: (401) 222-2827 ext. 113
Web: www.health.state.ri.us/hsr/professions/hair_barb.php

SOUTH CAROLINA
South Carolina Board of Cosmetology
Address: PO Box 11329, Columbia, SC 29211
Phone: (803) 896-4568
Web: www.llr.state.sc.us

SOUTH DAKOTA
South Dakota Cosmetology Commission
Address: 500 E. Capitol, Pierre, SD 57501
Phone: (605) 773-6193
Web: www.state.sd.us/dol/boards/cosmo

TENNESSEE
Tennessee State Board of Cosmetology
Address: 500 James Robertson Pkwy., Room 130, Nashville, TN 37243-
1147
Phone: (615) 741-2515
Web: www.state.tn.us/commerce/cosmetology/index.html

TEXAS
Texas Cosmetology Commission
Address: PO Box 26700, Austin, TX 78755-0700
Phone: (512) 454-4674
Web: www.txcc.state.tx.us

UTAH
Utah Board of Cosmetology
Address: 160 E. 300 South, PO Box 146741, Salt Lake City, UT 84114
Phone: (801) 530-6740; (801) 530-2233
Web: www.dopl.utah.gov

VERMONT
Vermont Board of Barbers & Cosmetology
Address: 26 Terrace St., Montpelier, VT 05609-1106
Phone: (802) 828-1134
Web: www.vtprofessionals.org

VIRGINIA
Virginia Board for Barbers & Cosmetology
Address: 3600 W. Broad St., Richmond, VA 23230-4917
Phone: (804) 367-8509
Web: www.state.va.us/dpor/bnc_main.htm

WASHINGTON
Washington Board of Cosmetologists, Barbers, Manicurists & Estheticians
Address: 405 Black Lake Blvd., PO Box 9026, Olympia, WA 98507-9026
Phone: (360) 664-6626
Web: www.wa.gov/dol/bpdcosfront.htm

WEST VIRGINIA
West Virginia Board of Barbers & Cosmetologists
Address: 1716 Pennsylvania Ave. #7, Charleston, WV 25302
Phone: (304) 558-2924
Web: www.state.wv.us/wvbc

WISCONSIN
Wisconsin Barbering & Cosmetology Examining Board
Address: 1400 E. Washington Ave., PO Box 8935, Madison, WI 53708
Phone: (608) 266-5511 ext. 42
Web: www.drl.state.wi.us

WYOMING
Wyoming State Board of Cosmetology
Address: 2515 Warren Ave. #302 Hansen Building East, Cheyenne, WY 82002
Phone: (307) 777-3534
Web: www.state.wy.us
U.S. TERRITORIES

GUAM
Guam Board of Barbering & Cosmetology
Address: PO Box 2816, Hagatna, GU 96932
Phone: (671) 735-7406
Web: N/A

PUERTO RICO
Puerto Rico Secretaría Auxiliar de Juntas Examindoras
Address: PO Box 9023271, San Juan, PR 00902-3271
Phone: (787) 722-2121
Web: www.estado.gobierno.pr

CANADIAN PROVINCES:

ALBERTA
Alberta Dept. of Advanced Education & Career Development/Beauty Consultant Division
Address: 10030 107th St., 7th flr. 7th St. Plaza, South Tower Edmonton, AB T5J 4X7
Phone: (780) 427-8517

BRITISH COLUMBIA
British Columbia Board of Examiners,
Cosmetologists Assn. of British Columbia
Address: 899 W. 8th Ave., Vancouver, BC V5Z 1E3
Phone: (604) 871-0222 ext. 303
Web: www.ciabc.net

MANITOBA
Manitoba Department of Education, Apprenticeship, Advanced Education
& Training
Address: 1010 401 York Ave., Winnipeg, MB R3C 0P8
Phone: (204) 945-5436; (877) 978-7233
Web: www.edu.gov.mb.ca/apprenticeship

NEW BRUNSWICK
New Brunswick Cosmetology Association
Address: 299 York St., Fredericton, NB E3B 3P2
Phone: (506) 458-8087

NEWFOUNDLAND
Newfoundland Industrial Training Division, Dept. of Youth Services &
Post-Secondary Training
Address: PO Box 8700, St. John's, NF A1B 4J6
Phone: (709) 729-5636
Web: www.gov.nf.ca/edu

NORTHWEST TERRITORIES
Northwest Territories Dept. of Education, Culture & Employment
Address: Career Centre, Box 1320, Yellowknife, NWT X1A 2L9
Phone: (867) 873-7357
Web: www.gov.nt.ca

NOVA SCOTIA
Nova Scotia Cosmetology Assn. of Nova Scotia
Address: 75 MacDonald Ave. #9, Dartmouth, NS B3B 1T8
Phone: (902) 468-6477; (800) 765-8757
Web: www.nscosmetology.ca

ONTARIO
Ontario Ministry of Education, Training, Colleges & Universities
Address: 900 Bay St., Toronto, ON M7A 1L2
Phone: (416) 325-2929
Web: www.edu.gov.on.ca

SASKETCHEWAN
Sasketchewan Dept. of Education/Apprenticeship Division
Address: 2140 Hamilton St., Regina, SK S4P 3V7
Phone: (306) 787-2444
Web: www.sasknetwork.gov.sk.ca

YUKON
Yukon Government of Yukon, Corporate Affairs
Address: PO Box 2703, C-6, Whitehorse, YK Y1A 2C6
Phone: (867) 667-5314
Web: www.gov.yk.ca/depts/community/corps

States that prohibit Credo blades/callus cutter implements for pedicures

Arizona	Maryland	Oregon
California	Massachusetts	Pennsylvania
Colorado	Michigan	Rhode Island
Connecticut	Nebraska	South Carolina
Delaware	New Jersey	Texas
Kansas	New Mexico	Washington D.C.
Kentucky	New York	
Maine	Ohio	

Appendix B
Grading of each state's cosmetology laws

State list / 100 pt test / state grade	EPA has grd registered disinfectant, tuberculocidal/sterilize plus/minus 5 pts	Allows callus cutter 20 pts	CEU required 10pts	10 minute immersion time or greater +10 points	Recommend or require steam Sterilization 10 pts	Allows Ultraviolet Light box as primary disinfection device minus 10 points	Has electric file protocol or has wire brush cleaned or soaked in acetone & disinfected 10 min 10 points	Lack of state published regulations 20 points	Discard Disposables posted rules 5pt	Score	Letter Grade 90 A, 80 B, 70 C, 60 D, 50 F
Alabama	yes+5 pts	yes-20	no-10	yes+10 pt	no-10 pts	no+10 pts	yes+10 pt	no+20	yes+5 pts	60	D
Alaska	sterilize +5pts	yes-20	no-10	Steril+10pt	yes+10 pts	no+10 pts	no-10 pts	no+20	no-5 pts	55	D-
Arizonia	EPA +5pts	no+20	no-10	yes+10 pts	no-10 pts	no+10 pts	yes+10 pt	no+20	no-5 pts	75	C+
Arkansas	EPA +5pts	yes-20	no-10	yes+10 pts	no-10 pts	no+10 pts	yes+10 pt	no+20	yes+5 pts	60	D
California	yes +5 pts	no+20	no-10	yes+10 pts	no-10 pts	no+10 pts	yes+10 pt	no+20	yes+5 pts	80	B
Colorado	yes +5 pts	no+20	no-10	no-10 pts	no-10 pts	no+10 pts	yes+10 pt	no+20	yes+5 pts	70	C
Connect	no rule -5pt	no+20	no-10	no-10 pts	no-10 pts	no+10 pts	no-10 pts	yes-20pts	no-5 pts	30	F---
Delaware	EPA +5pts	yes-20	no-10	yes+10 pts	no-10 pts	no+10 pts	no-10 pts	no+20	yes+5 pts	50	F
D.C.(Wash)	no imers -5pt	no+20	no-10	no-10 pts	no-10 pts	no+10 pts	no-10 pts	no+20	yes+5 pts	55	D-
Florida	EPA +5pts	no+20	yes+10	no-10 pts	no-10 pts	no+10 pts	yes+10 pt	no+20	no-5 pts	75	C+
Georgia	EPA +5pts	yes-20	yes+10	no-10 pts	no-10 pts	no+10 pts	no-10 pts	no+20	no-5 pts	45	F-
Hawaii	no EPA -5pt	yes-20	no-10	no-10 pts	no-10 pts	no+10 pts	no-10 pts	no+20	no-5 pts	30	F---
Idaho	EPA +5pts	yes-20	yes+10	no-10 pts	no-10 pts	no+10 pts	no-10 pts	no+20	no-5 pts	35	F---
Illinois	no EPA -5pt	yes-20	no-10	yes+10 pts	yes+10 pts	no+10 pts	no-10 pts	no+20	yes+5 pts	55	D-
Indiana	sterilize +5pts	yes-20	no-10	Steril+10pt	no-10 pts	no+10 pts	no-10 pts	no+20	no-5 pts	45	F-
Iowa	EPA +5pt	yes-20	yes+10	no-10 pts	no-10 pts	no+10 pts	no-10 pts	no+20	yes+5 pt	45	F-
Kansas	EPA +5pts	no+20	no-10	no-10 pts	no-10 pts	no+10 pts	yes+10 pt	no+20	yes+5 pt	80	B
Kentucky	mlt dis +5pt	no+20	yes+10	yes+10 pts	yes+10 pts	no+10 pts	no-10 pts	no+20	no-5 pts	85	B+
Louisiana	EPA +5pts	yes-20	no-10	yes+10 pts	no-10 pts	no+10 pts	yes+10 pt	no+20	yes+5 pt	50	F
Maine	no EPA -5pt	yes-20	no-10	yes+10 pts	no-10 pts	no+10 pts	no-10 pts	no+20	no-5 pts	45	F-
Maryland	EPA +5pts	no+20	no-10	no-10 pts	no-10 pts	no+10 pts	no-10 pts	no+20	no-5 pts	55	D-
Mass	ambig but+5pt	no+20	no-10	yes+10 pts	no-10 pts	no+10 pts	no-10 pts	no+20	no-5 pts	65	D+
Michigan	no EPA -5pts	no+20	no-10	no-10 pts	no-10 pts	yes-10 pts	no-10 pts	no+20	no-5 pts	45	F-
Minnesota	EPA +5pts	yes-20	no-10	no-10 pts	no-10 pts	no+10 pts	no-10 pts	no+20	no-5 pts	35	F---
Mississippi	EPA +5 pts	no+20	no-10	no-10 pts	no-10 pts	no+10 pts	yes+10 pts	no+20	yes+5 pts	70	C
Missouri	EPA +5pts	yes-20	no-10	no -10 pts	no-10 pts	no+10 pts	no-10 pts	no+20	no-5 pts	35	F---
Montana	EPA +5pts	no+20	no-10	no-10 pts	no-10 pts	no+10 pts	yes+10 pts	no+20	yes+5 pts	70	C
Nebraska	EPA +5pts	no+20	yes+10	yes+10 pts	no-10 pts	no+10 pts	yes+10 pts	no+20	yes+5 pts	90	A

State list 100 pt test state grade	EPA has grd registered disinfectant, tuberculocidal/sterilize plus/minus 5 pts	Allows callus cutter 20 pts	CEU required 10pts	10 minute immersion time or greater 10 points	Recommend or require steam Sterilization 10 pts	Allows Ultraviolet Light box as primary disinfection device minus 10 points	Has electric file protocol or has wire brush cleaned or scaled in acetone & disinfected 10 min 10 points	Lack of state published regulations 20 points	Discard Disposables posted rules 5pt	Score	Letter Grade 90 A, 80 B, 70 C, 60 D, 50 F
Nevada	EPA +5pts	yes-20	no-10	no-10 pts	no-10 pts	no+10 pts	yes+10 pts	no+20	yes+5 pts	50	F
New Hamp	EPA +5pts	no+20	no-10	no-10 pts	no-10 pts	yes-10 pts	yes+10 pts	no+20	yes+5 pts	60	D
New Jersey	EPA +5pts	no+20	no-10	no-10 pts	no-10 pts	yes-10 pts	no-10 pts	no+20	no-5 pts	45	F-
New Mex	no EPA -5pts	yes-20	no-10	yes+10 pts	no-10 pts	no+10 pts	no-10 pts	no+20	yes+5 pts	40	F--
New York	EPA +5pts	no+20	no+10	no-10 pts	no-10 pts	no+10 pts	yes+10 pts	no+20	no-5 pts	85	B+
N Carolina	EPA +5pts	no+20	yes+10	no-10 pts	no-10 pts	no+10 pts	no-10 pts	no+20	no-5 pts	65	D+
N Dakota	no EPA -5pts	yes-20	yes+10	no-10 pts	no-10 pts	no+10 pts	no-10 pts	no+20	no-5 pts	45	F-
Ohio	EPA +5pts	yes-20	no-10	no-10 pts	no-10 pts	no+10 pts	yes+10 pts	no+20	yes+5 pts	60	D
Oklahoma	EPA +5pts	yes-20	no-10	no-10 pts	no-10 pts	no+10 pts	yes+10 pts	no+20	yes+5 pts	50	F
Oregon	no EPA -5pts	yes-20	no-10	no-10 pts	no-10 pts	no+10 pts	yes+10 pts	no+20	yes+5 pts	45	F-
Penn	no EPA -5pts	no+20	no-10	no-10 pts	no-10 pts	no+10 pts	no-10 pts	no+20	no-5 pts	50	F
Rhode Is	EPA +5pts	no+20	no-10	no-10 pts	no-10 pts	no+10 pts	yes+10 pts	no+20	no-5 pts	55	D-
S Carolina	EPA +5pts	yes-20	yes+10	yes+10 pts	no-10 pts	no+10 pts	yes+10 pts	no+20	yes+5 pts	70	C
S Dakota	EPA +5pts	no+20	no-10	yes+10 pts	no-10 pts	no+10 pts	yes+10 pts	no+20	yes+5 pts	70	C
Tennessee	EPA +5pts	yes-20	no-10	yes+10 pts	no-10 pts	no+10 pts	no-10 pts	no+20	no-5 pts	45	F-
Texas	Sterilize+5pts	no+20	yes+10	yes+10 pts	yes+10 pts	no+10 pts	yes+10 pts	no+20	yes+5 pts	100	A+
Utah	Multiple+5pts	yes-20	no-10	yes+10 pts	yes+10 pts	no+10 pts	no-10 pts	no+20	yes+5 pts	60	D
Vermont	EPA +5pts	yes-20	no-10	yes+10 pts	no-10 pts	no+10 pts	no-10 pts	no+20	no-5 pts	55	D-
Virginia	EPA +5pts	yes-20	no-10	yes+10 pts	no-10 pts	no+10 pts	no-10 pts	no+20	no-5 pts	45	F-
Washington	EPA +5pts	yes-20	no-10	no-10 pts	no-10 pts	no+10 pts	yes+10 pts	no+20	yes+5 pts	40	F--
West Va	no EPA -5pts	yes-20	no-10	no-10 pts	no-10 pts	no+10 pts	no-10 pts	no+20	yes+5 pts	45	F-
Wisconsin	no imers-5pts	no+20	no-10	no-10 pts	no-10 pts	no+10 pts	no-10 pts	no+20	yes+5 pts	55	D+
Wyoming	EPA +5pts	yes-20	no-10	no-10 pts	no-10 pts	no+10 pts	no-10 pts	no+20	yes+5 pts	40	F-
Guam	no EPA -5pts	yes-20	no-10	no-10 pts	no-10 pts	yes-10 pts	no-10 pts	yes-20pts	no-5 pts	0	off scale
PuertoRico	no EPA -5pts	yes-20	no-10	no-10 pts	no-10 pts	yes-10 pts	no-10 pts	yes-20pts	no-5 pts	0	off scale

~~ TO ORDER *Death By Pedicure* ~~

ON LINE: Go to www.justfortoenails.com (PayPal only)

BY MAIL: Please supply credit card information, or send check/money order payable to Area Podiatry Center, 1225 Taft Hwy, Signal Mt, TN 37377 423-756-FOOT (3668)   Email address: rts9999999@aol.com

Name: _____

Shipping name/address:_____

_____

City _____ St. _____ Zip _____

Credit card type: ___ MC   ___Visa   ___Discover

Number: _____ Expires: _____

Signature _____ Phone _____

Death by Pedicure

Quantity ___ @ $24.95 $_____
Priority shipping for one book $6.95 $ 6.95
Shipping each additional book @ $1.95 $ _____
TN residents please add 9.25% sales tax/book $ _____

Death by Pedicure - Online Certification Course

Get certified as an Advanced Nail Technician after you read the book.
Go to www.Nailsaloninfectionsurvey.com and click MediNails Course
$ 99.00

Call about the new nail salon undercover video footage.

423-756-FOOT
(423-756-3668)

ONLINE CERTIFICATION COURSE $99.00

Get certified as an Advanced Nail Technician after you read the book.
Go to www.nailsaloninfectionsurvey.com and click MediNails Course

Area Podiatry Centers, 1225 Taft Hwy, Signal Mt, TN 37377
423-756-FOOT (3668)   Email address: rts9999999@aol.com
www.justfortoenails.com

Goudy on 50# BVG digital white; insert on 60# Carrara smooth
Type and design by Karen Stone